Leadership for Sustainability

Offering a bold and original perspective, *Leadership for Sustainability* explores how leadership can drive meaningful sustainability transitions through local and regional governance. The authors introduce an interpretive framework developed around the concepts of myth, metaphor and narrative, revealing sustainability as a highly productive fiction – one that enables communities to observe their environment differently and envision and organize long-term futures. Through critical analysis of sustainability narratives and a careful dismantling of common leadership myths, this book uncovers the functions and roles of leadership within governance systems. This approach illuminates how leadership can foster new modes of observation, understanding and organization that reconnect communities, governance and the environment. Featuring a clear and concise overview of key issues, tools, concepts and contexts for the understanding of leadership for sustainability, this is an essential insight for scholars and practitioners working in sustainability, environmental issues, leadership studies, public policy and administration.

KRISTOF VAN ASSCHE is Professor of Planning, Governance and Development at the University of Alberta. He is also affiliated with the University of the Free State in South Africa; Bonn University's Center for Development Research (ZEF) in Germany; and, in Canada, with Memorial University of Newfoundland's Harris Centre for Regional Policy and the University of Saskatchewan's Johnson Shoyama Graduate School of Public Policy.

MONICA GRUEZMACHER is Lecturer and Research Associate in Sustainability and Development at the University of Alberta and Adjunct Professor in Environmental Studies at the Environmental Policy Institute at Memorial University of Newfoundland.

In recent years, Monica and Kristof have been exploring the complexities of planning for long-term sustainability in rural communities across Western Canada and Newfoundland. Their collaborative work has resulted in the publication of several books, including *Crafting Strategies for Sustainable Local Development* (2022) and *Resource Communities: Past Legacies, Future Pathways* (with Lochner Marais and Xaquin Perez-Sindin, 2023). They are currently engaged in research and writing relevant for the reassessment of psychoanalytic perspectives in understanding governance.

Leadership for Sustainability

Myth, Metaphor and Narrative in Governance

KRISTOF VAN ASSCHE
University of Alberta

MONICA GRUEZMACHER
University of Alberta

CAMBRIDGE
UNIVERSITY PRESS

Shaftesbury Road, Cambridge CB2 8EA, United Kingdom

One Liberty Plaza, 20th Floor, New York, NY 10006, USA

477 Williamstown Road, Port Melbourne, VIC 3207, Australia

314–321, 3rd Floor, Plot 3, Splendor Forum, Jasola District Centre, New Delhi – 110025, India

Cambridge University Press is part of Cambridge University Press & Assessment, a department of the University of Cambridge.

We share the University's mission to contribute to society through the pursuit of education, learning and research at the highest international levels of excellence.

www.cambridge.org
Information on this title: www.cambridge.org/9781009620970
DOI: 10.1017/9781009620994

© Kristof Van Assche and Monica Gruezmacher 2026

This publication is in copyright. Subject to statutory exception and to the provisions of relevant collective licensing agreements, no reproduction of any part may take place without the written permission of Cambridge University Press & Assessment.

When citing this work, please include a reference to the
DOI 10.1017/9781009620994

First published 2026

Cover image: RLT_Images / DigitalVision Vectors / Getty Images

A catalogue record for this publication is available from the British Library

A Cataloging-in-Publication data record for this book is available from the Library of Congress

ISBN 978-1-009-62098-7 Hardback
ISBN 978-1-009-62097-0 Paperback

Cambridge University Press & Assessment has no responsibility for the persistence or accuracy of URLs for external or third-party internet websites referred to in this publication and does not guarantee that any content on such websites is, or will remain, accurate or appropriate.

For EU product safety concerns, contact us at Calle de José Abascal, 56, 1°, 28003 Madrid, Spain, or email eugpsr@cambridge.org.

Contents

List of Figures	*page* vii
Preface	ix

1	Basic Concepts: Leadership, Sustainability and Governance	1
	Introduction: Thinking and Organizing	1
	Leadership	4
	Governance	12
	Sustainability	18
2	Narratives and Interpretation	30
	Introduction: A Brief History of Interpretive Theory	30
	Narratives Create Meaning	36
	Narratives Connect Values, Ideas and Feelings	40
	Narratives Create Community	44
	Narratives Define Problems, Methods and Solutions	47
	Genre, Medium and Style	50
	Narrative and Time	54
	Concluding	59
3	Metaphors and the Amplification of Meaning	68
	Introduction	68
	Metaphor Revisited	69
	Roots and Families	74
	Stretching, Aging, Sliding and Traveling	78
	Metaphors and Complexity	82
	Leadership, Governance and Community	86
	Concluding	97
4	Metaphors and Narratives of Sustainability	105
	Sustainability as an Elusive Goal	105
	Narratives and Metaphors of Sustainability	109
	Negative Narrative Forces	114
	Mutual Metaphor Supports Society	118

	Narratives and Metaphors of Sustainability Governance	127
	A Normative Stance on Sustainability Governance	133
	Concluding	136
5	Five Myths of Sustainability Leadership	144
	Introduction	144
	Myth: Expertise Is Key in Sustainability Leadership	147
	Myth: Money Is Key in Sustainability Leadership	152
	Myth: Perfect Institutions Are the Key to Sustainability Leadership	157
	Myth: Morality Is the Key to Sustainability Leadership	163
	Myth: Innovation Is the Key to Sustainability Leadership	167
	Concluding: The Utility of Myths	171
6	Leadership for Sustainability	181
	Leadership Roles and Sustainability Governance	181
	Leadership Functions and Sustainability	189
	Leadership Roles in Rough Seas	201
	Concluding: Analyzing and Crafting Stories	207
7	Sustainability Leadership and Strategy	215
	Community Strategy and Narrative Leadership	215
	Naturalization, Reality Effects and Goal Dependencies	220
	Transitions and Trade-Offs	223
	Leadership Roles	225
	Roles, Stories and Metaphors	227

Glossary   233
Index   253

Figures

1.1	Sustainability leadership	*page* 5
1.2	Leadership roles	12
1.3	Blindness in governance perpetuated	13
2.1	Sustainability leadership and the power of stories	41
2.2	Master signifiers	43
3.1	Metaphor and target domain	70
3.2	Fabric of narratives	73
3.3	Metaphor family	75
3.4	Families of metaphors and role definition	77
3.5	Metaphors and complexity	83
3.6	Thinking and organizing	88
3.7	Stories, practices and roles	89
3.8	Leadership and governance fit	93
3.9	Leadership functions, roles and governance	96
4.1	Sustainability narratives and metaphor	113
4.2	Metaphor and narrative structure	119
4.3	Narrative and policy domains	120
4.4	Metaphor families and strategy	121
4.5	Sustainability narrative formation	132
5.1	Sustainability leadership and metaphor	145
5.2	Leaders as experts	148
5.3	Sustainability leadership and money	152
5.4	Sustainability leadership and institutions	157
5.5	Sustainability leadership and morality	163
5.6	Sustainability leadership and innovation	168
6.1	Sustainability governance	182
6.2	Sustainability governance and leadership	190
6.3	Leadership roles as bundles of functions	191
6.4	Stories and leadership functions	208
7.1	Strategy as narrative and institution	216

7.2 Sustainability strategy	217
7.3 Sustainability leadership and strategy	226
7.4 Metaphors and governance strategy	227
7.5 Stories, leadership and tensions	229
7.6 Discursive dynamics and the evolution of thinking and organizing	230

Preface

Leaders might have been compared with chefs, or chefs with leaders, but it makes little sense to think of recipes for leadership. Nevertheless, that's what one typically finds in cookbooks about leadership and strategy. Technicality is often confused with quality, simplicity with clarity and false promises with practicality and ambition. The same observation can alas be made about sustainability, a subject even more complex and elusive, but prone to promises of engineering and accounting. We're just three steps and two units away from achieving sustainability.

In this intellectual landscape, we believe there is enough unoccupied territory to think differently about sustainability, leadership and sustainability leadership. Our approach is both deconstructive and constructive, in the sense that we offer an interpretive frame which can be of assistance in deconstructing harmful myths about sustainability leadership, but also in analyzing the context in which leaders might find them. As such, it can assist in the construction of sustainability strategy and the discovery of leadership styles which fit both the challenge and the situation.

Our book, therefore, does not fall into the "how to" category, yet it is eminently useful for both analysts and practitioners of sustainability and sustainability transitions. It provides a new understanding of sustainability leadership in context, which can open the door to adapting both leadership style and context. We firmly place leadership for sustainability in governance, the process and system of public and private actors which structure the taking of collectively binding decisions. Leadership is thus not reduced to that of elected officials, nor of captains of industry, civil society heroes or responsible managers of organizations. Community leadership is emphatically presented as distributed and located in governance. We focus on local and regional governance, as it is here that most work must take place, yet the insights provided can support good sustainability governance and strategy at all levels.

Stories are the fabric of our lives, as we understand ourselves and the world through them. Stories shape our understanding of communities, how they should be governed and how they relate to their environment. Governance, meanwhile, cannot divest itself from leadership, as leadership is what makes it work and enables it to deal with its own imperfections. Leadership for sustainability in this book is focused on two main tasks: creating the conditions for good sustainability governance and guiding the creation and implementation of sustainability strategy. As we can articulate at least a few key features of good governance to redefine the relations between community and environment, and as we understand the demands of collective strategy, we can recognize a set of leadership roles and functions that can fit the bill.

Such roles can be played by leadership networks and collectives, as well as by individuals. In distributed leadership, roles can shift within groups and for individuals as institution building and strategizing progress. Strategy for sustainability is both a narrative and a set of institutions, so the crafting of stories that both fit and transform other stories is at the core of sustainability leadership. True sustainability strategy will aim at transformation of governance, beyond a mere redirection of policy, and leadership will be needed on the ground to move the community through this process as well. Hence, where sustainability is an issue – and it is an issue everywhere – addressing it can touch many stories and bring many leadership roles into existence. If institution building, strategizing and transformation are all required, as they will often be, leadership must transform itself as well, and this could be a literal change of guard, a reshuffling of networks or people taking up new roles.

Metaphors help us coin leadership roles we recognize as relevant for particular phases or aspects of transition, institution building and strategizing. No role can exist by itself, and no individual fits only one role. As narratives structure and reduce complexity, metaphors are even more powerful, explaining new or complex things in terms of better-known areas of life, condensing stories into images, systems into figures and ideologies into objects. Some metaphoric leadership roles get all the attention and are commonly glamorized by media and the leadership industry, catering to the masses who hope to transcend the masses. Visionary leadership is supposed to herald new futures, yet we would take claims of any savior role with a metaphorical grain of salt. We encounter a host of figures who perform leadership functions before and behind the scenes: builders, storytellers, translators, brokers, Machiavellians, therapists and others.

Such leaders can understand themselves through metaphors, or not, yet they cannot escape the power of metaphor. The communities they intend to lead and the governance systems they hope to guide do grasp themselves and the world through narrative frames. Storytellers they must be, and this implies more than the recounting of narrative. Good storytellers are listeners, gatherers, assemblers, tinkerers and crafters of stories, and if we recognize that telling is performing, we can see that other skills enter the stage. An interpretive perspective on leadership and sustainability touches the core business of leading.

Understanding the spaces delineated for leadership by traditions of thinking and organizing means becoming sensitive to the ways stories coevolve, the manner they mobilize emotion and the interweaving of stories, sometimes as ideologies, into institutions. The power of governance systems to naturalize, to make what is socially constructed and contingent look and feel like necessary and natural, is a blessing and a curse for anyone aiming to rebalance community and environment. One must recognize that power as the product of a unique coupling of stories and institutions, where stories can be crafted and turned into rules, and other stories blow in from the environment and return with the stamp of authority.

If we can know our relation to our environment only through stories, if that relation is regulated through governance and if governance can make it harder to see we are dealing with stories, understanding the actual functioning of narrative is all the more important. What strikes us as utterly hopeful, however, is that people can still believe in stories even if they know they're stories. Moreover, the same powers of governance can be harnessed by responsible leadership to craft strategies that settle fear of disaster, unmask false promises and orient calmly to imperfect yet sustainable futures.

1 Basic Concepts
Leadership, Sustainability and Governance

In this chapter, we get acquainted with the concepts of leadership, sustainability and governance, concepts we will need to develop our perspective on sustainability leadership. Leadership to move communities in a more sustainable direction will have to go through governance, through the process of collective decision-making that can place communities on a different development path. What amounts to good leadership will depend on the community, its stories about good governance and about leadership itself.

Introduction: Thinking and Organizing

Leadership for sustainability will have to create effects in thinking and organizing, and the relations between those two activities will be at the core of our story. Dealing with Grand Challenges requires coordinated action, organization, and governance to articulate the appropriate policies, plans and laws. We will speak of institutions, as policies, plans and laws all function as coordination tools in society (Van Assche et al., 2013). They enable the making and implementation of collectively binding decisions and, after a while, the guided transformation of communities and societies. Addressing such sustainability challenges also requires the creation of new stories about the good community, a desirable relation with the environment and a belief in the collective capacity to organize for the long term (Czarniawska, 2002; Kornberger, 2022).

Our idea of sustainability leadership hinges on the power of stories to create understanding and to engender change. This entails that we need to pay close attention to the influence of stories on modes of organization and vice versa. Not all stories have the same effect, and not all systems of governance create or reinforce stories in the same manner (Czarniawska, 2014). Thinking and organizing shape each other but can never be reduced to each other. In communities, the relation goes through governance, where some stories acquire prominence, and others are discredited or rejected. The selection of stories at the table has an impact on the selection of forms of knowing that come to bear on collective decisions and their implementation (Latour, 2009). The organization of the governance system will determine how expert stories and others enter governance, while some stories have the potential to transform governance, to build or dismantle it.

Thinking and organizing belong to different domains of human activity, and despite their intricate interweaving, they cannot be translated into each other perfectly. This is true in a double sense. Real forms of organization, and, by extension, community, cannot live up to their ideal imagined form (Seidl, 2016). Critical observations and stories about the system might hold true or not, yet as soon as the critique sparks actual reorganization, that new mode of organizing cannot perfectly address the issues observed. Next, we are bound to notice that several translations are always available. No story of a desirable community, of a sustainable future or even of good governance can produce only one form of organization (Bevir & Rhodes, 2005). The same system of governance, even the same decision, always leaves space for different interpretations, for different and new stories to develop about them.

A governance system, or, at a smaller scale, one organization, will always show traces of several stories, ideas and forms of knowing that went into its formation (Luhmann, 2018). Those perspectives can be coherent or less so. Different stories might have contributed to the evolution of the system over time or were influential in different domains of governance, in different departments or arenas (Howlett & Rayner, 2007). In democratic systems of governance, new stories can come in more easily, and a diversity of stories can more easily contribute, yet other polities, seemingly dominated by one voice, still reveal diversity and discontinuity in the stories structuring governance.

What helps to deepen our understanding of the relation between thinking and organizing, between stories and institutions in governance, is that governance is both *a form and a process* (Colebatch, 2014). This is not surprising, as organizing is a process, while the form it takes at one point in time, the structure that enables the process and is the result of it, is an organization. A governance system is marked by a process of organizing and by a structure of actors and institutions, its organization. Each community will develop its own structure and process, even if many aspects are prescribed by higher-level governments

(Brans & Rossbach, 1997). The process is always harder to observe than the structure, yet might be on a path to change that structure.

A department of nature conservation within a ministry of environment can be an actor in governance, when it has a voice, and can speak with one voice. The voice does not have to coincide with a formal mandate. Sometimes, the ministry will be an actor in dealing with other ministries, courts, producing institutions that need to coordinate with others. Sometimes, individuals within the department can influence decision-making in and outside that organizational setting. In the name of the department, the term "conservation" rather clearly indicates that what is aimed at is a process, and as conditions change, the governance of conservation also needs to reveal itself as a process, a process which relies on structures such as the department.

Stories can play a role in governance and its transformation because of structure and process, and they can transform both. New stories, though, need to be understood by and resonate with the community and with the actors in governance before they can make a difference (Yanow, 2000). They need to connect with a fabric of existing stories and the values, assumptions and emotions associated with it. At the same time, they need to be amenable to translation into the categories of governance: Are there actors that can identify with them? Can they be reformulated so they produce something that looks like a recognizable policy goal or a problem (Peters, 2018)? Do we have institutions and policy tools available to pursue the goal that is supported by the story or the capacity to enact such tools?

Stories, to gain traction, thus need to fit the worlds of thinking and organizing. They need to perform the double act of fitting into a world of other stories, and a world of policies, plans and laws, of organizational structures and processes that provide only limited access to newcomers (Van Assche et al., 2024). What makes this performance slightly easier is that stories are also in demand by governance; they are helpful to actors who might not know how to connect to the community, how to solve internal disagreement or how to recognize relevant goals and problems (Miller, 2012). Governance systems thus select, use and craft stories that allow them to keep doing their work.

Stories about poverty in the third world gained traction in the decades after the Second World War, as decolonization was underway, as media landscapes became more globalized, and as international organizations such as the UN expanded their agenda and mandate. Poverty was not a new concept, yet the third world was one, and the ideological competition between capitalist and communist blocs sparked a competition to support "development," where poverty was the most obvious first roadblock. Thinking and organizing on poverty in the global south thus coevolved, and were affected by other stories, on the right form of political organization and the correct understanding of progress. (Ziai, 2007)

The process, however, is never perfect, and we will encounter many reasons for this imperfection. Relations between governance systems, their communities and the encompassing ecological and material environment are never stable for long (Luhmann, 1989). Something always happens. There is the issue of translation between thinking and organizing, already hinted at. Conflicts might arise, resources could be scarce and the hopes, fears and desires of the community might shift in such a way that an immediate response through governance is not possible. Chapters 2 and 4 will illuminate that some stories are harder to change than others, even when they are long past their due, and that the same holds for institutions and organizations.

Leadership

Why Leadership?

Perfect governance systems, therefore, do not exist. They must adapt continuously, and they ought to be the subject of ongoing conversations about their improvement (Folke et al., 2005). Structures and processes might be the result of long deliberations, might find support broadly in the community, and they might have functioned reasonably well for a rather long time, yet that does not mean they are immune to the imperfections observed everywhere (Mansfield, 1979). If there is no space for self-reflection in the system, no conversation on its value and adequacy, things will go awry. If a system is too well adapted to its environment and seems perfect in that sense, chances are that the capacity to adapt to change has been overly constrained (Plummer & Armitage, 2010) (Figure 1.1). Moreover, structures might be in place, but making them work is a different issue: Implementation is so much more than pushing a button. Structure does not naturally engender or support process, while the available structures or processes might not easily assert their own suitability for pursuing a particular policy goal.

Leadership

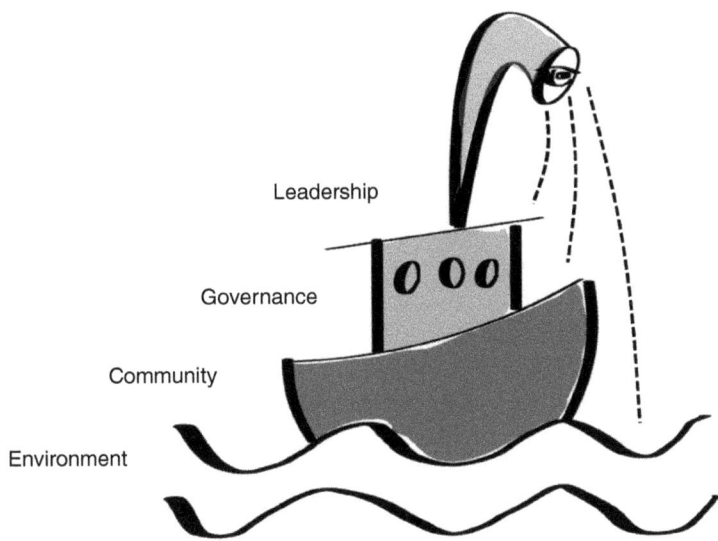

Figure 1.1 Sustainability leadership

Here, in our view, *leadership* comes in. Leadership is needed to make things work, and it is especially important when new problems barge in with new demands for governance. Even in communities where procedures, rules and regulations for seemingly everything exist, leadership is of the essence (Alvesson, 1996). This book starts from the observation that our planet is in deep trouble, that all communities are obliged to face sustainability challenges and it starts from the idea that our governance systems are not equipped to handle them. Stories about those challenges are not persuasive enough. In many parts of the world, people choose politicians and stories that evade or deny the issues.

Saying that we need strong leadership does not imply a reliance on old-fashioned strongmen. Rather, we understand leadership as *distributed*. By this we mean that it ought to be distributed over a group of people, in democracies, and we say that it always *is* distributed (Bolden, 2011). If we understand leadership as all the initiatives that go beyond procedures and routines, then leadership cannot be embodied by one person (Blaschke, 2015; Seidl et al., 2024). Even under a harsh dictatorship, commands from the Great Leader do not easily translate into chains of orders and actions that actually fulfill that command. Others need to understand what the leader might mean, how it could become reality, who should be mobilized, where resistance might be expected and how resources might be marshalled in unorthodox ways.

How leadership is distributed will differ per community and depend on what is possible and desirable there. Where direct participation in governance is deeply rooted, leadership tends to be distributed more widely and can shift more easily (Luhmann, 1990). Where expert-led administrations tend to wield power, political and economic actors can still be relevant, and their interplay might depend on the stability of the political scene (Fischer, 2000). The distributed character of leadership enables communities to manage complexity, develop administrative and political specialization and cultivate adaptive capacity. Distribution, however, does not always entail flexibility, as broad sharing does not always require flexible sharing. When new problems assert themselves, leadership might be able to navigate their imperfect governance systems and modify them perhaps, yet leadership itself is likely imperfect (Luhmann, 1997b). Hence, new forms of leadership might be called for.

Leadership can be distributed in many nonobvious ways, similar to the way obstacles to community development can be opaque for outsiders. Large landowners in a South American country can block any attempt at democratic reform and institution building and remain insensitive to critiques that they benefit from the colonial creation of large land holdings. The same class can hold the key to change, not only by managing their lands differently, but also by shifting stories in national politics and providing quiet support for larger land reform or withdrawing their backing of paramilitary groups destabilizing rural governance. (Fergusson et al., 2017)

Rather than trying to define one new form of leadership which is expected to perform better under new and trying circumstances, we argue it is more helpful to think of leadership *functions* which can be distributed in different ways. Communities might require a different or new combination of leadership functions at a given point, while some useful functions might not be available or might not be recognized as relevant.

Leadership Functions

Identifying a timeless set of leadership functions is a nonstarter, as the role of routines changes over time and place; hence, what goes beyond routines will vary. Yet, many leadership qualities and activities do recur. Leadership in governance tends to involve the *creative search for resources*, which can be money or anything. Even if nothing changes in governance, the resources needed for previously routinized operations might vanish or might become insufficient. When new initiatives materialize, chances are that they must draw on resources currently used elsewhere or simply not there. When administrative reform is a necessity to deal with new issues, this will take resources, and the resource distribution after the reform will differ from the old situation.

As we used the words "initiative" and "resources," we can immediately intimate that *taking initiative* and *reshuffling power relations* are priceless qualities for leaders (Flyvbjerg, 1998). Or, in our terms, they embody valuable leadership functions. Even when a community wholeheartedly desires a governance change, either a new policy direction or a change in procedure or structure, real obstacles might appear and vested interests might stand in the way. Even where a general direction might be agreed upon, a translation into policy initiatives might require, indeed, initiative. Mobilizing resources might mean that *re-relating inside and outside* is on the agenda, that leadership must establish new connections between governance and community and between different levels and systems of governance (Lichtenstein & Plowman, 2009).

Leadership, in the search for resources and support, might have to *re-relate formal and informal* institutions (Helmke & Levitsky, 2004). Indeed, if we understand formal institutions as policies, plans and laws, then we still need to acknowledge the existence of a world of informal coordination mechanisms. Sometimes, they can be parallel modes of coordination; elsewhere, they are better understood as traditions and habits embedding the formal institutions, enhancing their support and chances at implementation. Formal and informal institutions can respond to each other in myriad manners, and leaders ought to be aware of both formal and informal institutions, with an eye on managing their interplay. This means that leaders need to acquaint themselves with rules to break the rules, as well as rules to informally smoothen the application of other rules (Borins, 2000). They can benefit from knowledge of informal and formal tools enabling *quick action*, which is often necessary to keep long-term policies on track. Complementing strategy with tactics thus appears as another leadership function, while the *crafting of strategy* is a fundamental one that will prove key to sustainability governance (Carter et al., 2008).

Crafting strategy is a leadership function that assumes many qualities and activities, which could also be regarded as separate functions. For a strategy to work, there needs to be a *long-term perspective*, and leadership ought to consider it a task to either create long-term perspectives or create the spaces where they can emerge (Mintzberg, 1998). A persuasive perspective on the future will have to be a story, so finding, crafting and *telling stories* have their place in the toolbox of leadership (Throgmorton, 1996). One might object that many communities possess governance routines and entrenched habits of deliberating desirable and feared futures, but the point is that this is not true generally and uniformly. What leadership finds in terms of structure and process of governance, in terms of relations with community and environment, will vary greatly, so what is needed to make the system work will show the same variation.

Futures can become visible slowly in a community and its governance system. A Central European country might have a multi-tiered planning system in place, yet at a local level, this is felt as a series of restrictions on local action, and a legacy of a communist ideology that has lost its lustre. Local politicians with national connections, local administrators with academic backgrounds, in addition to some well-traveled entrepreneurs, grasp the benefits of coordinated action that can both preserve environmental and heritage assets and create a predictable and open business environment. As they all know each other, informal consultation comes easy, and an insight develops that plans and policies can actually support local agency, that interests can be compatible. (Elster et al., 1998)

In strategizing, and in the more daily activities of governance, leadership will need skills to identify *new policy tools* to pursue common goods or figure out how to use old tools in new ways (Grin et al., 2018). This requires a deep knowledge of system and environment, a knowledge which he or she might not possess, but could recognize in trusted allies and advisors. We arrive again at an advantage of distributed leadership, and, one can add, a difficulty in recognizing leadership, as formal leaders often live in the fiction that they are the only ones (Alvesson & Sveningsson, 2011). Administrative actors often fulfill leadership functions, without individuals or organizations ever willing to admit this, and the same can be said for corporate players, influential families, professional associations or civil society organizations playing an outsized role.

Strategy helps communities to *navigate risk and opportunity*, yet such navigation is part and parcel of other governance activities (Luhmann, 2017). Without leadership, many risks and opportunities might be missed, even when sophisticated procedures are in place to take care of navigation. It takes great interpretive skill to recognize problems and opportunities independently of current routines (Boin & Hart, 2003). New problems might rear their head, yet old problems might become slowly invisible for communities relying on procedural governance, and all too easily skip discussion or reflection. Risk and opportunity are assessed more adequately when both the governance system and its environments are sharply observed. In Chapters 6 and 7, we will argue that sustainability leadership is under considerable pressure in this function.

Environmental risk and economic opportunity cannot be balanced by mere calculation. What looks like an acceptable risk looks so in a story about opportunity and what appears as an amazing opportunity does so in a perspective of self and environment that supports an imagined future felt as desirable and realistic. A tourism future can take hold in a European region of coastal wetlands that hopes to emulate Palm Beach Florida, not calculating that climate, landscape, water quality, infrastructure, available space and investment potential all differ significantly. Leadership aware of this might temper the enthusiasm, maybe not for tourism, but for the American guiding example. This private reassessment of risk cannot sound publicly as a return to a self-image of low potential, and a new story is required, of a future maybe slightly less glamorous, but more reassuring, and with a greater local input and flavor.

Leadership functions become possible and desirable in a particular context, but all functions introduced above will prove useful for any community. If we say that leadership is always needed, because of the impossibility of perfect institutions, we do not suggest that leadership merely accepts such imperfection (Eggertsson, 2005). Working around routines, or finding ways to shake them up, modify them, have their place, but even distributed leadership cannot function on an ad hoc basis. Where new routines can be built, to deal with recurring problems, stable goals and provided of predictable resourcing and implementation tools, this ought to be favored (Howard-Grenville, 2005). Procedures engender blindness and rigidity, but they cannot be missed, as the alternatives of ad hoc governance and authoritarian centralization are decidedly riskier. Keeping an eye on the community and the diversity of voices and sentiments there helps to minimize blind spots, to prevent over-identification with the system of governance itself, its structures and processes (Kump & Scholz, 2022).

Leadership Roles

Leadership functions can be combined, or packaged, in various ways, and some packages can be aptly described as *roles*. Individuals can perform a function, but could also play a role, integrating different functions, a role that allows her to rise to the occasion. Roles can become fashionable or opportune, and fashions can change, so new combinations of leadership functions can become more prevalent (Alvesson, 2011). Changing roles can stem from new challenges, new practices or competition in academic and consultancy circles. Usually, a new leadership role crystallizes around several changes at the same time, with new ideas regarding leadership stemming from emerging practices, from academic reflection on figures that seem to perform well under new market and institutional conditions, sometimes individuals that seem to embody a future at the doorstep (Czarniawska, 1997, 2003).

Leadership roles can often be described in metaphoric terms, which, for now, we can understand as comparisons. A good leader can be presented as a captain or a gardener, as a commander under siege or in full attack mode. Each image of the leader is a role, and we have to understand that, in distributed leadership, several roles can coexist, while one person can shift roles depending on circumstances (Alvesson & Spicer, 2010). A role will favor or emphasize certain leadership functions and pay less attention to others. Attack modes favor tactics over strategy, while a gardener tends to embrace long-term perspectives, allowing continuous adaptation and an openness to initiative from elsewhere. We return to leadership metaphors in Chapter 3.

No role will fit all situations, and the current state of the world calls for new roles. This has been understood in much of the literature on leadership, on governance and sustainability (Chaffin et al., 2016). What is more problematic is that in swaths of that literature, this led to the uncritical embrace of a type of leadership that is supposed to solve all our problems. Speaking of transformative leadership and transformative governance, the assumption is that transformation is needed, hence leaders capable of catalyzing it. Which then leads to the creation of an ideal type of leader and the neglect of the diversity of starting points and challenges leaders must work with (Alvesson & Kärreman, 2016). Even where transformation of governance, towards a sustainability transition in society, is of the utmost importance, one cannot assume that an immediate focus on transformation will be productive. More fundamentally, the desire to move to rapid action embodied in the creation of such leadership concept, glosses over the fact that, even where reform is the focus, the skillset needed can differ radically from place to place.

What a sustainability transition would look like, and which leadership functions and roles would be helpful, cannot be formulated in the abstract. How much transformation would be involved, and how this would come about, cannot be coupled to one leadership role, to a fixed set of leadership functions, and attributes making them suitable to perform those functions. Thus, transformative leadership is not always good nor always possible, and what it means can vary so drastically that it cannot be delineated as a role. This is not surprising as the essence of the role is a generic goal of systems change, without too many indications with regards to leadership attributes or styles (Rosenhead et al., 2019).

A Central African town dominated by cement factories of colonial origin, controlled now by affiliates of the party in power nationally, is confronted with degradation of the local landscape, to the extent that much of the remaining limestone deposits are about to become unexploitable. Working conditions, moreover, are such that locals refuse to take up jobs in the factories, and management attracts workers from other regions and ethnicities. Nationally, leadership is aware of the risky dependence on one town for its ambitious infrastructure agenda. Forking paths appear: If sustainable development entails the construction of new infrastructure – and therefore increased cement production – should the response involve investment in the establishment of new cement factories across multiple regions? Or, alternatively, should the emphasis be placed on minimizing environmental harm and limiting further investment in cement, by directing national attention to the existing cement-producing region? This latter approach would involve reorganizing factory management and fostering new forms of collaboration with a strengthened local administration.

Other leadership roles burdened with high expectations ought to be scrutinized with the same stringency (Luhmann, 1997a). What could clarify the discussion might be a simple reminder that roles are

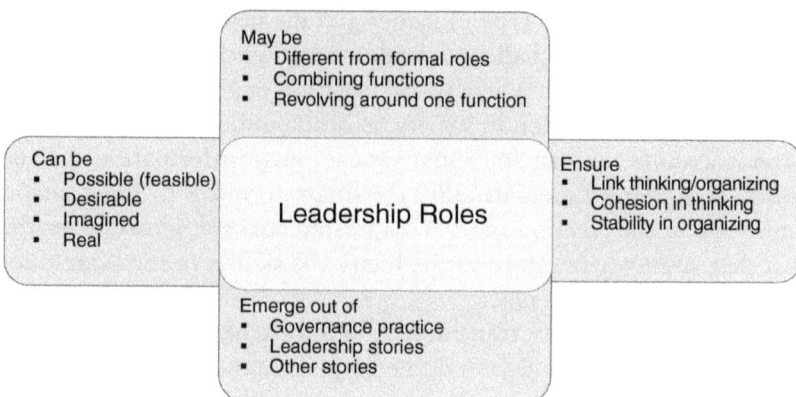

Figure 1.2 Leadership roles

constructions which emerge in a context and serve a purpose in that context. For sustainability leadership, that context is always triple: the governance system, the community and its ecological environment. Neither actors in governance nor community members have a perfect understanding of those nested systems, of the potential and limitations of governance to alter the relations between them. Problems that seem insurmountable can inspire calls for utopian or authoritarian leaders, and elsewhere to blind trust in participatory processes that replace insight in the real issues with overconfidence and over-identification with the community (Cooke & Kothari, 2001; Scott, 1998). Problems and opportunities, in other words, create problems and opportunities for governance, and for leadership. They bring out desires for leadership roles that may or may not measure up to the situation, and that may or may not find a place in the governance system (Figure 1.2).

Understanding governance, in other words, is of the essence, if we want to grasp what sustainability leadership could mean.

Governance

Governance is always there, in any community. Yet, the potential of governance to pursue collective goals, and to manage problems is not always used. If pursuing a more sustainable community has to be coordinated through governance, it makes sense to delineate the potential and limitations of governance systems themselves to effectuate change

Governance

(Van Assche et al., 2024). That change can be societal, it can pertain to the relation with the ecological environment and it can involve change in governance itself. Not all goals can be reached in the current organization of collective decision-making.

In fact, not every community, and not every environment is amenable to change to the same degree; each governance system has its own limits of steering. The modes of self-transformation available to a governance system are similarly constrained (Jessop, 1997). If we need more than trivial change or change that goes beyond the routines of self-transformation, we must invoke leadership again, in its different functions outlined above. Even with strong and creative leadership, limits will persist, and it is therefore of the utmost importance to locate those limits. Elections, public participation processes, policy assessments, procedures for policy coordination, opportunities for debate and deliberation are all valuable, and contribute to guided self-transformation, hence adaptation, of governance systems, but in many cases, they are not enough. In fact, they might reproduce an old blindness to problems, and they might easily introduce new blind spots (Foucault, 2007) (Figure 1.3). Transcending old limits of steering, where new problems would favor an expansion of the toolbox, does not necessarily occur, even where many adaptation mechanisms are in place. Why is this the case?

Figure 1.3 Blindness in governance perpetuated

Coevolution

Much can be ascribed to the *coevolutionary character* of governance systems.

First of all, we should understand governance configurations as subsystems of communities. They fulfill the task of coordinating collective action and regulating some individual behaviors. Both tasks involve collectively binding decisions, which can take the form of institutions: policies, plans and laws (Van Assche et al., 2013). Institutions regulate governance itself, while governance articulates new institutions, which need to fit the network of existing ones. Governance thus regulates itself, and it has the potential to shape communities (Hartley & Howlett, 2021). It can affect relations between the community and its ecological and material environment. Institutions guide the use of natural resources, the protection of natural areas, the building of infrastructures and so forth. We must distinguish therefore three coevolving systems: governance, community and the encompassing social-ecological system. One can speak of co-evolution, because one cannot understand the trajectories of the systems without reference to the others. They shape each other over time, although to different degrees and in different respects (Beunen et al., 2022). Wolves do not decide on villages the way the village council decides on pest control, yet village and wolves respond to each other, and a history of human interventions alters landscapes to such a degree that wolves find no place in them.

Second, actors and institutions co-evolve. We spoke of *configurations* because governance systems can be understood better when considering their unique combinations of actors and institutions, rather than by looking at each separately. This is the case for the rather obvious reason that actors and institutions are the product of the same evolutionary process, a process of emergence, where individuals and communities shape themselves and try to achieve things (North, 2006). For that, they develop forms of organization that delineate actors and institutions. Banks, bankers and banking tools appear at the same time; new banking tools enhance the position of bankers in communities, and at some point self-regulation within the profession gives way to governance, to rules governing the behavior of banks, the relations between bankers and the rest of society (Mahoney & Thelen, 2010).

Co-evolution does not require complete simultaneity. Things do not need to happen at exactly the same time. Rather, a change in one element of a co-evolving system is likely to trigger change elsewhere, and over time, the coupling between the elements can become tighter (Luhmann, 1995). New environmental regulations benefit certain sitting actors, can bring new actors to life, that is, within the orbit of governance, and they can reinforce the position of other policy tools or institutions, such as environmental plans. When this happens, it can reinforce the position of planning, and of planning experts in governance, either as consultants or in administration.

Third, knowledge and power co-evolve. We lean on Michel Foucault here, in emphasizing that knowledge is never neutral, certainly not knowledge that plays a role in governance. Governance embodies the promise of power, as aspirations, stories and ideas can generate decisions that bind the collective. Which means that they can shape the collective or even bring that collective into being (Foucault, 2012). As soon as an idea, a story, a perspective on reality enters governance, it changes color. It will be assessed by proponents and opponents on its possible influence on decision-making, which means its potential reshuffling of power relations in governance and community.

Knowledge, for Foucault and for us, is always produced in a frame that represents a particular ordering of the world, a particular set of power relations (Foucault, 2002). Any ordering of the world affects the production of knowledge in that frame, as well as the production of rules and regulations keeping that order in place. New understandings of the world have the potential to reshuffle power relations, as a shift in the construction of realities tends to bring about changes in what looks like a problem, an asset or a lofty aspiration. Expert knowledge cannot be isolated from these dynamics, as its presence in governance depends on the belief in its importance, which is in turn underpinned by a story about a reality where that particular expertise is important (Hillier, 2002).

Stories about problems, about the environment, about looming threats are not always welcome in governance or in the community. That is, they are accepted if they fit the fabric of existing stories and beliefs, which might be reinforced by expertise that is believed and believed to be relevant. Stories are given free entrance if it appears to actors that they represent something real and important for the community and could lead to decisions. If new policies are the result, the stories or derived expertise can achieve a prominent place in governance and community and might slowly take an appearance of neutrality (Miller & Fox, 2007).

In the former USSR, secret cities existed, inaccessible to foreigners and most Soviet citizens, not appearing on maps and in most policy documents. Those cities often accommodated industries deemed of national interest, industries that tended to come with a heavy environmental burden. Local actors have little influence on the future of such cities, except perhaps the management of the key industries, provided they had strong Moscow connections. In Moscow, few signals would be received from such communities, as they revolved around a few key players, interested in very few topics, and as Moscow elites expected to hear about those same things only. Environmental pollution, working conditions, rule of law would not make for stories registering in the capital, or finding a listening ear locally. (Rowland, 1996)

A story might look real enough for experts, but that holds no guarantee that it will have the same effect on the rest of us. Citizens might feel uncomfortable with the truths presented to them, actors in governance might feel their positions threatened, everybody might experience some difficulties in connecting the new problem or opportunity to the fabric of other stories that makes up their reality (Latour, 2009). The question of fit is not merely one of cognitive compatibility. People might see no logical reason to disagree yet still feel entirely unconvinced. The reasons can be manifold, but one important explanation is that what people want to be real, what they feel to be real and what they understand to be real are always blended (Zizek, 2019). For people, for organizations and communities, drawing hard distinctions between what they want, what they feel and what they believe amounts to a categorical impossibility. Neutral observation is not our forte, as humans, and in governance, where the specter of power is always present, where what we want might become reality, distinctions become blurred more easily (Van Assche & Gruezmacher, 2025).

Governance is never a level playing field for competing versions of reality, in other words, and altering the reality of governance systems will never entirely depend on new facts or additional expertise. The co-evolution of actors and institutions, of power and knowledge and of those two configurations ensures that new stories enter only selectively, that those stories are never just about new facts. It has the effect that some versions of reality and certain governance structures and processes keep each other in place. We speak of *rigidities* in governance evolution (Beunen et al., 2015).

Rigidities

Working towards sustainable communities must take notice of governance, as collectively binding decisions will be expected. Sustainability initiatives will likely necessitate a transformation of governance, based on new understandings of environmental problems (Berkes, 2017). We know by now that neither communities nor their governance systems are naturally amenable to self-transformation; merely presenting them with dramatic facts about a worsening environment tends to be insufficient. New stories are needed, and new forms of leadership, as the routines established over time will require fixing, and as stories hold greater potential to relate affect, desire and ideas in a way that can mobilize the community (Tewdwr-Jones, 2011).

For leadership, the understanding of rigidities in governance comes at a premium. Where leaders craft new stories, or when they focus on finding new policy tools to make a still cherished story reality, they need to be thoroughly familiarized with governance constraints. In evolutionary governance theory (EGT), we speak of *dependencies* and note that each governance path is marked by a unique combination of rigidity and flexibility (Van Assche et al., 2013). Rigidity is not to be vilified, as the dependencies also embody deeply held values, policy orientations, and as they perform the task of stabilizing governance and community. Simultaneously, what stabilizes limits adaptation, and delimits adaptive capacity, which is always the capacity to adapt to a circumscribed range of events.

Later in this chapter, we will introduce the idea of dependencies and throughout the book point out that leadership also consists in the observation and management of dependencies (Van Assche et al., 2021). What can be changed at what cost rarely transpires transparently from the formal description of the governance system (Easterly, 2006). Even long-time insiders retain blind spots in their observation of governance, and easily overestimate rigidities, taking too lightly the possibilities for disruption, the need for adaptation or, alternatively, overlooking the corrosion of trusted adaptation tools (Flyvbjerg, 2005). Leadership can assert itself in reassessing, in public or in private, what can be expected of the current system, and how it might be adjusted.

Governance systems have capacities to observe themselves and their environment, and they are able to articulate versions of past and future to orient their present operations. Not all systems realize this potential, and whether it happens or not is a matter of empirical observation (Voß & Kemp, 2006). In other words, one cannot take governance at its word. The self-description destined for outsiders and the self-understanding of governance systems are limited by the stories available to them, the values embraced, the positions defended (Czarniawska, 2002). If communities are serious about sustainability, the quality of observation and self-observation in governance takes on additional relevance.

A state government in the US might be inclined to fight inequality in new ways, and to stretch ideas of good governance and rule of law by considering affordable housing and health care as basic rights. It finds out quickly that inherited stories of individual freedoms and responsibilities, a court system based on common law, privileging jurisprudence and a federal government steeped in a diverging ideology constitute formidable obstacles for the envisioned reforms. Leadership then must carefully pick its battles, as it also relies on federal government through a variety of programs, and as some legal rigidities are easier to reinterpret than others. (Platt, 1996)

Without an image of the future, of futures feared and desired, long-term policies and strategies are not in the cards, while some problems and goals will warrant coordination over the long term. Without an understanding of the past, learning from that past, from the origins of problems, and the difficulties to strategize earlier, will be tenuous (Van Assche et al., 2023; Van Assche & Gruezmacher, 2025). And without observation and self-observation, any pursuit of common goods will be blind (Alvesson et al., 2016). Leadership might focus on fixing some of these issues, if they represent structural obstacles to sustainability strategy, rather than on crafting workarounds, finding resources or other leadership functions. We will speak of leaders as builders and storytellers.

Sustainability

The absence or presence of versions of the future in governance systems and the quality of observation make a difference for the range of options available to governance and its leadership (Adger & Jordan, 2009). Which self-understanding is in place, which lessons are drawn from history and which futures are deemed desirable and susceptible to steering are relevant for the assessment of policy options and reform risk (Bennett & Howlett, 1992). These questions become even more pertinent in considering the rigidities that might support or jeopardize sustainability policy. If systems operate on the basis of problematic understandings of self and environment, or lack interest in collective futures, this severely hampers the space to maneuver. Observing such situation does offer pointers for what might need repair before anyone can embark on a sustainability journey.

Yet, what is sustainability? The question cannot be dismissed merely because it supposedly has been answered so often. We know that sustainability thinking emerged in the 1970s, that it was popularized under the auspices of the Club of Rome, who called the attention of the world to the limits of growth ideologies, both capitalist and communist. Swedish Prime Minister Gro Brundtland chaired the writing of a report for the United Nations. Under the title *Our Common Future*, the report sparked a flurry of policy formulation towards sustainability, and it recognized the importance of economic and social sustainability, besides the environmental concerns that were the impetus of the writing (Seefried, 2015).

Meanwhile, a group of Canadian and European ecologists had coined the concept of *resilience*, as the capacity of ecosystems to bounce back after shocks and explored its relevance beyond the discipline. Hence, the concept of social-ecological systems, and the idea that communities and ecologies could damage each other beyond repair but also find a relation whereby shocks could more easily be tolerated. Whereas much of the early sustainability rhetoric still aimed for sustainable *development*, resilience thinking is less clearly positioned in the corner of softened capitalism (Brown, 2012). Robust systems and damage control take center stage and the influential Stockholm Resilience Centre, representing a core group of resilience researchers, has worked with great zeal towards governance systems engendering more resilient system states (Steffen et al., 2015).

In 2015, the United Nations adopted a list of seventeen sustainable development goals (SDGs) which could further the coordination within and between countries. The SDGs show an expanded understanding of sustainability compared to the Brundtland report and reveal the influence of resilience thinking. In this book, we will refer often to the SDGs, in the main narrative and especially in examples and vignettes, as they frame much of the current sustainability thinking, not only in international politics but also at the level of organizations, where universities now target sustainability rankings, to name one thing.

Sustainable development goals and their definition:

1. No Poverty: End poverty in all its forms everywhere.
2. Zero Hunger: End hunger, achieve food security and improved nutrition and promote sustainable agriculture.
3. Good Health and Well-being: Ensure healthy lives and promote well-being for all at all ages.
4. Quality Education: Ensure inclusive and equitable quality education and promote lifelong learning opportunities for all.
5. Gender Equality: Achieve gender equality and empower all women and girls.
6. Clean Water and Sanitation: Ensure availability and sustainable management of water and sanitation for all.
7. Affordable and Clean Energy: Ensure access to affordable, reliable, sustainable and modern energy for all.
8. Decent Work and Economic Growth: Promote sustained, inclusive and sustainable economic growth, full and productive employment and decent work for all.
9. Industry, Innovation and Infrastructure: Build resilient infrastructure, promote inclusive and sustainable industrialization and foster innovation.
10. Reduced Inequalities: Reduce inequality within and among countries.
11. Sustainable Cities and Communities: Make cities and human settlements inclusive, safe, resilient and sustainable.
12. Responsible Consumption and Production: Ensure sustainable consumption and production patterns.
13. Climate Action: Take urgent action to combat climate change and its impacts.
14. Life Below Water: Conserve and sustainably use the oceans, seas and marine resources for sustainable development.
15. Life on Land: Protect, restore and promote sustainable use of terrestrial ecosystems, sustainably manage forests, combat desertification and halt and reverse land degradation and halt biodiversity loss.
16. Peace, Justice and Strong Institutions: Promote peaceful and inclusive societies for sustainable development, provide access to justice for all and build effective, accountable and inclusive institutions at all levels.

17. Partnerships for the Goals: Strengthen the means of implementation and revitalize the global partnership for sustainable development.

While a fair share of the academic literature on sustainability and resilience aims to capture more sustainable system states in quantitative terms, our perspective underlines the importance to understand sustainability as a spectrum of possible system relations, a spectrum moreover which will differ between social-ecological systems (Scoones et al., 2007). The problems facing communities diverge, and the answers available to them, partly in terms of governance responses, are similarly varied.

Besides the diversity of possible system relations we could call sustainable, and besides the unique path and goal a community must define for itself, we must recognize another issue. What sustainability could mean for a community and which specific sustainability path to choose cannot be ascertained directly. Creative interpretation is involved, stories are needed to pin down an actionable meaning. In fact, images, analogies and stories were part and parcel of sustainability discourse from its inception. Even if early advocates of sustainability and resilience policy were not entirely aware of it, they too needed narrative support to stabilize their new and cherished concepts. They found that support in images of stability and shock absorbance, in narratives of harmonious relations between humans and nature, while later authors branched off into new narrative realms, finding new images to further articulate what sustainability might mean in diverse fields of application (Larson, 2011).

An East African nation plagued by civil war for decades and coming out of a history of incomplete governance reforms, is looked upon in the western world as primarily suffering from hunger. Support, some of it under the banner of sustainability, hopes to prevent future famine. National elites, meanwhile, frame the situation differently, attributing hunger to conflict and machinations by competing factions. In rural areas, not all affected by the conflict, the major obstacle to sustainability manifests itself as the fragmented and incoherent governance that resulted from wave after wave of reform. Sustainability itself thus appears sometimes as a positive goal yet elsewhere emerges as a product of problems. A problem starts to look as an obstacle to something, to a sustainable state that only then becomes defined. (Kemmerling et al., 2022)

In Chapters 2 and 3, we unpack the nature of narrative and metaphor, which helps to understand why they prove so useful in grasping what eludes our grasp, to structure ideas and ideals, fears and other feelings about our relationship with the natural environment. After which, in Chapter 4, we can productively return to the theme of sustainability, how it has been steeped in stories and our effort to interpret the interpretive base of sustainability will enable us to delineate more sharply what sustainability leadership could mean. Because the landscape of literature on sustainability and leadership has been cluttered with mythologies, we devote Chapter 5 to the deconstruction of these myths, as they are unhelpful at best and obstruct the view on both sustainability and sustainability leadership.

Chapter 6, then, presents our perspective on sustainability leadership, marking the centrality of sustainability strategy, and the leadership and governance capacities that need to be in place to render strategy and its implementation realistic. We identify several leadership roles that might prove key to efforts at sustainability strategy and its enabling governance transformation. Recognizing the diverse forms of and paths towards sustainability, the associated variety of governance configurations, we nevertheless distill characteristics of good governance that are especially partial to the pursuit of sustainability goals and derive beneficial leadership roles and functions from these requirements of good sustainability governance.

In our discussion of sustainability governance, we first impress on the reader the importance of long-term perspectives in governance, and the systematic coupling with understandings of the past (Hajer & Oomen, 2025). If little interest in the future, in collective goods that can be pursued over the longer term, can be traced, or if governance unduly constrains itself in their pursuit, any leadership interested in sustainability must step in. Where the past remains blurry, or captured in self-aggrandizing or victimizing mythologies, the construction of sustainable futures remains highly unlikely (Asad & Sadler-Smith, 2020).

Second, we stress the centrality of observation and self-observation, the diversity of observations available to governance. Especially relevant is the observation of always shifting systems relations, between governance, community and environment. The mutual effects of the social and ecological environment on each other, and the implications for system stability and the further evolution of the relations, deserve close attention (Luhmann, 1989). Observation without self-observation leads to dead ends, as both the reasons for and effects of observations within the system cannot be assessed without a cultivation of reflexivity.

Third, we reiterate our belief in strategy, so the capacity of governance systems to articulate strategy deserves our interest. Leadership can greatly contribute to the formation and implementation of strategy, through the crafting and telling of stories, the integration of policies and, fundamentally, the strengthening of community. If people do not feel there is a community worth defending, arguments assuming common interests become significantly less persuasive (Leopold, 1970). If the common interest is reduced to the prevention of the same sort of harm to all individuals, sustainability strategy will shrink and shrivel to the point of irrelevance.

For sustainability strategy to emerge, governance will have to do more than cultivating observation and self-observation, and the image of good governance, as in enabling sustainability transition, will be detailed in subsequent chapters. We will make a broad-stroke distinction between situations where most features of good sustainability governance are in place, and others where even basic requirements are not met. What leaders should do, which functions and roles would be helpful under such different conditions, is bound to diverge, yet the answer in concrete cases is complicated by the fact that the most effective leadership roles in terms of problem-solving might not be the ones desired by the community or supported by the governance system.

Our final chapter, Chapter 7, further elaborates the idea of sustainability strategy, the difficulties for leadership in navigating dilemmas posed by any sustainability transition, and the value of interpretive perspectives on sustainability leadership. If we can elucidate the narrative construction of sustainability and leadership and locate effective and legitimate sustainability leadership within governance configurations that always shape themselves through stories and institutional structures, then the importance of narrative will appear inescapable. Recognizing and crafting narrative, performing stories and discreetly assessing other performances transcend "soft skills"; they are at the core of sustainability leadership.

Sustainability can only be comprehended productively as emerging from a tangle of stories, stories about ourselves, the real community and the real world, stories about past and future, about threats and opportunities appearing in the relation with our environment (Descola & Palsson, 2003). Sustainability issues can only be addressed when a second set of stories is considered, stories about good and acceptable leadership and about the governance structures and processes we prefer to solve problems and grasp opportunities. If our understanding of governance is self-limiting to the extent that common goods, shared futures and broader system relations are excluded from the picture, our futures are bleak indeed. If, on the other hand, we accept a collective future, and leadership mobilizing governance systems measuring up to the Grand Challenges of our day, optimism cannot be written off as fantasy (Pestoff, 2014). Stories and metaphors structure what is and what could be, for leaders and for everyone else. Before we get carried away too much, let us take a closer look at what narratives can achieve.

References

Adger, W. N., & Jordan, A. (Eds.). (2009). *Governing Sustainability*. Cambridge University Press.

Alvesson, M. (1996). Leadership studies: From procedure and abstraction to reflexivity and situation. *The Leadership Quarterly*, 7(4), 455–485.

Alvesson, M. (2011). Leadership and organizational culture. In Bryman, A., Collinson, D., Grint, K., Jackson, B., & Uhl-Bien, M. (Eds.). *The SAGE Handbook of Leadership* (pp. 151–164). SAGE Publications.

Alvesson, M., & Kärreman, D. (2016). Intellectual failure and ideological success in organization studies: The case of transformational leadership. *Journal of Management Inquiry*, 25(2), 139–152.

Alvesson, M., & Spicer, A. (2010). *Metaphors We Lead By: Understanding Leadership in the Real World*. Routledge.

Alvesson, M., & Sveningsson, S. (2011). Management is the solution: Now what was the problem? On the fragile basis for managerialism. *Scandinavian Journal of Management*, 27(4), 349–361.

Alvesson, M., Sveningsson, S., & Blom, M. (2016). *Reflexive Leadership: Organising in an Imperfect World*. SAGE Publications.

Asad, S., & Sadler-Smith, E. (2020). Differentiating leader hubris and narcissism on the basis of power. *Leadership*, 16(1), 39–61.

Bennett, C. J., & Howlett, M. (1992). The lessons of learning: Reconciling theories of policy learning and policy change. *Policy Sciences*, 25(3), 275–294.

Berkes, F. (2017). Environmental governance for the anthropocene? Social-ecological systems, resilience, and collaborative learning. *Sustainability*, 9(7), Article 7.

Beunen, R., Van Assche, K., & Duineveld, M. (2015). *Evolutionary Governance Theory: Theory and Applications*. Springer.

Beunen, R., Van Assche, K., & Gruezmacher, M. (2022). Evolutionary perspectives on environmental governance: Strategy and the co-construction of governance, community and environment. *Sustainability*, *14*(16). 9912. https://doi.org/10.3390/su14169912

Bevir, M., & Rhodes, R. A. W. (2005). Interpretation and its others. *Australian Journal of Political Science*, *40*(2), 169–187.

Blaschke, S. (2015). It's all in the network: A Luhmannian perspective on agency. *Management Communication Quarterly*, *29*(3), 463–468.

Boin, A., & Hart, P. 't. (2003). Public leadership in times of crisis: Mission impossible? *Public Administration Review*, *63*(5), 544–553.

Bolden, R. (2011). Distributed leadership in organizations: A review of theory and research. *International Journal of Management Reviews*, *13*(3), 251–269.

Borins, S. (2000). Loose Cannons and rule breakers, or enterprising leaders? Some evidence about innovative public managers. *Public Administration Review*, *60*(6), 498–507.

Brans, M., & Rossbach, S. (1997). The autopoiesis of administrative systems: Niklas Luhmann on public administration and public policy. *Public Administration*, *75*(3), 417–439.

Brown, K. (2012). Policy discourses of resilience. In M. Pelling, D. Manuel-Navarrete, & M. Redclift (Eds.). *Climate Change and the Crisis of Capitalism*. Routledge.

Carter, C., Clegg, S. R., & Kornberger, M. (2008). *A Very Short, Fairly Interesting and Reasonably Cheap Book About Studying Strategy*. SAGE Publications.

Chaffin, B. C., Garmestani, A. S., Gunderson, L. H., Benson, M. H., Angeler, D. G., Arnold, C. A. (Tony), Cosens, B., Craig, R. K., Ruhl, J. B., & Allen, C. R. (2016). Transformative environmental governance. *Annual Review of Environment and Resources*, *41*, 399–423.

Colebatch, H. K. (2014). Making sense of governance. *Policy and Society*, *33*(4), 307–316.

Cooke, B., & Kothari, U. (2001). *Participation: The New Tyranny?* Zed books.

Czarniawska, B. (1997). *A Narrative Approach to Organization Studies*. SAGE Publications.

Czarniawska, B. (2002). *A Tale of Three Cities, or the Glocalization of City Management*. Oxford University Press.

Czarniawska, B. (2003). Forbidden knowledge: Organization theory in times of transition. *Management Learning*, *34*(3), 353–365.

Czarniawska, B. (2014). *A Theory of Organizing*. Edward Elgar Publishing.

Descola, P., & Palsson, G. (2003). *Nature and Society: Anthropological Perspectives*. Routledge.

Easterly, W. (2006). *The White Man's Burden: Why the West's Efforts to Aid the Rest Have Done So Much Ill and So Little Good*. Penguin Books.
Eggertsson, T. (2005). *Imperfect Institutions: Possibilities and Limits of Reform*. University of Michigan Press.
Elster, J., Offe, C., & Ulrich, K. P. (1998). *Institutional Design in Post-communist Societies: Rebuilding the Ship at Sea*. Cambridge University Press.
Fergusson, L., Molina, C., Robinson, J., & Vargas, J. F. (2017). *The Long Shadow of the Past: Political Economy of Regional Inequality in Colombia* (SSRN Scholarly Paper 2932228).
Fischer, F. (2000). *Citizens, Experts, and the Environment: The Politics of Local Knowledge*. Duke University Press.
Flyvbjerg, B. (1998). *Rationality and Power: Democracy in Practice*. University of Chicago Press.
Flyvbjerg, B. (2005). Machiavellian megaprojects. *Antipode*, 37(1), 18–22.
Folke, C., Hahn, T., Olsson, P., & Norberg, J. (2005). Adaptive governance of social-ecological systems. *Annual Review of Environment and Resources*, 30, 441–473.
Foucault, M. (2002). *The Order of Things: An Archaeology of the Human Sciences*. Psychology Press.
Foucault, M. (2007). *Security, Territory, Population: Lectures at the College De France, 1977–78*. Palgrave Macmillan UK.
Foucault, M. (2012). *Discipline and Punish: The Birth of the Prison*. Knopf Doubleday Publishing Group.
Grin, J., Hassink, J., Karadzic, V., & Moors, E. H. M. (2018). Transformative leadership and contextual change. *Sustainability*, 10(7), Article 7.
Hajer, M. A., & Oomen, J. (2025). *Captured Futures: Rethinking the Drama of Environmental Politics*. Oxford University Press.
Hartley, K., & Howlett, M. (2021). Policy assemblages and policy resilience: Lessons for non-design from evolutionary governance theory. *Politics and Governance*, 9(2), 451–459.
Helmke, G., & Levitsky, S. (2004). Informal institutions and comparative politics: A research agenda. *Perspectives on Politics*, 2(4), 725–740.
Hillier, J. (2002). *Shadows of Power: An Allegory of Prudence in Land-use Planning*. Routledge.
Howard-Grenville, J. A. (2005). The persistence of flexible organizational routines: The role of agency and organizational context. *Organization Science*, 16(6), 618–636.
Howlett, M., & Rayner, J. (2007). Design principles for policy mixes: Cohesion and coherence in "New Governance Arrangements." *Policy and Society*, 26(4), 1–18.

Jessop, B. (1997). The governance of complexity and the complexity of governance: Preliminary remarks on some problems and limits of economic guidance. In A. Amin & Hausner (Eds.), *Beyond Market and Hierarchy* (pp. 95–128). Edward Elgar Publishing.

Kemmerling, B., Schetter, C., & Wirkus, L. (2022). The logics of war and food (in)security. *Global Food Security*, 33, 100634.

Kornberger, M. (2022). *Strategies for Distributed and Collective Action Connecting the Dots*. Oxford University Press USA – OSO.

Kump, B., & Scholz, M. (2022). Organizational routines as a source of ethical blindness. *Organization Theory*, 3(1), 86–105.

Larson, B. (2011). *Metaphors for Environmental Sustainability: Redefining Our Relationship with Nature*. Yale University Press.

Latour, B. (2009). *Politics of Nature*. Harvard University Press.

Leopold, A. (1970). *A Sand County almanac: With Other Essays on Conservation from Round River*. The Random House Publishing Group.

Lichtenstein, B. B., & Plowman, D. A. (2009). The leadership of emergence: A complex systems leadership theory of emergence at successive organizational levels. *The Leadership Quarterly*, 20(4), 617–630.

Luhmann, N. (1989). *Ecological Communication*. University of Chicago Press.

Luhmann, N. (1990). *Political Theory in the Welfare State*. De Gruyter.

Luhmann, N. (1995). *Social Systems*. Stanford University Press.

Luhmann, N. (1997a). Limits of steering. *Theory, Culture & Society*, 14(1), 41–57.

Luhmann, N. (1997b). The control of intransparency. *Systems Research and Behavioral Science*, 14(6), 359–371.

Luhmann, N. (2017). *Risk: A Sociological Theory*. Routledge.

Luhmann, N. (2018). *Organization and Decision*. Cambridge University Press.

Mahoney, J., & Thelen, K. (2010). A theory of gradual institutional change. In *Explaining Institutional Change: Ambiguity, Agency, and Power* (Vol. 1). Cambridge University Press.

Mansfield, H. (1979). *Machiavelli's New Modes and Orders*. Cornell University Press.

Miller, H. T. (2012). *Governing Narratives: Symbolic Politics and Policy Change*. University of Alabama Press.

Miller, H. T., & Fox, C. J. (2007). *Postmodern Public Administration*. ME Sharpe.

Mintzberg, H. (1998). Covert leadership: Notes on managing professionals. *Harvard Business Review*, 76, 140–148.

North, D. (2006). *Understanding the Process of Economic Change*. Routledge.

Pestoff, V. (2014). Collective action and the sustainability of co-production. *Public Management Review, 16*(3), 383–401.

Peters, B. G. (2018). *Policy Problems and Policy Design*. Edward Elgar Publishing.

Platt, R. H. (1996). *Land Use and Society: Geography, Law, and Public Policy*. Island Press.

Plummer, R., & Armitage, D. (2010). Integrating perspectives on adaptive capacity and environmental governance. In D. Armitage, & R. Plummer (Eds.). *Adaptive Capacity and Environmental Governance* (pp. 1–19). Springer.

Rosenhead, J., Franco, L. A., Grint, K., & Friedland, B. (2019). Complexity theory and leadership practice: A review, a critique, and some recommendations. *The Leadership Quarterly, 30*(5), 101304.

Rowland, R. H. (1996). Russia's secret cities. *Post-Soviet Geography and Economics, 37*(7), 426–462.

Scoones, I., Leach, M., Smith, A., Stagl, S., Stirling, A., & Thompson, J. (2007). *Dynamic Systems and the Challenge of Sustainability* [Report]. The Institute of Development Studies and Partner Organisations.

Scott, J. C. (1998). *Seeing Like a State: How Certain Schemes to Improve the Human Condition Have Failed*. Yale University Press.

Seefried, E. (2015). Rethinking progress: On the origin of the modern sustainability discourse, 1970–2000. *Journal of Modern European History, 13*(3), 377–400.

Seidl, D. (2016). *Organisational Identity and Self-transformation: An Autopoietic Perspective*. Routledge.

Seidl, D., Ma, S., & Splitter, V. (2024). What makes activities strategic: Toward a new framework for strategy-as-practice research. *Strategic Management Journal, 45*(12), 2395–2419.

Steffen, W., Richardson, K., Rockström, J., Cornell, S. E., Fetzer, I., Bennett, E. M., Biggs, R., Carpenter, S. R., de Vries, W., de Wit, C. A., Folke, C., Gerten, D., Heinke, J., Mace, G. M., Persson, L. M., Ramanathan, V., Reyers, B., & Sörlin, S. (2015). Planetary boundaries: Guiding human development on a changing planet. *Science, 347*(6223), 1259855.

Tewdwr-Jones, M. (2011). *Urban Reflections: Narratives of Place, Planning and Change*. Policy Press.

Throgmorton, J. A. (1996). *Planning as Persuasive Storytelling: The Rhetorical Construction of Chicago's Electric Future*. University of Chicago Press.

Van Assche, K., Beunen, R., & Duineveld, M. (2013). *Evolutionary Governance Theory: An Introduction*. Springer.

Van Assche, K., Beunen, R., & Gruezmacher, M. (2024). *Strategy for Sustainability Transitions: Governance, Community and Environment*. Edward Elgar Publishing.

Van Assche, K., Duineveld, M., Gruezmacher, M., & Beunen, R. (2021). Steering as path creation: Leadership and the art of managing dependencies and reality effects. *Politics and Governance*, *9*(2), 369–380. https://doi.org/10.17645/pag.v9i2.4027

Van Assche, K., & Gruezmacher, M. (2025). *Psychoanalysis and Governance: Discourse and Decisions, Identities and Futures*. Taylor & Francis.

Van Assche, K., Gruezmacher, M., Marais, L., & Perez-Sindin, X. (2023). *Resource Communities: Past Legacies and Future Pathways*. Taylor & Francis.

Voß, J.-P., & Kemp, R. (2006). Sustainability and reflexive government: Introduction. In J.-P. Voss, D. Bauknecht, & R. Kemp (Eds.) *Reflexive Governance for Sustainable Development* (pp. 3–28). Edward Elgar Publishing.

Yanow, D. (2000). *Conducting Interpretive Policy Analysis* (Vol. 47). SAGE Publications.

Ziai, A. (2007). *Exploring Post-Development: Theory and Practice, Problems and Perspectives*. Routledge.

Zizek, S. (2019). *The Sublime Object of Ideology*. Verso Books.

2 | Narratives and Interpretation

In this chapter, we delve deeper into the realm of stories, or narratives. This endeavor is particularly worthwhile if we acknowledge that our knowledge of the world is largely shaped by narratives. We discuss several functions of narratives that are relevant to our study of sustainability leadership, in and through governance. Narratives create meaning, they define problems, solutions and methods, and they connect values, feelings and ideas. Even more fundamentally, narratives create community, which involves patterns of openness and closure, of inclusion and exclusion. We develop a succinct theory of interpretation to extend our understanding of stories and their roles in governance and community, with special emphasis on the concepts of genre, audience and medium, the structuring of time through stories and the position of stories that select other stories and keep them in place: master narratives.

Introduction: A Brief History of Interpretive Theory

People know themselves and the world through narrative. They construct the past and the future in narrative form (Antze & Lambek, 2016). Organizations orient themselves towards their environment based on identity narratives, and governance systems constitute themselves based on stories about legitimate distributions of power, of good governance and the real community (Czarniawska, 2002). What we want to see as important enough in our communities and governance that it ought to be maintained can be seen as such because of stories, stories about the real community, its core values, quality of life and environment (Sandercock, 1998).

The idea that we understand ourselves through stories is the starting point of narrative theory, of interpretive approaches to policy and society. An early form of narrative theory can be found in Vladimir Propp's seminal work *Morphology of the Folktale* (2015), originally published in 1928, where a grammar of the folk tale is reconstructed based on a broad selection of Russian fairy tales. For Propp, what he found applied to more than his Russian stories. He believed he discovered a set of rules governing other cultural expressions, rules for structuring compelling stories, populated with recognizable heroes and villains, episodes and climaxes and even sidekicks. In the anthropology of the post-war decades, Claude Levi-Strauss applied this form of analysis to any cultural product and expression, to cultures as a whole (Leach, 1989). He recognized recurring structures and elements in mythologies around the world and shared with Propp a conviction that he had found a logic of culture, expressed in a long list of books, among them, notably *Structural Anthropology* (1968).

In the 1950s *semiotics*, or the general theory of interpretation, emerged, a movement across disciplines which aimed to establish rules of interpretation and guide the exploration of meaning in different communicative contexts. Semiotics sought to better understand how culture operates through its various forms of expression and sign systems, while also delineating the limits of interpretation. (Deely, 2003). Where stories veiled less comfortable truths, where they made no sense anymore, they became of great interest to interpretive critics and theorists. An iconic example was Roland Barthes, a French intellectual interested in virtually anything he could grasp through the lens of his early semiotics – which was a lot (Berger, 2014). Influential work appeared from the 1950s to the 1970s, but his best-known book remains the *Mythologies* (1957), where he paid attention to wrestling matches, steak and fries, travel magazines and laundry detergents to unveil mythologies of capitalist bourgeois society, stories largely unnoticed, nevertheless fulfilling a crucial function: keeping hierarchies and power relations in place (Chandler, 2001).

The Italian semiotician and novelist Umberto Eco, who passed away in 2016, contributed greatly to the development of semiotics, drawing on ideas from different disciplines and enhancing our understanding of processes of interpretation in different sign systems and different contexts. Language might be the most developed sign system we have access to, yet Eco, and the semiotic tradition more broadly, would recognize music, architecture, but also cooking, gestures and painting as sign systems, marked by their own principles of production and interpretation (Eco, 1976). Sign systems can interact and complement each other, as when a person wearing something unfashionable enters a high-concept building and starts to sing something incomprehensible. Roland Barthes analyzed fashion as a sign system, in his 1967 work *Systeme de la mode* (Barthes et al., 1990), building on earlier work by the Prague school of cultural semiotics in the 1930s (Winner, 1979). Both came to the conclusion that sign systems such as fashion are shaped by a double evolutionary logic: New expressions refer to existing ones, using current rules of signification, and slowly transforming them, while they also orient themselves toward contexts external to the sign system. This can be specifically another sign system (fashion referring to art) and it can be a broader reference to changes in society.

The semiotics of Umberto Eco helps to guide us through the broader landscape of interpretive theory in this chapter. One point taken from Eco we underline here is that the idea of signs making up our reality, and the idea of stories as primary tools to structure signs and signification do not deny the existence of an external reality. Rather, our understanding of reality is mediated through signs, and more often than not, through stories that confer meaning on those signs and guide their selection. (Eco, 2000). As soon as we say something, we use signs; as soon as we think about something, we are in the realm of signs and interpretation. Thinking transcends words, and images, feelings and desires, conscious and unconscious, mix and mingle with logical operations, yet, whatever the entangling at a given moment, if we try to make sense of our feelings and ideas, we cannot circumvent the world of signs. We interpret everything, including ourselves (Hook, 2003).

Some stories are more persuasive than others, some are plainly wrong. We can distinguish four main reasons why an interpretation is wrong: *first* is overinterpretation, meaning that it goes beyond what the signs, given current rules of interpretation, are willing to say. *Second*, we might be dealing with a wrong application of grammatical or logical rules. *Third*, there might be no immediate flaws in interpretation, but the story contradicts others that are more firmly rooted in accepted reasoning and observation. *Fourth*, the interpretation fails for reasons unknown to us, for reasons of a reality unbending to the signs available to us at the moment (Eco, 1994). Psychoanalyst Jacques Lacan would speak here of an intrusion of the Real. It might be clear from this succinct presentation that several flaws might coincide, and, conversely, that what looks like an incorrect interpretation might be revealed later to be correct or convincing (Zizek, 2015).

An interpretive approach does not therefore mean that all interpretations are created equal. Nor does it give permission to isolate stories on one subject from other topics, just as one cannot, a priori, exclude the relevance of other sign systems when interpreting expressions and events in one system-say art (Bal, 2002). One can still choose to focus on one sign system, one topic, one narrative, one site of observation (such as an organization) and suspend judgment on the truth value of any narrative. Studying the functioning, migration, transformation of stories or looking carefully at their effects in terms of power relations, resource distributions, inclusion and exclusion or on the production of new narratives can be highly valuable, say, for people interested in governance and its long-term achievements (Yanow, 2000).

Trust is a more important precondition for communication and interpretation than anything else. Before anyone can believe anything, trust must be established (Luhmann, 1995). Rather than inquiring about the truth value of a sign or a story, people and communities first check, often unconsciously whether they trust it or not. And that process is rather involved, as what needs to be trusted is a multiplicity. One needs to trust the source, the person or medium revealing the sign. When dealing with a person, one ought be sure that the person is capable of producing such signs, and that she can produce it with sincere intentions (Rodríguez-Ferrándiz, 2019). If one encounters the sign somewhere unexpected, one must ascertain whether the medium can hold the message. Furthermore, one needs to believe that the sign system is capable of conveying such message, and that neither medium nor sign system are corrupted (Eco, 1984b). One must understand the message itself, before believing it, as nonunderstanding can undermine trust not only in one's own interpretive competence, but also in the source. Finally, trust in the reality of the situation taken as starting point for the communication needs to be established or taken for granted.

Which brings us to the importance of a *shared encyclopedia*. Before anything can be interpreted and believed, before the distinction between truth, fiction and lies can be made, a significant amount of shared understanding must exist between the reader and author, speaker and audience, between leadership and community (Eco, 1984a). Not only shared cultural knowledge, linguistic expertise, general understanding of the situation is involved, but in governance, a basic knowledge of the governance system, its tools and roles, its acceptable power relations and appropriate modes of behavior. Where detailed knowledge is not expected from the audience, trust takes on a greater importance: trust in the law, in the governance system, in the truthfulness and value of experts figuring in the process of governance (Dellepiane-Avellaneda, 2010).

Where that trust is lost, and where, perhaps only partly by chance, citizens understand less and less of a governance system telling stories that do not ring relevant, simply increasing the flow of information will not restore it (de Vries et al., 2019). New modes of participation in a system otherwise unchanged will not make much of a difference. Where experts take up roles that are not understood by others, where powerful actors deploy experts to pursue opaque goals or where experts are suspected of privileging their own agendas, tensions are bound to emerge, and vulnerable groups and perspectives will find themselves excluded (Cooke & Kothari, 2001). Many marginalized stories will not come to the surface, while others will remain silently encoded in the structures and tools of governance (Bevir, 1999).

If any talk of gender inequality is coded as leftist ideology by a large part of the population, and if a bureaucracy perceiving itself as neutral, but observed as covertly leftist, comes up with a new initiative to promote science education and technology jobs to girls, this initiative will not be taken to resolve any real problem by many. Any claim to neutrality will be distrusted. Other initiatives, not openly linked to gender by government, can still founder because of the same distrust, as secret intentions can be read into them. Where entrenched interests oppose new policies, this creates two distinct openings for them: mobilizing opposition to the supposed ideological goal and capitalizing on the more general distrust towards government. (Rosanvallon & Goldhammer, 2008)

Such insights have become more commonplace since the 1970s, when Michel Foucault, a friend of Roland Barthes, had been conducting his fine-grained studies of prisons, hospitals, mental illness and scientific figures of thinking for some years. For Foucault, knowledge always shifts power relations, while power comes with implications for the interpretation of the world, both by those in power, and those subjected to it. He speaks of *power/knowledge*, indicating that neither side can be understood in isolation. For Foucault, meaning appears in *discourse*, which may or may not take on a narrative form (McHoul & Grace, 1995). Discourses are conceptual structures that make an aspect of reality accessible, by delineating certain elements, relations, processes as relevant, and simultaneously leaving alternative delineations in the shadow. Discourse thus simultaneously creates and hides realities. Discourses can fragment, lose persuasive capacity; they can travel, transform, recombine and coevolve (Foucault, 1979).

The ideas of Michel Foucault, Roland Barthes, Claude Levi-Strauss often blended into a powerful discourse that travelled across the world and across disciplinary boundaries. Later, and to a somewhat lesser extent, the same happened to Umberto Eco's semiotics. Their inspiration combined with more localized influences to create *interpretive turns*, in a variety of disciplines (Rabinow & Sullivan, 1987). In anthropology, history and sociology, they can be observed in the 1970s, in geography and politics slightly later, and in the more applied world of policy, planning and administration it only happened in the 1990s (Miller, 2002). In environmental studies, in places of reflection where sustainability began to look like something real and desirable, one had to wait even longer before the spell of natural sciences weakened enough to allow space for interpretive alternatives (Van Assche et al., 2014). Management and organization studies, with creative minds like Barbara Czarniawska and Mats Alvesson, proved a fertile ground for the study of narrative and its centrality to social and organizational identity (Alvesson, 1987; Czarniawska, 1997).

Interpretive turns look different in different contexts (Yanow, 2007) As one can suspect, stories take a central place. This book owes much to these turns, and where some disciplines have taken a few other turns in the meanwhile, we remain convinced that many insights produced are still valid and valuable. We are also convinced that connecting the dots again, combining narratively inspired insights from different fields is more than worth the effort. Indeed, where geographers and architects might have focused on the interpretation of space, on spatial semiotics and the grafting of stories in the landscape, and where historians and anthropologists devoted their energies to the unveiling of social constructions, of narratives of the powerful and the weak, in the writing of history and culture, disciplinary boundaries often stood in the way of writing bigger stories on the power of stories (Bal, 2002; Fuller, 1991).

If we consider affordable and clean energy systems a sustainable development goal appertaining to engineers and the ministries they dominate, we create boundaries in thinking and organizing that immediately limit our understanding of possible pathways. The disciplinary and professional boundaries of engineering make the topic sensitive to the roles and hierarchies in the profession and in the ministries. These boundaries introduce a selectivity in terms of topics, methods and data, reinforce assumptions regarding good governance and the role of technology commonly held where engineers rule. If we expand the scope of our thinking by looking at the "clean" aspects through an environmental science lens, this on the one hand carries over some of the engineering assumptions, on the other hand, introduces new blind spots, regarding the nature of the social, and possible ways of organizing society-environment interactions. Where we try to complete our image of energy problems by conducting anthropological and sociological studies, different methodological and ideological fault lines assert themselves, and if we call in administrative or management experts, the fashions and models of the moment can easily slip into the robes of universal truth. Sustainability leadership, then, entails the understanding of disciplinary boundaries, and the continuous labor of managing blind spots and perspectival limitations. Put differently: the needed interdisciplinary work requires leadership, not only piecing together knowledge in a team of experts. (Lam et al., 2014)

But what do narratives actually do? In the following sections, we will discuss several functions of narrative. *First*, narratives create meaning, which is their primary function. Without this benefit, the others would not accrue. *Second*, they define problems and solutions and can select the methods involved and accepted. *Third*, stories are connectors. They connect ideas, feelings, values, and *fourth*, they create identity. Individual, organizational and social identities are primarily a matter of narrative. Narratives are not always persuasive. They do not fulfill their functions in each and every situation. Sometimes, one function undermines the others, and sometimes, they lose their hold over people altogether, making space for new stories, for new realities and promises.

Narratives Create Meaning

We follow Michel Foucault and look at narratives against the background of discourse. Not every discourse can be recognized as narrative, but every narrative structures discourse and reveals a variety of discourses (Foucault, 2002). Without narrative, much discourse would be less comprehensible and cohesive, and the potential of discourse to convey meaning would be limited. We will add later in this chapter that its capacity to convey emotion would be hampered as well. Discourse can be convincing, yet narrative adds much to its persuasive power. Stories can make something look and feel true, and they can increase the impression of relevance (Eco, 2025).

Aligning with the semiotic tradition, we argue that narrative holds sway over people because of two reasons: it provides structure, and it guarantees access to a world of other stories. Indeed, a story rarely explains itself fully, and meaning comes to fruition through a web of linkages with other stories. The structure a narrative can bring to discourse is from the start more than structure, as the patterns and the elements only make sense because of a context and a history of patterns already interpreted, of stories already circulating (Culler, 2002). A hero figure can be identified because other heroic stories abound; an anticlimax can be appreciated because expectations have been formed in a history of storytelling.

Stories allow individuals and communities to recognize things in the world because of recognition of the stories themselves, and this works through content and form, through the familiarity of figures, facts and episodic structures (Barthes & Duisit, 1975). Many types of stories evolved over time, coupled to occasions and environments. The *telling* of stories, or their performance, would similarly increase its variety, with new roles in society emerging together with new stories and styles of storytelling (Baetens, 2018). The *visibility* of stories showed more diversity, as complex societies developed stories that were able to hide themselves, in socially inaccessible corners, or finding shelter behind other stories (Baecker, 2006). Where stories appear to be absent, they are hiding. Where neutrality reigns, and the facts seem to speak for themselves, one needs to look harder for the stories structuring the facts.

Narratives thus familiarize through their familiarity. This has the paradoxical effect that, when the opposite is aimed at, when defamiliarization is desired, one ends up with stories as the way to go (Miall & Kuiken, 1994). If new and outlandish stories are told, if precise expectations are subverted, assumptions about reality might be questioned. Hence the power of art to make people look differently, and, beyond art, the importance of storytelling in politics (Davis, 1979). What can be estranging can be the performance, the combination of sign systems involved, adding unexpected music to a commonplace story playing out in an unusual place. It can be the appearance of a startling new metaphor (see Chapter 3), a blurring of typologies of stories, a detective story playing out in a medieval setting, a research method emulating Sherlock Holmes.

Types of stories develop their own logic, and if that inherent logic is not adhered to, confusion follows. Meaning does not flow from a universal logic, yet from contextual modes of reasoning that fit the structure and content of story, the occasion of storytelling (Eco, 2025). Which brings us to another reason why truthfulness is not the main criterion in storytelling and in the construction of our realities: *stories do things*. More precisely: they are expected to do things. Without trust, no truthfulness can ever be established; without grasping the expected role of a story, its reality and its value can never be assessed (Rorty, 1989). People perform stories and stories perform roles in society. They fit occasions, and they mark occasions. Hence, some stories draw attention to themselves, while others move in the background; some emphasize individual authenticity, others serve to underline social unity (Maggio, 2014).

Stories can change when their role changes, or when their believability suffers. That believability, as one can expect, is tied to the function again, as something is believable in a certain role and context. If the story changes, it can increase its chances of survival, as nonadaptation can more easily lead to the story being relinquished altogether. The evolution of stories can hinge on the presence of other stories, which hinder or support the story in question, or the role it performs (Bietti et al., 2019). Social change can redefine functions and the occasions where these functions might be performed.

To spice up things further, we add that that both discourse and narrative can travel, expanding the space for and diversity of possible expression and interpretation. In those voyages, they tend to adapt to changing contexts (Bal, 2002). They might also alter those contexts, in terms of other discourses and stories affected, transformed and reinterpreted, and in terms of new modes of organization that can come about. We speak here of *discursive or narrative migration and* can say plainly that these are among the most common phenomena in our socially constructed worlds (Foucault, 1971). Stories do stabilize social relations and forms of governance, but they are untrustworthy allies of whoever places their conservative trust in them. They change color, move and transform, can disintegrate, with each fragment starting to lead its own life, as the Greek hydra. Entire stories can travel, individual concepts or discursive fragments, and the peripatetic life of whatever is traveling can entail the crossing of multiple boundaries, the boundaries of disciplines, of literary genres, of art and science, stretching up the limits of interpretation in each new domain (Swyngedouw, 1992). Everyday life can be interpreted through stories containing fragments stemming from classical mythology, more recent mythologies about the power of science, psychoanalytic theories never consciously encountered and religious principles officially forgotten (Cutchins, 2017; de Certeau, 1984).

Stories of sustainable production and consumption can ease the minds of worried consumers. They change with increasing insight in our environment and with innovation in production methods, but also because they integrate new fragments of narrative, create new links with stories about the good life, justice, good governance and identity. National pride can be caressed, as we can feel more sustainable than others, old stories about a return to nature gain new currency. Sustainability can combine with beliefs in technological progress to create a new consumer subjectivity, a belonging to a group of, likely urbane, sophisticates with new reasons to feel superior. (Ferkany, 2015)

Governance is only possible because it occurs against a background of a tapestry of stories (Bevir, 2011; Miller, 2012). The tapestry metaphor points at their cohesion, the weaving of threads keeping each other in place. Stability is a key objective of any governance system, and the warp and weft of narrative, in governance and community, greatly enhances that stability. We can say now that this stability is never absolute, and, in fact partly illusory. Some stories stabilizing governance are simply stories stating that stability, in the hope that they have a stabilizing effect. Ancient kings traced their lineage back to the Gods, expecting that the connection with a divine order of things, and with the power creating that order, would guarantee stability (Scott, 2017). Even so, discourse is restless, and people, ideas and goods moving around, circumstances changing, powers losing their lustre can diminish the persuasive power of the stories and the social order they maintain (Duineveld et al., 2013).

French philosopher Gilles Deleuze coined the term *rhizome* for the creativity inherent to the world, the ongoing self-transformation of everything we encounter (Deleuze & Guattari, 1987). What he refers to goes beyond stories. For him, the world is imbued with creative capacities: new connections between material objects and environments, discourse and beings can always appear, as in the rhizomatic root systems of reeds. Places come about through interactions between people, stories and materiality; new processes of organization rearrange and redefine places, people and ideas (Massey, 2005). A basic insight we can distill is that discourse travels and has productive potential. Stories are mobile, trigger new mobilities, of people, ideas, goods, forms of organization, yet they can also generate new stories seemingly without much intervention or movement (Gabriel, 2015). New interpretations suddenly appear, almost out of nowhere, and what might have triggered can be a minute occurrence, a new relation, that can hardly be traced.

Narratives Connect Values, Ideas and Feelings

Rhizomes make connections, and stories are amazing catalysts to establish new linkages. This activity transcends the production of meaning, as what can be connected is more than ideas. Feelings and values can be integrated through stories, associated with ideas and people can connect through stories (Hogan, 2011). As can be expected, what can unite can divide, and stories are also deployed to establish boundaries, to separate people, ideas and values, to disconnect other stories. Both connecting and dividing can happen consciously, can be used strategically, yet intentionality need not be involved (Linde, 1993) (Figure 2.1a).

We can distinguish two distinct mechanisms of connectivity at work. Stories can be constructed as connectors between disparate elements, those elements aggregating into a narrative structure. Second, those elements might not be associated into narrative directly but find connectivity through other stories. Certainly, both mechanisms can be combined, and stories can exert an influence on the construction of others, which connect previously loose elements (Figure 2.1b). The narrative fabric that makes up our reality, and that makes governance possible, is often involved here, as some stories do not only uphold others, but also have a hand in the emergence of new stories (Foucault, 1976). This can happen through analogy and association, of ideas, affects, values and social identity.

New stories can thus appear through the influence of others that are not immediately apparent or considered relevant (Sandercock,

Narratives Connect Values, Ideas and Feelings 41

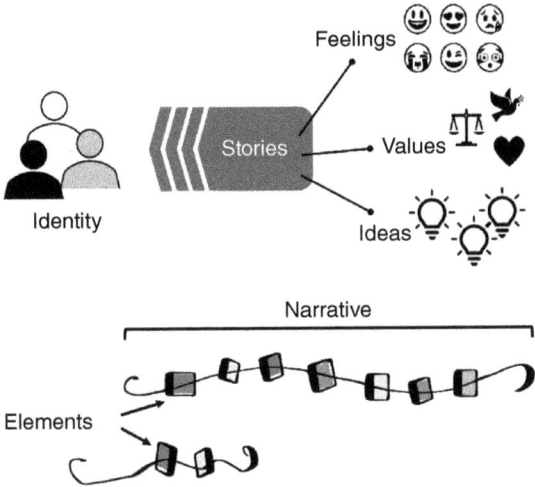

Figure 2.1 (a) Sustainability leadership hinges on the power of stories to create understanding and to engender change. Addressing sustainability challenges requires the creation of new stories about the good community, a desirable relation with the environment and a belief in the collective capacity to organize for the long term. Therefore it is important to understand the way stories bind feelings, values, ideas and identity. (b) Stories can connect disparate elements (ideas, feelings, etc.) into a narrative structure. In addition, those elements might not be associated into narrative directly but find connectivity through other stories. Both mechanisms can be combined, and stories can exert an influence on the construction of others, which connect previously loose elements.

1998). They can be indirectly connected, through a chain of ideas or feelings, through similarities that are less obvious. An atmosphere can be recalled, a connection with a shared history can be at work, a structural similarity might become productive (Pile, 2013). In some cases, the chain of associations can be reconstructed with relative ease, while elsewhere, it takes great effort, and there, it makes sense to speak of an unconscious association. Stories can pop up seemingly without rhyme or reason, but they do rhyme with something. This can happen to individuals, and it happens to groups and communities that share stories and histories (Van Assche & Gruezmacher, 2025).

One of the reasons why unexpected associations occur, why new narrative is structured without too much understanding of the driving force, is that key stories upholding the reality, observed and desired, of a community, are not observed themselves (Foucault, 1970). Grounding values and their stories might be enshrined in a constitution, religion or ideology, but they might have lost their binding value, while others, old or not, might have taken their place. Even where they still have a structuring power, observing them might not be easy. Thus, what we call *master narratives*, stories underpinning and connecting many others, possess not only a stabilizing but also a productive function (Lyotard, 1984). Master narratives can select, hide, highlight, deconstruct and build others.

If we embrace full and productive employment and decent work as a sustainable development goal, this can be upheld by stories of work as a right and as key to human dignity, and by stories predicting social unrest when not enough people are gainfully employed. In the USSR, ideology did not allow for the acknowledgment of unemployment, so one had to deny its existence, blame its lingering existence on laziness and capitalist obstruction, or create virtually meaningless jobs. Under capitalism, reducing regulation and taxation might create more jobs, yet many of those are what David Graeber has called "bullshit jobs," meaningless, repetitive, and disposable, while the story on innovation and the "knowledge society" that was supposed to bring more and better jobs, is actively veiling the destruction of work by machines. The meaning and implication of full, productive and decent work emerges through master narratives which are imperfect at best. Which is no reason to abandon the goal, but a compelling argument to see it as a driver of conversations: What do we see as work, as productive and meaningful? (Alvesson, 2004; Graeber, 2018)

In their various functions, master narratives rely not only on their structural position in cultures and organizations, but also on certain signs that play an outsized role, even if they cannot always be discerned. We speak of *master signifiers*, a concept borrowed from psychoanalyst Jacques Lacan (Hook & Vanheule, 2016). Master signifiers tend to feature in master narratives, and, as those narratives, they can be conscious or unconscious, acknowledged or disavowed. We argue that they can exert their power seemingly by themselves, when encountered or used in isolation, yet such power ultimately derives from master narratives, latent or overt. What is this power? First of all, it is the power to connect other stories, and to connect individuals and organizations that want to connect, that want to believe they are connected (Fink, 2017). They can smooth over differences and uncertainties stemming from the difficulty of communication itself, and from the

Narratives Connect Values, Ideas and Feelings 43

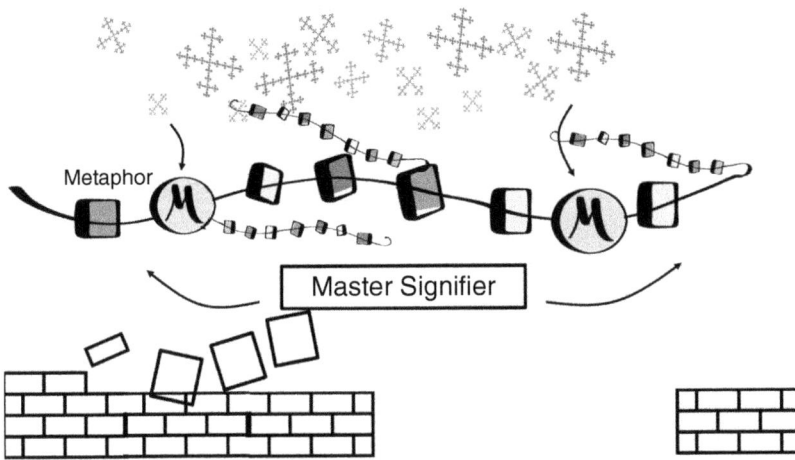

Figure 2.2 Master signifiers are words for big things which are hard to conceptualize. They can be used to create the impression of shared understanding, even if we do not know exactly what is meant, and even when we mean different things. Sometimes, they are metaphoric, but not necessarily so. Master signifiers can structure narratives that then help to make understandable what eluded us before. "Sustainability" is such a master signifier, and "innovation" another one. The master signifier "sustainability" can anchor several sustainability narratives, and the identification of "innovation" as a master signifier helps to see how the seemingly sturdy construction of our reality (the brick wall in the illustration) reveals its fragility when we take a closer look. The anchoring provided by each master signifier is always partly fictional; layering such fictions (master signifiers supporting others) and developing them (into narratives) does not change the character of sustainability narratives as productive fictions.

real differences and complexities one desires to ignore. Master signifiers thus work as a powerful glue and at the same time as eraser. Their use can both trigger and indicate a form of magical thinking where a new unity, hence a new reality, is willed into being through the use of the talisman of the signifier (Bracher, 1993) (Figure 2.2).

The power of master signifiers and narratives signals that something else is going on beyond connecting ideas. Affect and desire are involved, and, by extension, values. Values only work when they can be shared, in a community, and their propagation through narrative is a process of community creation. Desire is a driver of becoming, of individuals and groups and hence an engine of narrative production and dissemination (Sztompka, 1991). Individuals and communities, but also organizations can desire, a desire becoming effective and driving change through narrative, and, in fact, coming to life through narrative. As individuals learn how and what to desire through embedding in a community, communities shape their desire through participation in a world of narrative production and consumption (McGowan, 2012).

Stories can play such diverse and powerful roles because they do more than generating content, more than connecting ideas. Their structuring effect entails the connection of concepts and affects, and, through this weaving, the expression and pursuit of desire. Moods can be structured into affects and explained through stories which link these affects to history and context. A narrative structuring thus assists in interpreting oneself, and the situation one finds oneself in; what appears real can feel real, while the story simultaneously delineates what one feels (Linde, 1993). Once affectively laden stories circulate, others can recognize themselves in them, so the affect reproduces itself through the story (Young & Frosh, 2018). Context and performance make a difference: A believable story is a well-told story, and what counts as persuasive storytelling crucially depends on the situation, and the kind of stories and telling expected.

The behavior of people and organizations can confirm or deny the reality and relevance of stories, and if stories are told or sold by actors in governance that cannot be mapped onto their actions, this is a problem if those actors are trying to pursue the common good (Fairclough, 2005). Possibly, their actions do not translate the values shared narratively with the community well enough, possibly there's a lack of sincerity. Alternatively, new stories reared their head in the community, unbeknownst to governance, and actions previously looking neutral or positive now appear in a negative light.

Narratives Create Community

Narratives thus connect yet their connectivity cannot be taken for granted. They can unite and divide, and what appeared to be uniting can polarize later. We can distinguish several mechanisms through which narratives can create and support community. *First*, stories literally connect people through telling, where togetherness in listening can create bonds between the listeners. *Second*, people can share an understanding of reality by subscribing to the same narrative construction of that reality. This can happen through conceptual, affective and structural analogies. *Third*, narratives can enroll new listeners through transformation, so evolving stories can extend community. *Fourth*, stories *about* the collective can create the collective as in "this is what we are, this is what we do" (Geertz, 1973; Rappaport & Simkins, 1991).

We would like to emphasize this last point, that is, that stories about the community are only one way for stories to create social links. We know already that not all stories are immediately visible in their uniting or divisive workings, so the strength of social ties is not easy to ascertain; even the existence of community should not be taken for granted. Any community is imagined, but can come into being through that imagination, through the telling of stories about communities present and hoped for (Anderson, 2006). Those stories can engender modes of organization, structures and processes of governance that assume the existence of the community and help to perpetuate it, but perfect performativity and stability cannot be guaranteed (Putnam, 2000). Governance, in other words, is always precarious, as the community it is supposed to serve might only exist in an administrative sense or might see itself quite differently from the image lingering with actors.

European Union projects under the INTERREG program hope to reduce disparities between regions in Europe by promoting cross-border collaborations at regional level. An implicit longer-term goal is also to reinforce regional governance and identities, and relatively weakening the national level, in the vision of the "Europe of the regions." What actually happens in such projects, whether they achieve their own objectives, and support the objectives of the EU, depends on a variety of factors, not in the least the nature of the existing regional boundaries, the relation with regional identities, and the powers of regional government and governance. (During, 2010)

As usual, the multiplicity of stories in community and governance can offer support, can work as a stabilizing factor. Governance and community can share more than they are aware of, and channels might exist, beyond formal representation and participation, through which narratives can travel, connect, transform each other (Verdery, 2003). A few stories play a particular role, however, in the stabilization of community and the relation with governance. There are the master narratives with which a community can identify itself, enshrining core values, and there are stories about past and place.

Narrative identity, as the stories delineating the collective, tends to support itself through stories about the past, through constructing and embracing a version of history (Eriksen, 2010). A group identifies key moments in its past, high points and reversals of fortune and recognizes itself in a narrative which is always selective (Certeau, 1988). Neighbors and relatives, allies and enemies feature in such stories and without those, the community has difficulties in grasping its own cohesion. Stories can be institutionalized as history, become the official history disseminated or enforced by the state and they can survive as alternative or competing versions of the past, cultivated by groups perhaps not agreeing with the identity narratives crafted by state or elite (Scott, 2009).

Spatial identity, as the stories about a place shared in a community, is not always tightly linked to social identity, but, in the other direction, social identity tends to require spatialization as well as a temporal dimension (Shields, 2013). Communities routinely imbricate stories about self, place and history, in a triad that enhances stabilization. Yet, the same entangling offers new routes for change, as alterations in one story, or changing affective investments in one of them, most likely come with consequences for the others, or for their mutual support (Barnes & Duncan, 1992). If they unravel, the sense of community can weaken, if they reshape each other, it might transform.

Creating community by telling stories about the community is not an easy matter, even if the storytellers hold the power over education and regulation. If everybody in France must identify as French first and foremost, and if this implies one must speak French, go to a Catholic church, drink wine and eat baguettes, then not all those elements might feel as relevant, and some might be resented to the extent that one resolutely refuses to be French. It took the French state several centuries to get rid of minority languages and religions. Regarding the culinary examples, the issue of Frenchness was solved by embracing all local and regional variations, and de facto claiming half of the cuisines of the neighboring regions as French. (Robb, 2008)

Existing identities, as variations of and alternatives to a new official story, make a difference. Creating community by imposing stories and practices (explained by those stories) hinges not only on the nature of the story so dear to the powers that be, but also on the stories already in place, and the differences between old and new that new is trying to erase. Thus, the Romans, aware of this, conquered brutally, yet also accepted the Gods of the conquered areas as their own, and gave citizenship easily. A difficulty, even for the Romans, was that the significance of some differences was not always apparent to them, so when the Jewish population of the near east rose up, they did not fully understand why, lost their patience beyond measure and created rifts that were not healed for centuries (Eisenberg, 2007).

Narratives Define Problems, Methods and Solutions

What appeared to the Romans as a Jewish problem did so because of their ignorance of Jewish religion, the interweaving of cultural and religious identity, more intricate than elsewhere in the classical world. Roman administration relied on a rudimentary and inadequate story regarding the Jewish people, the product of Roman assumptions and institutional traditions, and a story regarding the role of religion in community life that did not allow them to observe Jewish realities (Turcan, 2013).

Problems never appear out of nowhere. Something becomes a problem from a perspective, and that perspective does not exist without stories. What applies to problems, applies to solutions and to methods of analyzing problems and finding solutions (Fischer, 2003). A few different causalities can be distinguished, however. Some stories define both problem and solution, while others delineate a problem, while relying on others to find the solution. Some methods of problem analysis are tightly coupled to a master narrative regarding the state of the world, others can operate under varied master signifiers (Van Assche et al., 2023). Certain methods of problem solving are directly prescribed by an ideology envisioning the good society and its enemies, others are to a large degree the correlative of the methods chosen to analyze problems (Béland & Howlett, 2016).

These different relations between problems and solutions, as mediated by methods and stories, are not neutral in governance. They have different effects with regard to possible interventions in society, possible reforms of governance itself and the selection of expertise and policy tools to address an issue (Latour, 2004). We will encounter diverse understandings of sustainability, of good governance, of the real community and relevant environments and the implications for sustainability strategy are significant.

A community is always faced with problems of various sorts, and the more ambitious the governance system, the higher the expectations of life, the more differentiated and specialized governance and community become, the more problems can be observed (Luhmann, 1990). Complexity engenders a more fine-grained image of reality and its deficiencies, hence a multiplication of problems. That same complexity can imagine more diverse solutions, leaning on an ever-increasing array of expert knowledges available to governance, and a bewildering variety of stories. Some of those stories enter governance through political representation and participation, others through the experts and managers in the governance system. We mention managers as guardians of organizational identity, and experts as representatives of disciplinary and professional identities, each identity a coagulation of stories cohesive enough to become a story itself (Sveningsson & Alvesson, 2003).

In governance systems reliant on a diversity of expert knowledges, the integration of this knowledge is only possible by maintaining the myth of the "fact." If we can believe in objectively delineated facts that assert their relevance in an objective way, we can come to objective problem definitions, and all experts can contribute their piece. The fact that these pieces almost never fit together, indicates the missing narrative. Where they do fit, there is an unacknowledged shared narrative – an ideology, a nationalism, an elite culture. Disagreement tends to be attributed to personalities, power relations, or over-specialization, all of which might be there, but not explaining the structural impossibility to define facts and combine them without discourse and narrative. "The environment" can certainly not be assembled into a concept without underlying stories that select the features we would recognize as "environmental" and as governable. (Cairney, 2016; Luhmann, 1989)

Not every story in the governance system is compatible with all others, and not every story is emotionally laden to the same degree. Yet, governance systems do need a semblance of cohesion to operate, and they need a minimal affective investment to retain the loyalty of the community (Van Assche & Gruezmacher, 2025). The structure and processes of the governance system, we know, select stories, as they transform and produce stories, some for internal use, others directed at the community it serves. Each element of governance affects the selectivity of narrative consumption and production. Not only the dominant stories selectively accepting others, but also the set of actors and their power relations, the accumulated and narratively tinged institutions have a bearing on narrative selectivity (Jessop, 2014).

Which stories are behind a particular problem definition, or support a deep emotional awareness of a problem, might be hard to ascertain. Affect might have traveled between different actors, in discursive chains, might be product of the process of governance, of the use of certain institutions, and the sorts of stories and expert perspectives included and excluded in decision-making. The problem definition might be enshrined in tradition, anchored in grounding institutions, or rather the result of contingent encounters in the hallways of power (Bacchi, 2009). What ends up on the table of decision-makers as a problem and a solution, is molded in a journey that bear little resemblance to the official description of the decision-making process.

Power/knowledge in governance thus operates in and through the tapestries of stories we spoke of, but those tapestries are more intricate than meets the eye. In the story governance tells about itself, what is often emphasized is either "the facts," likely established by exerts, or "the voice," the will of the people, represented by politicians, assisted by administrations and their experts. Of course, neutrality, as in the absence of stories defining facts, has no place in governance. Stories are always there, in the voices of people yelling at their politicians, demanding the recognition of different problems, in the interpretation of those voices by politicians, administrators and other actors, and in the reinterpretation of the situation by experts inside and outside governance (Czarniawska, 2010).

An objective starting point for the designation of a situation as a problem does not exist, as communities can be blind to something that is horrible for others or even find it a confirmation of its core values. Maybe we need to suffer since we are punished for our collective sins? Maybe this is not suffering, but a prelude to enlightenment? Mapping community needs on to a hierarchy of needs cannot be satisfactory for long, as what really counts is not need but desire, and since the need itself is framed in stories where desire is at work (Kapoor, 2014). Communities can trip over an impossible desire for something seemingly irrelevant for any outside observer (Dalrymple, 2004). Where an emotional investment finds its origin can only be established after a careful unraveling of master narratives, and a patient search for the reasons why something becomes, in Lacanian terms, an *objet a*, an expression and a replacement object for a deeper aspiration that is harder to recognize (Gunder & Hillier, 2009). New stories will form around such *objet a*, since it is encircled by desire.

What is resilient for some, amounts to an acceptance of unnecessary suffering to others. What appears as resilient in one perspective, looks like a pitiful reconstruction of a problematic regime from a different angle. The problematic regime might be acceptable for many residents, because they do not believe western stories about participatory democracy, because their desire might be captured by very different stories, of national greatness, of suffering caused by ancient opposing forces. (McGowan, 2022)

Quantification, or the assigning of numbers to situations, problems and solutions does not alter this basic truth of governance. Communities do not know why they want something; they become absorbed by ever shifting attractors of desire. A new park might be the shining future, embodying something desirable that resists naming. Desires captured in seemingly unrelated stories can attach themselves to an earlier parks story, invest it with affect that was not there before, that might be hard to comprehend even by the proponents of the park. Numbers might be alluring, in their promise of clarity, their promise of banishing stories and unstable desires, but they cannot deliver on these promises. Narrative and desire always lurk behind indicators, statistics, models and forecasts (Muller, 2018).

Genre, Medium and Style

The issue of trust in numbers in governance, of their power to hide their own narrative underpinning, brings us to the insight that narratives have effects not only through their performance, not only through their connectivity to other narratives and their role in governance, but also through their *packaging*. We rely on this crude term to introduce the concepts of *genre* and *medium*. The way stories are packaged influences their options for linking to other stories, for *intertextuality*, as the package partly determines the associations that can be made in interpretation.

In art and literature, where the term stems from, a genre is a category of creations that display certain formal, substantive and material features (Baxandall, 1979). A genre is about form and content, about features of the stories that can be told in the genre, and the style of the narration, or representation (Eco, 2025). A detective story will find some resistance with audiences if written in the style of Joyce or Dante, and have its readers puzzled when there's no mystery to solve, or when there's nothing to read, when it's transposed to the medium of painting (Eco, 1979; Vanbergen, 1993).

A *medium* tends to be more long-lasting than a genre or style and includes material aspects of the signifier. Newspapers, radio and TV are media, but so is the printed word or image and oil paintings. Each material appearance of a collection of signs becomes susceptible to interpretation in a different way, and enables circulation according to different principles, in different networks (Latour, 2005). Media affect the content they convey, and the patterns of circulation they achieve, the audiences reached and created, can, in the other direction, reshape form and content carried by the medium (Kittler, 1999). Some genres appear on TV rather than in movie theaters, although that example already illustrates that media and style coevolve.

Style is, in the broadest sense, a way of doing things. For cultural theorist Mikhail Bakhtin, an early semiotician, style is also a category that blurs the boundaries between form and content (Williams, 2005). The style of a writer has syntactic and semantic aspects, can be recognized in the way words are ordered, in the structure of a sentence, of a text. One can say that stories can be told in different styles, and that the author can be recognized in some of those styles. A style can also be identified by its themes and topics, its emotional register, its web of assumptions and tacit references to worlds outside the text. Some styles can only be understood through deep familiarity with the history of art, of cinema (as with Quentin Tarantino), while others rely more on knowledge of the social or natural worlds. All sign systems are capable of producing styles, even ones where the content seems harder to grasp (as with architecture).

For Bakhtin, some genres could be *polyphonic*, meaning that different views on the world are copresent, sometimes in a conflict that becomes a theme. Elsewhere, the author takes seemingly no position, and different realities simply coexist. Those voices could appear in different styles, as when characters speak and behave in quite distinct manners, or when episodes of a story appear in a different setting, conveyed in distinct modes of expression (Schuster, 1985). Even where polyphony was not the intention of an author, not the result of careful composition, for Bakhtin it can occur in texts, or, by extension, expressions. This, for him, results from the *dialogic character* of language, where a text is always interpreted in a cultural context, and in a history of previous expressions. Which means that a reader *makes* a cultural expression dialogic and might infer an intention by the author that is possibly not there. Telling an old and very well-known story in a slightly mocking tone might be read in a specific way if the mockery is recognized, if there is an image of the author, an understanding of the traditional audience, role and context of the story. Thus, an informed reader might experience a dialogic text, containing the voices of an (authoritative) tradition and a (mocking) individual author. Readers unfamiliar with the author, or identifying with tradition differently, might either miss the mockery, or might read mockery into everything that is not literal reproduction (Bakhtin, 2010).

Relevant for our story is that style, genre, medium and story itself cross the boundaries of form and content. Stories told and performed will display features of style, genre, medium. What can be told and how it is interpreted depends on all of these modes of structuring and packaging. A different way of thinking about this is to say that both form and content require structure, and that each manner of structuring generates its own audience, its own reader or interpreter, through manipulating the chances of encountering and understanding such packaging. Specialized knowledge comes often in specialized genres, tends to be dressed in styles familiar to the specialist. Familiar stories, on the other hand, might appear in a variety of styles and genres, and might produce a wide array of new interpretations when appearing in new guises in new places (Barthes, 1957; Frye, 2009).

For Umberto Eco, signs contain other signs, and any aggregation of signs has the potential to become a sign for something else (Eco, 1976, 2000). What is interpreted is never a word in isolation, but a word in a sentence, which can already suggest style. That sentence features in a story in a book or a TV show, where the choice of genre and medium contributes to the interpretation of every expression read or watched. A genre comes to stand for something, acquires meaning for itself, a set of expectations regarding form and content, and anything that deviates from those expectations will draw attention (Todorov, 1975). When the meaning of something is not clear, not only might new stories be constructed, old ones tried for fit, but also different styles, genres, media might prove useful to come to a meaningful interpretation. If science cannot be a simple reading of reality, it needs to become a detective novel.

Communicating sustainability where it has not been communicated before brings experts inside and outside governance, politicians and activists, to creative storytelling, to experiments with medium, genre, style. Retelling sustainability stories where they have been ideologically tainted before, might take a different rhetoric. An English–Romanian project in the Danube Delta worked with children in the Delta Villages to discover stories and meanings of the creatures and the places of this vast wetland region, through coproduction of puppet theatre. Rather than lecturing residents about sustainability and why they must care, the project tried an unusual medium to experiment with a new genre and unveil to people that they already had their sustainability stories. This only works, though, if those interested in sustainability are willing to think in terms of stories, and willing to reconsider their own story in the process. (Lowery et al., 2020)

Organizations and governance systems operate on the basis of a bewildering variety of communications. Ministries might not produce paintings or detective movies, yet their semiotic functioning relies on the production and consumption of stories that can entail many sign systems, a pallet of styles, genres and media, reflecting the complexity of society and governance itself. Actors in governance, depending on their roles, have access to different aspects of reality, through different stories, and communicate with each other, with leadership and with others in the social environment in distinct manners (Fischer, 2003). Defining problems, finding solutions, investigating what is true or worthwhile, takes place in ways marked by and expressed in distinct styles.

Some will foreground storytelling; others tend to veil the story or truly believe there is none. Some genres will be more accepted in certain circles in society and governance, particular styles will look suspicious in certain cultures when associated with actors in governance (Mosse, 2005). Speaking in parables might be acceptable for leadership in some cultures but would be met with hostility elsewhere. Even where it is generally understood to be useful, an engineering department is not expected to speak in parables or produce a music video as yearly report. Private sector management fashions rendered the subgenre of the executive summary more important than the rest of a governmental report or policy document, and the common accusatory story about slow and wasteful government does not incline managers to spend time reading the rest. Performing speed and action outweighs thoughtful and careful decision-making (Rosa, 2013).

Transforming governance, and changing society through governance, cannot meaningfully happen without understanding unique patterns of stories, styles, genres and media, their hierarchies, their expected role and distribution. What stories can do, depends crucially on package and performance, and we understand now that the packaging tends to affect the gift more than superficially. Communicative traditions in domains of governance, in society, those governing the interactions between governance and society, always enable and constrain the ideas and affects that circulate and could alter what looks and feels real. Power relations, between not only actors and their stories, but also between styles, genres and media can, rather immediately, tinge the reception of new stories about emerging problems (Stone, 2012).

If local stories about an environment, expressing local knowledge and place attachment, are dismissed as marginal to the real, i.e. expert-driven definition of sustainability problems, if children's theatre is accepted only to translate and disseminate established scientific or bureaucratic truths, then we close ourselves off for meaningful participation by parents and children alike in the construction of locally viable versions of sustainability. If such dismissal of genres, media, styles and their audiences continues, participation becomes less likely, and resistance against technocratic domination can turn easily into aversion of sustainability discourse, or against coalitions of experts and bureaucrats more generally. (Jasanoff, 2004)

When affect spreading like wildfire cannot be contained, and produces stories with an emotional investment that can easily undermine the stability of society, without offering realistic alternatives, the response by governance has to consider that more than old formal agreements, more than apparently objective facts, a reinterpretation of stories is required, and that, in this effort, every aspect of packaging and performance can count. The wrong suit might be enough to be dismissed.

Narrative and Time

What Time Does to Stories?

Stories do something to time and time does something to stories. Stories make it easier to look backward and forward in time, to access experiences of other times (and places) in a way that transcend the relaying of facts and certainly the limits of individual experience (Certeau, 1988). Looking forward as a community, bringing desirable and undesirable futures within grasp, requires stories. Those stories cannot be entirely disconnected from existing stories, and this limits the repertoire available to those who wish to make a future shared, and orient collective action towards that future (Van Assche et al., 2024). Connections between system and environment, between past, present and future can be elucidated through stories.

Meanwhile, stories can outlive their functionality and become, using a term from cultural theorist Juri Lotman, *ossified*. Ossification here means a loss of relevance for a community, before forgetting or rejection sets in (Lotman et al., 1978). Ossified stories might represent a loss of considerable importance to communities, if they are still useful to address real problems, yet not noticed or believed anymore. The term ossification points at another feature: ossified stories stopped changing, hence adapting. When communities stop noticing the relevance of a narrative, that story stops adapting to changing circumstances. A loss of relevance, therefore, often means a disconnect from relevant conversations, those conversations that seep into governance and make a difference in decision-making (Chaffin et al., 2014; Makaryčev & Jacyk, 2017).

When the stories central to long-term strategies become ossified, there is a problem. It might mean that the strategy itself is nonadapted, or otherwise irrelevant, that political or cultural context, as well as the nature of the problems and opportunities envisioned have shifted beyond recognition. In that case, immediate action is required, as the strategy in place ought to be abandoned, possibly replaced. Keeping it in place undermines the legitimacy of the whole governance system and reduces chances that future strategies can solve anything. Possibly, the strategy in place still represents an adequate way to address the future, but became black-boxed or otherwise isolated, removed from public discourse (Latour, 1996). If that is the case, moving the strategy back into the spotlight of public discussion is commendable, as both adaptation and continued support are essential.

People might gradually lose motivation to do what is presented as the right thing by governance, and sometimes, ossification is the culprit. Risky behavior, endangering one's health and that of others can be appealing, can become gradually normalized in a permissive environment. Besides these forces, ossification might be at work, a loosening grip of old narratives. Ossification of a communist narrative on social responsibility and collective action can occur together with the appearance of attractive narratives of freedoms but it might also happen independently (Verdery, 1996). Perception of hypocrisy can intensify ossification of government-sponsored narratives, as when state – owned factories are the worst polluters, while government discourse underlines wise resource use and environmental conservation. Stories that were convincing in the early days of an ideology might get bogged down in the practicalities of governance and lose their binding power. When the Soviet regime presented cigarettes as a capitalist problem and lure, while profiting of their production, few people paid attention to the health message and Soviets smoked more than any other nation. (Starks, 2022)

Where stories cannot be described as ossified, they can still erode or silently shift. By which we mean that they can lose persuasive power, or transform in the shadows, without much public scrutiny or awareness in governance (Luhmann, 2012). Both processes occur naturally and are not harmful per se. Things become more problematic when master narratives upholding the discursive fabric of governance either lost support or changed quietly, creating rifts in that fabric, discursive and affective tensions, institutional incoherence, more variegated patterns of support.

Master narratives and master signifiers can evolve without much notice. They might not openly feature in discourse and institutions, while declining attention to stories once they are institutionalized, turned into policies, laws or plans can create problems over time. When stories underpin structure or process of the governance system, governance features might survive long beyond the embrace of new values and stories in society, leading to unfortunate path dependencies. In a different scenario, however, an initial grounding story, translated into key governance features, can evolve, remain recognizable, yet without causing a rethinking of governance. In both scenarios, a difference between master signifiers and the current policy tools silently developed, and older and newer features of governance might be compatible only in name (Van Dijk, 2006)

What Stories Do to Time?

Stories are subjected to time, and they create time. Taking cues again from Umberto Eco and systems theorist Niklas Luhmann, we distinguish between *narrative time, experiential time and systems time* (Eco, 1984b, 2025; Luhmann, 1995).

Narrative time is the time as structured in the world of the story. It is the time as experienced by the characters. Those characters can tell their own stories, evoking other times, marked by their own rhythms, changing intensities, dramatic climaxes and reversals, recounted versions of fast and slow, exciting and boring. A character shows up again after then years, on the next page. A few paragraphs later, she recounts a distant past that could be either history or mythology (Eco, 2025).

Experiential time is the time experienced by an individual, marked by events and cycles which are not conjured up by that individual, but intruding in life through biology, the natural environment and society. Which means that stories do contribute to the shaping of experiential time, starting with stories of the self, the good life, the well-adjusted life (Ricoeur, 1979). Experiential time can reflect a work–life balance (or imbalance) that integrates the need to sleep and eat and do things that generate some form of income in a more or less acceptable way. What is felt as natural to an individual stems from habit, from observing and emulating others, from internalizing others, from pursuing and repressing desire (Adam, 2013).

Systems time is the time as needed and produced by social systems, either organizations or governance systems (as politics in the broad sense), by the other function systems, such as law, the economy, religion, art and science (Luhmann, 1995). Society as the overarching social system can impose a standard time, supporting the coordination of various systems and activities, but this does not erase the difference between system temporalities. Governance, in daily routines and its more strategic activities, is obliged to consider the differences in temporality between systems, strive for partial coordination, but is bound to remain lacking in the effort. Which means that the work never ends. Governance needs to manage its internal complexity, with a web of organizations resisting full integration into the same temporality and, with that, agenda (Luhmann, 1990). It enters into conversation with external actors of the organized sort, and it cannot escape the impossible duty of coordinating law, economy and politics. In modern societies, a reference to science for at least some policy directions is traditional, while in traditional societies, religion could be more influential, with politics aiming to instill religious principles into the other function systems. Organizations are obliged to develop a sophisticated systems time that is both unique and integrated into society (Luhmann, 2018), with some rhythms reflecting couplings to other systems (tax season!) and others its idiosyncratic evolution (Taco Tuesday; board meeting first Tuesday of the month).

For climate change policy, both time and space presented problems. Global changes tend to remain abstract, and the systems temporalities involved are far removed from our own experience of time. The drama of climate change helped to resolve the disjuncture in temporalities, in a double sense: a diversity of stories quickly assembled, and the speed of climate change and omnipresence of its effects brought the phenomenon within the grasp of more people. Right now, the speed of climate change is such that we are dealing with an inverse of the original problem: our governance processes render it difficult to respond quickly enough. One reason being the slowness stemming from debate and checks and balances, another reason, which we will discuss in this book, is that many systems must develop their capacity to assess long-term perspectives, and institutional capacity more broadly. (Beckert, 2024; Marquardt & Delina, 2021)

Systems time, narrative time and experiential time relate in a variety of ways. Stories can be traced in every structuring of time, and once a structure exists, it might feature in new stories. Noncoordination of these manifestations of time is usually not a problem, unless a person or organization is prevented from functioning, cannot fulfill obligations, does not recognize itself or enters a state of utter confusion. Individuals live in society, and that entails encounters with various systems times and narrative times. Some rhythms will be internalized, others consciously followed and many can be safely ignored. For governance systems, especially of the more ambitious sort, life is not that easy. Governance needs to organize itself for a job that is always changing, with demands that tend to multiply. It might try to impose its temporality on society, but that is a recipe for disaster, as systems might collapse or lose their identity, thus their functionality (Jessop, 2006).

Governance systems can invoke their capacities for organizing and thinking, their power to craft stories imagining futures desired and feared, to legitimize present or future institutions and interventions (Beckert, 2016). Stories can make different futures understandable, imaginable and can make them feel worth working for. Such narrative effort will require a *congruence* of temporalities. Ideally, a new narrative, translated into new institutions, can enhance the congruence, a similarity real enough to allow for a practical fit, between different systems times and between experiential and systems times. At the very least, the narrative time appearing in governance discourse ought to bring temporalities relevant for problem solving into the picture, and this means rendering it understandable for a new audience (Hajer & Oomen, 2025).

Working on congruent temporalities is finding ways to tell stories that make something relevant by bringing it into the world of others in a very specific way. Making things feel real by moving them forward or backward in time, speeding up or slowing them down, translating them to different rhythms, condensing and summarizing, highlighting key events, allows to show starting points now and in the past that were not noticed before, processes that were not visible, implications not considered relevant. We have here an experiment with structure which makes the content more persuasive, sometimes rendering the message visible for the first time, sometimes adding urgency to a story vaguely or duly noted but not taken too seriously. Congruence between experiential and systems time via narrative time can open up windows for people to understand systems anew; it might also create support for a remaking of systems.

Concluding

Stories are everywhere, and this is not surprising, as we construct our world through narrative. Narrative structures time and space, distinguishes interior and exterior forces, locates agency and creates meaning. In doing so, it connects ideas, values and affect and brings people together, through the act of storytelling and the content of the stories. Stories make community, in other words, so governance must know and avail itself of important stories in the community, while cultivating the craft of storytelling, to organize itself and the community.

Leadership, we know, can overcome some of the imperfections of governance systems, and help them to fulfill their potential. Crafting and telling stories become valued leadership skills, but we would add now that insight in the diverse functions and features of stories can support those skills. We are not speaking of theoretical knowledge necessarily, as what brought people into leadership roles was often their intuitive grasp of these principles. Practical wisdom, judgment or *phronesis*, in terms of Aristoteles (and more recently Bent Flyvbjerg (1998)) cannot easily be circumscribed, but we would argue that one of its core components is the ability to read and navigate the narrative landscape in and around governance, which we now understand a bit better.

In Chapter 3, we add an important element to our theory of narrative and interpretation, that is, we elaborate the story of metaphors, figures which considerably extend the functionality of stories. Metaphors open new conceptual and affective vistas, and render hitherto incomprehensible, or rather, boring and seemingly too well-known phenomena, into something new, interesting and understandable. This will lay the groundwork for Chapter 4, where we grapple with narratives and metaphors of and for sustainability.

References

Adam, B. (2013). *Timewatch: The Social Analysis of Time*. Chichester, United Kingdom: John Wiley & Sons, Ltd.
Alvesson, M. (1987). *Organizations, Culture, and Ideology*. International Studies of Management & Organization.
Alvesson, M. (2004). *Knowledge Work and Knowledge-Intensive Firms*. Oxford: Oxford University Press.
Anderson, B. (American C. of L. S.) (2006). *Imagined Communities: Reflections on the Origin and Spread of Nationalism* (3rd ed., p. 240). Verso Books.
Antze, P., & Lambek, M. (Eds.). (2016). *Tense Past* (0 ed.). Routledge.
Bacchi, C. L. (2009). *Analysing Policy: What's the Problem Represented to Be?* Pearson.
Baecker, D. (2006). Niklas Luhmann in the society of the computer. *Cybernetics & Human Knowing*, 13(2), 25–40.
Baetens, J. (2018). Stories and storytelling in the era of graphic narrative. *Stories*, 12, 27–44.
Bakhtin, M. M. (2010). *The Dialogic Imagination: Four Essays*. University of Texas Press.
Bal, M. (2002). *Travelling Concepts in the Humanities: A Rough Guide*. University of Toronto Press.
Barnes, T. J., & Duncan, J. S. (1992). *Writing Worlds. Discourse, Text and Metaphor in the Representation of Landscape*. Routledge.
Barthes, R. (1957). *Mythologies*. Éditions du Seuil.
Barthes, R., & Duisit, L. (1975). An introduction to the structural analysis of narrative. *New Literary History*, 6(2), 237–272.
Barthes, R., Howard, R., & Ward, M. (1990). *The Fashion System*. University of California Press.

References

Baxandall, M. (1979). The language of art history. *New Literary History*, *10*(3), 453–465.

Beckert, J. (2016). *Imagined Futures: Fictional Expectations and Capitalist Dynamics*. Harvard University Press.

Beckert, J. (2024). *How We Sold Our Future: The Failure to Fight Climate Change*. John Wiley & Sons, Ltd.

Béland, D., & Howlett, M. (2016). How solutions chase problems: Instrument constituencies in the policy process. *Governance*, *29*(3), 393–409.

Berger, A. A. (2014). Semiotics and society. *Society*, *51*(1), 22–26.

Bevir, M. (1999). Foucault, power, and institutions. *Political Studies*, *47*(2), 345–359.

Bevir, M. (2011). Public administration as storytelling. *Public Administration*, *89*(1), 183–195.

Bietti, L. M., Tilston, O., & Bangerter, A. (2019). Storytelling as adaptive collective sensemaking. *Topics in Cognitive Science*, *11*(4), 710–732.

Bracher, M. (1993). *Lacan, Discourse, and Social Change: A Psychoanalytic Cultural Criticism*. Cornell University Press.

Cairney, P. (2016). *The Politics of Evidence-Based Policy Making*. Springer.

Certeau, M. de. (1988). *The Writing of History*. Columbia University Press.

Chaffin, B. C., Gosnell, H., & Cosens, B. A. (2014). A decade of adaptive governance scholarship: Synthesis and future directions. *Ecology and Society*, *19*(3), 13. www.jstor.org/stable/26269646.

Chandler, D. (2001). *Semiotics for Beginners* [Webpage].

Cooke, B., & Kothari, U. (2001). *Participation: The New Tyranny?* Zed Books.

Culler, J. (2002). *Barthes: A Very Short Introduction*. Oxford: Oxford University Press.

Cutchins, D. (2017). Bakhtin, intertextuality, and adaptation. In T. Leitch (Ed.), *The Oxford Handbook of Adaptation Studies*. Oxford: Oxford University Press.

Czarniawska, B. (1997). *A Narrative Approach to Organization Studies* (Vol. 43). Sage Publications.

Czarniawska, B. (2002). *A Tale of Three Cities, or the Glocalization of City Management*. Oxford: Oxford University Press.

Czarniawska, B. (2010). The uses of narratology in social and policy studies. *Critical Policy Studies*, *4*(1), 58–76.

Dalrymple, W. (2004). *From The Holy Mountain: A Jou*. Penguin Books India.

Davis, R. G. (1979). Benjamin, storytelling and Brecht in the USA. *New German Critique*, *17*, 143–156.

de Certeau, M. (1984). *The Practice of Everyday Life*. University of California Press.
de Vries, J. R., van der Zee, E., Beunen, R., Kat, R., & Feindt, P. H. (2019). Trusting the people and the system. The interrelation between interpersonal and institutional trust in collective action for agri-environmental management. *Sustainability, 11*(24), 7022.
Deely, J. (2003). The word semiotics: Formation and origins. *Semiotica, 2003*(146), 1–49.
Deleuze, G., & Guattari, F. (1987). *A Thousand Plateaus: Capitalism and Schizophrenia*. Continuum.
Dellepiane-Avellaneda, S. (2010). Good governance, institutions and economic development: Beyond the conventional wisdom. *British Journal of Political Science, 40*(1), 195–224.
Duineveld, M., Van Assche, K., & Beunen, R. (2013). Making things irreversible. Object stabilization in urban planning and design. *Geoforum, 46*, 16–24.
During, R. (2010). *Cultural Heritage Discourses and Europeanisation: Discursive Embedding of Cultural Herigate in Europe of the Regions*. Wageningen University.
Eco, U. (1976). *A Theory of Semiotics*. Indiana University Press.
Eco, U. (1979). *The Role of the Reader: Explorations in the Semiotics of Texts*. Indiana University Press.
Eco, U. (1984a). Metaphor, dictionary, and encyclopedia. *New Literary History, 15*(2), 255–271.
Eco, U. (1984b). *The Role of the Reader: Explorations in the Semiotics of Texts* (Vol. 318). Indiana University Press.
Eco, U. (1994). *The Limits of Interpretation*. University of Indiana Press.
Eco, U. (2000). *Kant and the Platypus: Essays on Language and Cognition*. HMH.
Eco, U. (2025). *Six Walks in the Fictional Woods*. Harvard University Press.
Eisenberg, R. (2007). Divided we fall: The roots of the Great Jewish Revolt against Rome. *Hirundo The McGill Journal of Classical Studies, 5*, 147–160.
Eriksen, T. H. (2010). *Ethnicity and Nationalism: Anthropological Perspectives: Third Edition*. Pluto Press.
Fairclough, N. (2005). Discourse in processes of social change: "transition" in central and eastern Europe. *B.A.S. British and American Studies, 11*, 9–34.
Ferkany, M. (2015). Is it arrogant to deny climate change or is it arrogant to say it is arrogant? Understanding arrogance and cultivating humility in climate change discourse and education. *Environmental Values, 24*(6), 705–724.

Fink, B. (2017). The master signifier and the four discourses. In D. Nobus (Ed.). *Key Concepts of Lacanian Psychoanalysis* (pp. 19–37). Routledge.

Fischer, F. (2003). *Reframing Public Policy: Discursive Politics and Deliberative Practices*. Oxford University Press.

Flyvbjerg, B. (1998). *Rationality and Power: Democracy in Practice*. University of Chicago Press.

Foucault, M. (1970). *The Order of Things*. Pantheon Books.

Foucault, M. (1971). Orders of discourse. *Social Science Information*, *10*(2), 7–30.

Foucault, M. (1976). *Histoire de la sexualité. Tome 1: La volonté de savoir*. Paris: Gallimard.

Foucault, M. (1979). *Discipline and Punish: The Birth of the Prison*. Penguin Books.

Foucault, M. (2002). *Archaeology of Knowledge* (2nd ed.). Routledge.

Frye, N. (2009). Anatomy of criticism. In D. J. Hale (Ed.), *The Novel: An Anthology of Criticism and Theory 1900–2000*. John Wiley & Sons, Ltd.

Fuller, S. (1991). Disciplinary boundaries and the rhetoric of the social sciences. *Poetics Today*, *12*(2), 301–325.

Gabriel, Y. (2015). Narratives and stories in organizational life. In Y. Gabriel *The Handbook of Narrative Analysis* (pp. 273–292). John Wiley & Sons, Ltd.

Geertz, C. (1973). *The Interpretation of Cultures: Selected Essays*. Basic Books.

Graeber, D. (2018). *Bullshit Jobs: A Theory*. Simon & Schuster.

Gunder, M., & Hillier, J. (2009). *Planning in Ten Words or Less: A Lacanian Entanglement with Spatial Planning*. Ashgate Publishing, Ltd.

Hajer, M. A., & Oomen, J. (2025). *Captured Futures: Rethinking the Drama of Environmental Politics*. Oxford University Press.

Hogan, P. C. (2011). *Affective Narratology: The Emotional Structure of Stories*. University of Nebraska Press.

Hook, D. (2003). Language and the flesh: Psychoanalysis and the limits of discourse. *Pretexts: Literary and Cultural Studies*, *12*(1), 43–63.

Hook, D., & Vanheule, S. (2016). Revisiting the master-signifier, or, Mandela and repression. *Frontiers in Psychology*, 6. Published Online: 2016-01-19. https://doi.org/10.3389/fpsyg.2015.02028

Jasanoff, S. (2004). *States of Knowledge: The Co-Production of Science and the Social Order*. Routledge.

Jessop, B. (2006). Spatial fixes, temporal fixes and spatio-temporal fixes. In N. Castree & D. Gregory (Eds.), *David Harvey: A Critical Reader* (pp. 142–166). Blackwell Publishing.

Jessop, B. (2007). From micro-powers to governmentality: Foucault's work on statehood, state formation, statecraft and state power. *Political Geography, 26*(7), 34–40. https://doi.org/10.1016/j.polgeo.2006.08.002.
Kapoor, I. (2014). Psychoanalysis and development: Contributions, examples, limits. *Third World Quarterly, 35*(7), 1120–1143.
Kittler, F. A. (1999). *Gramophone, Film, Typewriter*. Stanford University Press.
Lam, J. C. K., Walker, R. M., & Hills, P. (2014). Interdisciplinarity in sustainability studies: A review. *Sustainable Development, 22*(3), 158–176.
Latour, B. (1996). *Aramis, or The Love of Technology*. Harvard University Press.
Latour, B. (2004). *Politics of Nature: How to Bring the Sciences into Democracy*. Harvard University Press.
Latour, B. (2005). *Reassembling the Social: An Introduction to Actor-Network-Theory*. Oxford: Oxford University Press.
Leach, E. (1989). *Claude Levi-Strauss*. University of Chicago Press.
Lévi-Strauss, C. (1968). *Structural Anthropology (1–2)*. Allen Lane.
Linde, C. (1993). *Life Stories: The Creation of Coherence*. Oxford University Press.
Lotman, Yu. M., Uspensky, B. A., & Mihaychuk, G. (1978). On the semiotic mechanism of culture. *New Literary History, 9*(2), 211–232.
Lowery, B., Dagevos, J., Chuenpagdee, R., & Vodden, K. (2020). Storytelling for sustainable development in rural communities: An alternative approach. *Sustainable Development, 28*(6), 1813–1826.
Luhmann, N. (1989). *Ecological Communication*. University of Chicago Press.
Luhmann, N. (1990). *Political Theory in the Welfare State*. Mouton de Gruyter.
Luhmann, N. (1995). *Social Systems*. Stanford University Press.
Luhmann, N. (2012). *Theory of Society, Volume 1. Cultural Memory in the Present*. Stanford University Press.
Luhmann, N. (2018). *Organization and Decision*. Cambridge University Press.
Lyotard, J. F. (1984). *Postmodern Condition: A Report on Knowledge*. Manchester University Press.
Maggio, R. (2014). The anthropology of storytelling and the storytelling of anthropology. *Journal of Comparative Research in Anthropology and Sociology, 5*(02), 89–106.
Makaryčev, A. S., & Jacyk, A. V. (2017). *Lotman's Cultural Semiotics and the Political*. Rowman & Littlefield International.
Marquardt, J., & Delina, L. L. (2021). Making time, making politics: Problematizing temporality in energy and climate studies. *Energy Research & Social Science, 76*, 102073.

Massey, D. B. (2005). *For Space*. Sage Publications.
McGowan, T. (2012). *The End of Dissatisfaction?: Jacques Lacan and the Emerging Society of Enjoyment*. State University of New York Press.
McGowan, T. (2022). *Enjoyment Right & Left*. Sublation Media.
McHoul, A., & Grace, W. (1995). *A Foucault Primer: Discourse, Power and the Subject*. Melbourne University Press.
Miall, D. S., & Kuiken, D. (1994). Foregrounding, defamiliarization, and affect: Response to literary stories. *Poetics, 22*(5), 389–407.
Miller, H. T. (2002). *Postmodern Public Policy*. SUNY Press.
Miller, H. T. (2012). *Governing Narratives: Symbolic Politics and Policy Change*. University of Alabama Press.
Mosse, D. (2005). *Cultivating Development: An Ethnography of Aid Policy and Practice*. Pluto Press.
Muller, J. Z. (2018). *The Tyranny of Metrics*. Princeton University Press.
Pile, S. (2013). *The Body and the City: Psychoanalysis, Space and Subjectivity*. Routledge.
Propp, V. (with Pirkova-Jakobson, S.). (2015). *Morphology of the Folktale* (L. Scott, Trans.). Martino Fine Books.
Putnam, R. D. (2000). *Bowling Alone: The Collapse and Revival of American Community*. Simon & Schuster.
Rabinow, P., & Sullivan, W. M. (1987). *Interpretive Social Science: A Second Look*. University of California Press.
Rappaport, J., & Simkins, R. (1991). Healing and empowering through community narrative. *Prevention in Human Services, 10*(1), 29–50.
Ricoeur, P. (1979). The human experience of time and narrative. *Research in Phenomenology, 9*, 17–34.
Robb, G. (2008). *The Discovery of France*. Picador.
Rodríguez-Ferrándiz, R. (2019). Faith in fakes: Secrets, lies, and conspiracies in Umberto Eco's writings. *Semiotica, 2019*(227), 169–186.
Rorty, R. (1989). *Contingency, Irony, and Solidarity*. Cambridge University Press.
Rosa, H. (2013). *Social Acceleration: A New Theory of Modernity*. Columbia University Press.
Rosanvallon, P., & Goldhammer, A. (2008). *Counter-Democracy: Politics in an Age of Distrust*. Cambridge University Press.
Sandercock, L. (1998). *Making the Invisible Visible: A Multicultural Planning History*. University of California Press.
Schuster, C. I. (1985). Mikhail Bakhtin as rhetorical theorist. *College English, 47*(6), 594–607.
Scott, J. C. (2009). *The Art of Not Being Governed: An Anarchist History of Upland Southeast Asia*. Yale University Press.
Scott, J. C. (2017). *Against the Grain: A Deep History of the Earliest States*. Yale University Press.

Shields, R. (2013). *Places on the Margin: Alternative Geographies of Modernity*. Routledge.

Starks, T. (2022). *Cigarettes and Soviets: Smoking in the USSR*. Northern Illinois University Press, an imprint of Cornell University Press.

Stone, D. (2012). *Policy Paradox: The Art of Political Decision Making* (3rd ed.). W.W. Norton & Co.

Sveningsson, S., & Alvesson, M. (2003). Managing managerial identities: Organizational fragmentation, discourse and identity struggle. *Human Relations*, 56(10), 1163–1193.

Swyngedouw E., M. Dunford (Ed.), & G. Kafkalis, G. (Ed.) (1992). The Mammon quest. "Glocalisation," interspatial competition and the monetary order: The construction of new scales. In *Cities and Regions in the New Europe. The Global-Local Interplay and Spatial Development Strategies* (pp. 39–67). Belhaven Press.

Sztompka, P. (1991). *Society in Action: The Theory of Social Becoming*. University of Chicago Press.

Todorov, T. (1975). *The Fantastic: A Structural Approach to a Literary Genre*. Cornell University Press.

Turcan, R. (2013). *The Gods of Ancient Rome: Religion in Everyday Life from Archaic to Imperial Times*. Routledge.

Van Assche, K., Beunen, R., & Gruezmacher, M. (2024). *Strategy for Sustainability Transitions: Governance, Community and Environment*. Edward Elgar Publishing.

Van Assche, K., Duineveld, M., & Beunen, R. (2014). Power and contingency in planning. *Environment and Planning A*, 46(10), 2385–2400.

Van Assche, K., & Gruezmacher, M. (2025). *Psychoanalysis and Governance: Discourse and Decisions, Identities and Futures*. Taylor & Francis.

Van Assche, K., Verschraegen, G., Beunen, R., Gruezmacher, M., & Duineveld, M. (2023). Combining research methods in policy and governance: Taking account of bricolage and discerning limits of modelling and simulation. *Futures*, 145, 103074.

Van Dijk, T. (2006). How the hands of time mould planning instruments: Iterative adaptation pushing limits in rural areas. *European Planning Studies*, 14(10), 1449–1471.

Vanbergen, J. (1993). The text-analytical study of art criticism: A model for establishing the complexity and specificity of cultural communication. In A. Rigney & D. W. Fokkema (Eds.), *Utrecht Publications in General and Comparative Literature* (Vol. 31, pp. 217–226). John Benjamins Publishing Company.

Verdery, K. (1996). *What Was Socialism, and What Comes Next?* Princeton University Press.

References

Verdery, K. (2003). *The Vanishing Hectare: Property and Value in Postsocialist Transylvania*. Cornell University Press.
Williams, J. M. (2005). Bakhtin on teaching style. *Written Communication, 22*(3), 348–354.
Winner, T. G. (1979). Some fundamental concepts leading to a semiotics of culture: An historical overview. *Semiotica, 27*(1–3).
Yanow, D. (2000). *Conducting Interpretive Policy Analysis* (Vol. 47). Sage Publications.
Yanow, D. (2007). Interpretation in policy analysis: On methods and practice. *Critical Policy Studies, 1*(1), 110–122.
Young, L. S., & Frosh, S. (2018). Psychoanalysis in narrative research. In K. Stamenova, & R. D. Hinshelwood (Eds.). *Methods of Research into the Unconscious* (pp. 199–210). Routledge.
Zizek, S. (2015). *Absolute Recoil: Towards A New Foundation Of Dialectical Materialism*. Verso Books.

3 | Metaphors and the Amplification of Meaning

In this chapter, we explore the creation of meaning through metaphor. We pay special attention to the expansion of meaning through metaphors, establishing connection between semantic domains, explaining one phenomenon in terms of others, while carefully articulating the trade-offs always involved. Metaphors, just as narratives, can travel, sometimes conspicuously without their narratives, sometimes accompanied. They can gain and lose strength, and they can encounter resistance. We then consider the importance of metaphoric understandings of leadership, community, environment and good governance, concepts central to the understanding of sustainability leadership.

Introduction

Life is full of metaphors, and we understand life through metaphor. Didn't we just say that we understood ourselves through narrative? Indeed, but those narratives are so much more powerful in their explanation of phenomena because of metaphors. We understand things in many ways through *analogy*, through a comparison that is often silent. In ancient rhetoric, a metaphor is nothing more than such silent comparison, yet more recent theory has illuminated their deeper workings (Gunderson, 2009). Analogy is one of the most elementary tools to understand something, as something we already are familiar with can serve to explain something else. This saves us time and effort, and it brings in the unfamiliar into the sphere of familiarity.

The analogy we invoke, however, is likely the result of a history of other invocations – we understand something in terms of other terms that came about by pointing further back at things we are supposed to know. This only works because we forgot, collectively and individually, that older analogies structure the new ones proving so useful (Foucault, 2002b). The reality of always receding explanations, of solid ground remaining out of sight because of endless analogies, cannot be calculated, as this would hamper social life. Analogic movement never stops, a situation analogous to the semantics of words and any other sign. Signs require other signs to define them, signs which mean something because of more signs, etc. Semiotician C.S. Peirce speaks here of *infinite semiosis*, and we can distinguish already two meanings of that concept: Finding solid ground in interpretation is impossible, as touching reality is impossible, and second, that *new* meanings will always show up, in new contexts, with new interpreters who bring new associations to bear on the sign encountered (Eco, 1976).

As words and other signs cannot be pinned down objectively, and as they will generate new signs in new interpretive situations, analogies cannot escape this symptom of the way we craft our realities. Words refer to other words, signs to other signs, and analogies to other analogies, linking up not just words but spheres of reality that have been described in words and stories before. Thus, cultures can self-organize; they can establish groups through building worlds out of thin air. Group and world harden in the same process, a process of meaning-making and social formation, where the existence of the group serves as reference point and truth guarantee for the version of the world built, and the truth of the world undergirds the reality of the group (Barth, 1998; Strathern, 1988). Within budding societies, groups and roles can differentiate which further solidify the developing truth, by guaranteeing and possibly imposing it, a process that is necessarily tautological: *it is so because we say so, because it is so* (Luhmann et al., 2004).

Metaphor Revisited

Metaphors, in this perspective, are nothing more than structured and productive analogies. By this we mean that they are capable of producing meaning because of a pre-existing structure in a different semantic domain, an already established field of recognizable meanings, to which can be related (Lakoff & Johnson, 2008). This prestructuring generates a potential for connections between concepts in the new domain, the one to interpret for the first time, or find new meanings in. Old explanations might be inadequate, looking less real and metaphors might shed a new light on them.

The operation of metaphor can work two ways: they familiarize and defamiliarize. One can resort to new metaphors to find new meaning, and one can rely on them to find structure in what was confusing and new (Ricoeur, 2006). Old metaphors might be rejected and replaced by new ones, or metaphors might appear where they were not immediately apparent. As with narrative, they might find acceptance and dissemination for a variety of reasons, and they can travel through various means. People might not know why they are attracted to a new metaphor, or why the new story that emerges through its use is so alluring; they might also not be aware of the metaphor, or the way it travelled (Gibbs, 1994; Ricoeur, 1996).

The old domain of meaning, the one already structured, we call the *source domain*, and the one we try to structure or grasp anew, is the *target domain* (Figure 3.1). Target domain and source domain can't be too different, as nobody would understand the metaphor, or would likely see it as a purely artistic expression if the domains appear unrelated. In other words, it must be possible for enough people to recognize analogies between the domains (Lakoff & Johnson, 2008). Interestingly, the attempt at metaphor can *make* analogies that were not considered before. Once one connection between domains

Figure 3.1 Metaphors attempt to comprehend a concept within one domain of life (target domain) by drawing parallels to a different domain (source domain) where the concept is already understood. By employing various metaphors to explain the same concept, such as "community" and drawing insights from different source domains, we can obtain diverse perspectives in the target domain. Consequently, our inferences about what we must collectively do to maintain and preserve the community, as well as its essence, will vary.

is established, others might follow. Sometimes, an analogy between domains already circulates in the culture, so metaphors follow easily; in other cases, it is rather the metaphor that establishes a broader analogy – which can then support new metaphors.

If the target and source domain already appear too similar, the power of metaphor to generate new insights is limited. One might feel oneself more at home in the world or the subject matter, if new metaphors do not add much. This might be most relevant in situations where that world is under threat (Lakoff, 2016). When discovery or reinterpretation would be advantageous, such layering of self-similar metaphors connecting domains already close, is an issue. Not only does it add little, it also renders the discursive world in question less open to questions, more immune to change.

Different metaphors highlight different features in a phenomenon through the connection with different source domains and, certainly, the selection of analogous traits used in that connection. Thus, when metaphors change in culture or subculture, when various metaphors coexist in parts of society, in organizations or professions, alternative insights in the target domain, or the object, practice, idea of special interest in that domain are at stake (Charteris-Black, 2005). Which might be a problem, or not. Old and new are compared or unknowingly blended if different discourses meet each other, and if key concepts are silently considered through different metaphorical lenses, this might become an issue. People and organizations might think they speak of the same thing, but they are not. Consequences for governance can be significant, as the policy implications of different metaphorical conceptions of "community," "governance," "health," "environmental quality" and of course "democracy" can diverge beyond measure (Semino, 2008).

One can consciously apply several metaphors to the same issue, in the hope to elucidate a subject from different angles and find synergies or, perhaps superior angles. This phenomenon can occur within a research team, even within an individual, or one can perceive the web of disciplines as a proliferation of metaphors. Consequently, interdisciplinary work can be interpreted as an effort to combine metaphors and amplify insights. (Ortony, 1993; Toulmin, 2003). In governance, one can see the value of multiple metaphors in participatory processes, where voices can appear which are grounded in different metaphoric universes (Peters & Peters, 2018). Yet also the cultivation of truly different perspectives within the governance system, and the possibility for them to confront and learn, rather than be integrated in predefined schemes, can be understood as harnessing the power of combined metaphors (Dryzek, 2013).

The spaceship earth metaphor draws out different analogies, compared to the earth as metaphorical mother. They also draw on different narrative traditions and produced different stories. The earth was known as a mother figure to the ancient Greeks and many other cultures, yet, for the Greeks, Gaia wasn't much of a caring figure, and the Gaia of the twentieth century counter-culture, as a harmonious unity, an organism itself, didn't dwell much on the conflict that constituted our world for the Greeks, let alone her rather vindictive tendencies. The same counter – culture that saw Gaia coming back from the dead, in a better mood than her ancient manifestation, saw the birth of actual spaceships, and the experience of fragility and radical dependence and interdependence in space travel. Each metaphor highlights aspects of our relationship to the planet, associates with specific emotions and generates policy orientations. Within the same metaphor, different interpretations remain possible, as there are many mother figures imaginable, and as a spaceship can suggest dependence or rather control, steering and the amazing power of technology. (Boulding, 2011; Höhler, 2015)

Governance systems and their communities do not rely on single metaphors to understand something, just as they cannot be fully integrated under one narrative that would explain all. Metaphors come and go, coexist and compete, just as narratives mix and mingle, transform each other and keep each other in place. In the narrative fabric of our lives, and the one upholding governance systems, metaphors can play the special role of *connectors of narratives* (Figure 3.2). Stories can support each other through shared metaphors, as when stories are nested, kept in place by ideologies, as grand stories providing us with metaphors that can pervade a great many other stories (Ricoeur, 2006). Religious or secular worldviews ("enlightenment") can support stories about the good life, justice, the real and good community. Those stories can sneak similar metaphors into specific policies, ideas on structure and process of governance.

Stories can thus connect through shared metaphors, while metaphors can produce new stories fitting fit the narrative fabric of governance and community, and either questioning or reinforcing it, by providing new connectivity. New stories appearing in public discourse might bring new metaphors closer or endow old ones with new

Metaphor Revisited 73

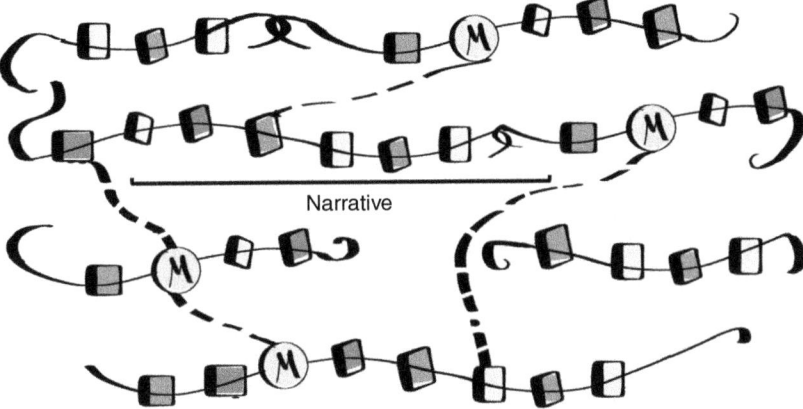

Figure 3.2 Governance and communities don't rely on single metaphors or narratives. Instead, we can comprehend the realities constructed within communities and presented in governance as a fabric of interconnected narratives, nested within each other. Ideologies and religious worldviews can reinforce narratives of good governance and the good community, which then support stories about specific policy domains. Metaphors can establish connections between narratives at the same level and between levels through direct sharing, logical compatibility, or affective resonance. The layering and coupling of narratives reinforce our perception of a natural order, a reality that is challenging to question or alter.

persuasive power (Luhmann, 2000). In governance, metaphors can establish couplings between narratives at the same level and between levels. By this we mean that stories can be nested in other, bigger, stories through shared metaphors, and that they can connect to stories that are not encompassing but just related (Van Assche et al., 2021, 2023). Master narratives can contain metaphors that assist in keeping many other stories in place, and this can be at different levels of abstraction (more things are explained). Hence, stories of good governance underpin many others, as many things make less sense if there is no implied understanding of good governance (Ferguson, 1990; Mosse, 2005). Yet, stories about several topics in governance can be coupled through shared metaphors, even if there is no clear overarching story from which they both derive.

A shared metaphor can be explicitly articulated, wherein the metaphor serves as a common conceptual framework inviting reflection because of its visibility. In this case, the underlying structure or logic provided by the metaphor exhibits noticeable similarities across the two narratives, thereby facilitating a meaningful linkage between them. Alternatively, the metaphor is not evident in either story, but the stories show logical compatibility which stems from the presence of identical or related metaphors. A similar line of reasoning follows from the same metaphorical font. A third form of connectivity stems from shared affect. Here, too, the shared metaphor might not be apparent, but an affective resonance, a shared sensibility between stories might stem from similar metaphoric understandings of a phenomenon relevant to both stories (Ahmed, 2014; Kövecses, 2003).

The weaving of stories, and the layering of metaphors, the multiple connections between stories stabilize our reality. What appears as a natural order does so because of stories about order, about nature and because of metaphors in those stories that pervade many others (Barthes, 2006; Barthes et al., 1990). Metaphors appear and reappear as sources of stability and instability, of conservatism and discovery. Of course, what happens does not primarily depend on the nature of metaphor, but rather on the specific content and coupling of stories about the world.

If we believe in an unchangeable order, changing that order through policy is not in the cards. If we start from an idea, as the ancient Greeks, that the world we live in is one where the Gods are already losing importance, and where each generation of humans has to do a bit better than the previous ones, then a greater diversity of stories and metaphors envisioning progress might drive progress.

Roots and Families

Metaphors become possible when a semantic domain is already fairly structured, when more is understood than the immediate object of comparison. A set of relations has been established, a number of objects delineated in this different plane of signification, and this creates the potential to attribute meaning to more than one thing in the target domain (Lakoff & Johnson, 2008). Analogies between the objects of comparison can lead to analogies observed in a broader domain of meaning, which can then create offspring, or *families of metaphors* (Figure 3.3). If we understand an object or concept through a metaphor, the explanatory power can extend from the whole to the parts, to similar wholes, to a context, possibly to larger wholes (Foucault, 2002b).

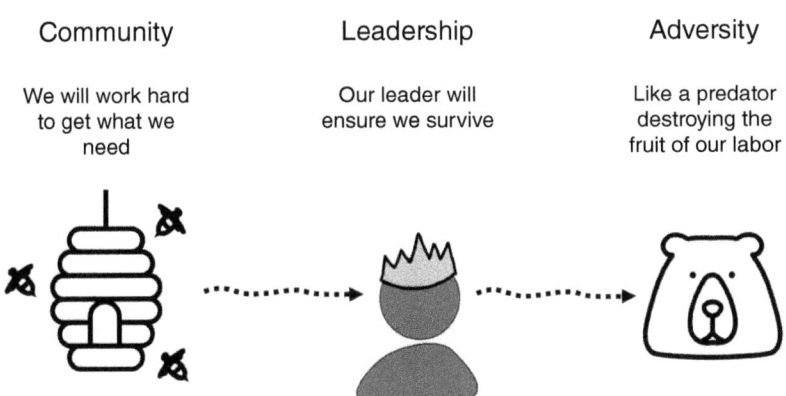

Figure 3.3 Metaphors, when widely used, often give rise to a family of metaphors. In this context, viewing the community as a beehive introduces specific ideas on roles, values, leadership, problems and solutions. A general understanding of adversity can influence the conceptualization of specific problems and, often unconsciously, guide the search for solutions. However, if a family of metaphors is prevalent, they are used as a lens for understanding a wide range of phenomena and questioning them, and shifting to alternative perspectives becomes challenging.

Offspring can come about through the recognition of new analogies, and this will be guided by what is considered relevant and what is already structured in the domain of the metaphor (Eco, 1986). If a metaphor derives from a cultural domain or topic that is established, from an important economic activity, from a landscape that is well-known, then many other metaphors can appear, as the landscape is familiar and extensive. Once something appears as a suitable metaphor, it can guide conversation and thinking, the formation of narratives and the borrowing of selective others. And it opens opportunities for new metaphors to appear. A path might have been well trodden, every nook and cranny of a building might be familiar, yet they only acquire metaphoric potential, when the house or the path are recognized as a useful metaphor.

The productivity further depends on the complexity and importance of what is to be understood, as that for which a metaphor is sought. Understanding society, the good life, justice, moves people to find metaphors, and the question of values, roles, leadership appears immediately on the horizon. Staying in the metaphor can bring out stories, and new metaphors might appear. If the beehive is society, then it is an organized one, with clearly defined roles, a common interest, yet also some mobility, maybe with an authority not lightly questioned. If bad luck is like a storm, then many things can be affected by it. Maybe unconsciously, preparing for a storm, fixing the damage of a storm will take a certain route (Semino, 2008).

Complexity can be explored but also produced by metaphors. New distinctions might be introduced which were not feasible before. If the community is imagined as a ship, it suggests the capacity for change, direction and collective navigation. In contrast, if it is conceived as the rigid and divinely ordained domain of a Pharaoh – a god-like ruler – imagination and flexibility are constrained. Viewing the community as a ship allows for a broader range of comparisons, explanations and metaphors than understanding it as something static and self-contained, like an orange. Families of metaphors, if prevalent, can become a lens for the understanding of a wide variety of phenomena, which also render questioning hard, if they establish an order felt as natural, and if few alternative angles are available (Kövecses, 2003) (Figure 3.3).

Families can derive from a basic or *root metaphor*. Root metaphors are those who already procreated abundantly, and structure a set of phenomena of importance to a society (Figure 3.4). Root metaphors can become enshrined in social structures, governance systems, but also in academic disciplines or cultural genres (Lakoff & Johnson, 2008). As roots, root metaphors can grow deep or shallow, provide more or less anchoring, and support plants big and small. They can uphold the fabric of society, or the lifeworld of a subculture. One and the same metaphor can grow deep roots, and grow a big tree, in one community, while elsewhere it moves to the margins of culture (Bakhtin & Iswolsky, 2020). If leadership is important, chances are that it is explored through various metaphors but also that some become root metaphors. Branching out becomes more likely (Alvesson, 1996).

If we understand poverty through the metaphor of life as a punishment for past sins, and the metaphor of society as a rigidly structured beehive, then we will find inequalities natural, possibilities for change limited, and fighting poverty as a possible in itself. We can, as the medieval mendicant orders, the Franciscans and Dominicans, decide to change our attitude towards

Roots and Families 77

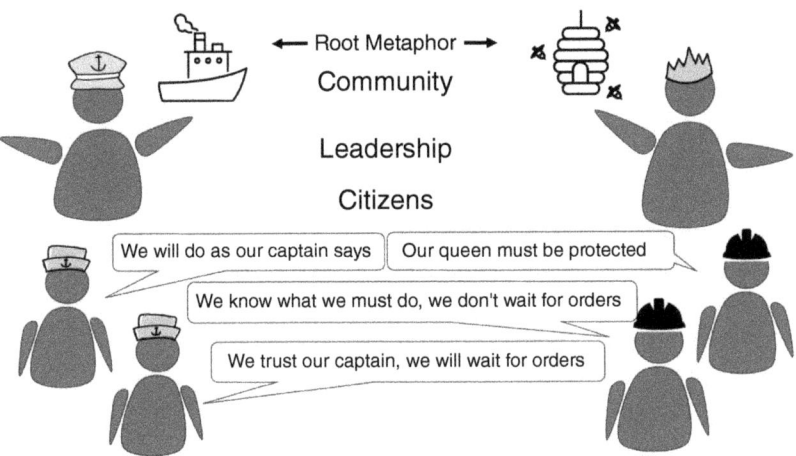

Figure 3.4 Families of metaphors can originate from a fundamental, or "root" metaphor. Different metaphors of the community can lead to varying concepts of role distribution in society, different ideas of citizenship, administration and leadership. These differences can also extend to differences in loyalty, identification with leadership and the community.

cities, and stop seeing them as cradles of sins, so we can take care of the spiritual needs of the urban poor. Which can happen without questioning the social order. Where spiritualities related to the Franciscans attempted to question social inequalities, the hierarchies and riches of the church, they were branded as heretics and relentlessly persecuted. Commiserating with the poor was all good and well, but where that led to criticizing the social order giving rise to this poverty, problems arose. God could not endorse a social order and simultaneously condemn its consequences, so poverty had to be treated by the mendicants as a positive condition, which they could emulate themselves. Poverty was seen as a sign of similarity to Christ, and the simple life a gateway to the spiritual life. (Eco, 2002; Swanson, 1999)

Tracing the root metaphors at work in governance systems and societies can be a worthwhile effort. It can clarify why the same stories appear, why decisions go in the same direction, why alternative explanations are a hard sell (Baumgartner & Jones, 1993; Stone, 2012). Metaphors and stories are likely connected, and the relation between root metaphors and master narratives deserves close attention (Miller, 2012). We do believe it is worth our time, as different metaphors of community will generate diverse ideas on ideal role distributions, on leadership, the common good. Ideas of citizenship might sprout from the same ideas, stories on diversity and the management of conflict. By extension, root metaphors can affect loyalty to, identification with leadership and the community.

We spoke earlier of the connective function of metaphors for narratives, and we can add now that the coupling between root metaphors and master narratives in governance and society deserves tracing. Not all metaphors feature in a narrative context, and not all master narratives are overly metaphorical, but chances are that some couplings are relevant for governance to maintain its stability and legitimacy (Hajer, 1995). Master signifiers can be root metaphors, yet not every master signifier is metaphoric. One can distinguish between *tight and loose coupling*, where some master signifiers can hardly exist outside certain narratives, and without invoking root metaphors, while others retain their function in only the loosest association with a pre-existing narrative or metaphor (Glynos & Howarth, 2007). Rather, they seem to produce ever new ones.

Master narratives, root metaphors and master signifiers do not exist in a stable relation, in other words. Their connectivity greatly contributes to the stability of a world and a world of organization, however, in positive and negative ways. If we live in a world facing new problems, mired in questions of adaptation, challenged to find new solutions, then the rigidity coming with root metaphors, master narratives and signifiers and their couplings needs to be understood. Adaptive capacity, or transformative leadership, cannot be adequately envisioned without finding the roots and the masters, the rigidities that go beyond more obvious issues, such as lack of resources and slow democratic processes.

Stretching, Aging, Sliding and Traveling

As anything else in this world, metaphors change and age. Which brackets their utility in terms of stability or innovation, but also reframes the risk involved in relying on them. Grasping this evolutionary fact opens the door to newer metaphors and urges us to keep the conversation open on important social topics. Like narratives, metaphors can *ossify*, move to the margin of culture and harden, lose their adaptivity and productivity by becoming disconnected from relevant conversations. They can be forgotten, can lose their innovative function by ceasing to spur curiosity, or their stabilizing function by losing prestige, noteworthiness, or connectivity with evolving stories (Eco, 1986).

Metaphors can lose validity when important stories they uphold are not believed anymore, or when social, political and economic structures compatible with their view of the universe collapsed or lost credibility. In times of suffering, conflict, when fissures in the community appear, metaphors can polarize, as condensed points of resistance, summaries of what one does not like anymore (Lakoff, 2014). As they can figure in stories with a wide variety of functions, what happens to those stories, and the forms of organization derived from them, affects the metaphors. Just as metaphors can bestow credibility and intelligibility on something in the world, what happens in the world will affect the reception and use of the metaphor (Charteris-Black, 2005).

Two further mechanisms can be distinguished which typify the transformation of metaphor: *metaphoric stretch* and *metaphoric slide*. A measure of success of a metaphor, similar to the creation of offspring, is the expansion of that what can be explained through metaphor or *stretch*. If people succeed in distilling new meanings from their experience through metaphor, they tend to apply the metaphor to other experiences (Kövecses, 2003). Over time, the field of application of the metaphor can grow, and the perception of success by other people can lead to further adoption, to travel and to stretching (Bal & Marx-MacDonald, 2002). The same analogy can be discovered in other places, different analogies can be found in the same metaphor. What often happens simultaneously is that the analogy becomes ever more tenuous. Metaphors can explain more and more things, until they become meaningless (Lakoff & Johnson, 2008). A distinct mechanism can kick in then, where the metaphor acquires a talismanic character, and what is invoked is not so much understanding as ritualistic agreement. The metaphor comes into its own as a Master Signifier (Zizek, 2019). This mechanism does not always come into play, and more commonly, the metaphor will just lose its allure.

Stretching a metaphor can easily undermine its functionality when novelty was a main attraction of the metaphor in question, and when repetitive and broader application is more obviously self-defeating (Barthes et al., 1990). When feeling at home in the familiar world is what is expected from the metaphor, finding it in more places does not lead as easily to an overstretching. When machines became prevalent in the nineteenth century, they became a symbol for a rapidly changing world, for progress, or for destruction of all things traditional, depending on one's point of view (Benjamin, 1935; Mumford, 2010).

One could be for or against the age and the world of the machines, and the metaphoric force of machines has stayed with us ever since, expressed in popular culture, in science as well as in policy.

While we project meanings and analogies on machines, machines were also used to explain more and more things in life and more aspects of life: the body is a machine, the mind, daily life can be structured in machinic manners. In this metaphor, the mind is easily understood as a machine, hence more easily reduced to the brain. The machinic metaphor thus appears to be a very elastic one, which reflects the importance of machines in society and our fascination with them. One explanation might be that the machine, its increasing complexity and capacity offers more and more analogies to body, mind and society, and that the metaphor remains helpful to explain ourselves to ourselves, in a manner that is not overly confrontational. (Von Bertalanffy, 1967)

When metaphors are successful in the other sense, when their offspring can be found in many places, it can stretch the root metaphor, as the diversity of this offspring, always offering more possible analogies than the parent itself, can reflect back on the parent. The family, in other words, allows people to see the parents in a new way and to bring them to new places. Traveling offspring can bring this about more easily, as the diversity of contexts where they land quickly engenders new uses of the offspring, with consequences for the reinterpretation of the parent. Certainly, there are limits to this process, as root metaphors might be more enshrined and culturally or institutionally stabilized than others.

Metaphoric slide needs to be distinguished from stretch and has little to do with its success. A similarity with stretch is that the metaphor becomes gradually less effective, yet the reason here is that the analogies harnessed by the metaphor seems to lose their allure (Charteris-Black, 2005). What felt meaningful starts to feel empty. For Lacan, the worlds we construct are never entirely stable or coherent, and this stems from the *slippage* of signifiers. In semiotic terms, one could say that the signs, or signifiers, never lock onto signifieds and onto the world outside sign systems in a stable manner (Zizek, 2009). A sign is never perfect in its reference to a concept, and sign and concept together cannot fully grasp, or capture for a long time, the phenomenon out there we are trying to understand and navigate. Lacan assigns the world outside language more agency, and what he calls the Real, is not a passive, though slippery substrate receiving most meanings, yet an active force that can suddenly reject established meanings.

Anything that weakens the analogies on which the metaphor rests, can cause slide, difficulties in the connection between target and source domain. Changes in the target domain, or in the source domain can be pointed at or the slide can be associated with the way analogies are recognized, which can in turn reveal the influence of narrative shifts (Semino, 2008). Often, however, it is virtually impossible to pinpoint the reason for a loss of persuasive power of the metaphor, and we argue that *slippage* in the Lacanian sense is more than likely at play here. When signifiers in either target or source domains lose their grip, the metaphor will feel different. When stories establishing analogies between the domains encounter an unwilling Real, those analogies can crumble, hence, the metaphor. Explaining metaphoric slide in a particular case is often not easy and might not be worth the effort. What is important, is noticing the fact of sliding itself.

Metaphors can travel, as stories, discourse and concepts do. Discursive migration can entail the mobility of every discursive form and figure (Foucault, 1971). Ideas can move without taking their whole narrative context with them, and the same applies to metaphors. Of course, something needs to travel; using a metaphor requires some understanding of a target and source domain, enough to recognize the value of an analogy. We can distinguish two forms of travel, one where the metaphor wanders and triggers effects in new contexts, and one where a metaphoric model finds new target domains, where analogies can be discovered. If we recall the machines, then the metaphor "the mind is a machine," can trigger new effects in new places easily, in new narrative and social contexts, while the "machine" model can attract new buyers, so to speak, new phenomena where machinic analogies can be discovered (Latour, 1999).

If a healthy body is a functioning machine, and a well-governed polity is a healthy body, then good governance is like the maintenance of a machine, and ideas can travel freely between the realms of politics, engineering and health. Public health can be reimagined as bio-politics, using engineering analogies, and social issues can be interpreted readily as maladies or symptoms thereof. This then opens the door to moralizing stories about policies that make society sicker or healthier, and if problem groups can be identified, they can be blamed for causing the disease. Religious ideas upholding a prevalent morality can find easy access to political discourse – ideas of sinners and saints, punishments and rewards. (Foucault, 2020)

Traveling concepts can trigger new metaphors in new contexts, and metaphors can travel on the back of successful narratives. Cultural change, as the spread of new master narratives, tends to entail metaphoric shifts as well. In science, big shifts, often called paradigm changes, tend to associate with deconstruction and reconstruction of root metaphors (Hesse, 2017). Important to note, for our story, is that the boundaries of science, culture and politics are often irrelevant in the meandering ways of metaphors and narratives (Keller, 2000). The idea that these boundaries are hard, and that ideas do not move beyond them, makes it harder to observe their movements (Latour, 1987). In reality, religious metaphors might structure artistic discourse, old scientific knowledge can appear as folklore, and political ideology easily pervades scientific discourse smugly claiming neutrality (Foucault, 2002b).

Metaphors and Complexity

When we claimed that analogy is the most elementary mechanism driving the building of metaphor, the recognition of features in a target domain that seem similar enough to something in the source domain, then we might have been simplifying matters. Analogy builds explanation, but this is supported by a second feature of metaphor: *simplification*. One could argue that not every metaphor is simple, and certainly that metaphors open complex lines of reasoning, which could, as we know, entail new metaphors. True, metaphors allow us to find new patterns, yet this is, at first, a move of complexity reduction. Afterwards, complexity can be rebuilt from a new base, the new metaphor, and possibly the narratives it can mobilize.

Meaning is generated by metaphors through simplification of elements and relationships within the subject to be explained. This process may involve discarding existing discourse and start anew, or, where little explanation exists, it offers support to start from scratch (Schön, 2017). Complexity reduction is at the heart of metaphorical thinking. It can be a matter of building ideas where not much structure is perceived, or a task of decluttering, of finding one's way through an overwhelming mess of associations and ideas (Figure 3.5a). Since we live in cultures, and make sense of our world through shared stories, we do encounter similar problems of attributing meaning, and we tend to grasp for similar solutions, among them metaphors (Sahlins, 2009).

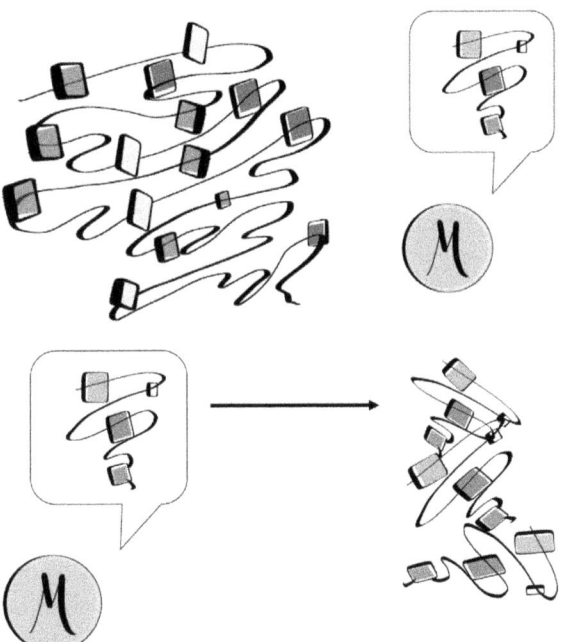

Figure 3.5 (a) While metaphors and other language devices help us to simplify realities to bring them within grasp of our thinking, this simplification can become problematic. Metaphors and narratives can be inappropriate if they offer incorrect simplifications, which do not reflect what we are trying to understand, making actions based on them less effective. The myths of sustainability leadership discussed in later chapters are examples of this: they are stories that are not explaining. (b) Not all metaphors are adequate, and some hit the boundaries of their functionality; simplification can become problematic when trying to rebuild or understand the initial complex situation.

Establishing analogies and reducing complexity, with the aim to rebuild complexity, are thus part and parcel of the same metaphoric operations. Analogies allow us to see structure, find clarity in what is too much, likely incoherent, structure, or too little structure in an environment intuitively grasped as complex (Luhmann, 1995). Complexity reduction supports analogy and vice versa. A general starting point is hard to identify, as real people live in a world that is already cultural, already full of meaning, and as history cannot take us back to the first metaphors. A minor beginning, where a new metaphor comes in, is more easily identifiable, and here, the work of Michel Foucault provides again powerful hints at the processes at work. For Foucault, analogic thinking is historical, meaning that it was not always the same, and that its importance fluctuated over time (Foucault, 2002b, 2003a). Which means that metaphoric thinking evolves, that root metaphors do not have the same fertility everywhere.

Basins appeared in water management as a metaphor capable of radical complexity reduction, yet one that enabled a reconstruction of complexity that could guide new coordination in water policy, and new forms of policy integration beyond water. Many invisible connections in the water system become traceable, through the metaphor of a simple basin, where an outflow determines the unity to be delineated. A basin idea could generate new complexity because it was linked to the concept of a system, where a set of relations can be envisioned that keep a process going. Thus, rivers, creeks, wetlands, lakes and ponds and aquifers could be connected into closed systems with a shared drain, where water moved in flows often unseen. (Molle, 2009)

What remains universal, in Foucault's and our view, is that something new cannot appear naked. It will be dressed in narrative, might be grasped through metaphor, might produce new metaphors. Analogic thinking can wax and wane in importance, yet analogies cannot be missed. An initial structure might be perceived in the target domain thanks to other metaphors, because of existing stories, and modes of reasoning building on them, and this fragile beginning might enable similarities with a better-known semantic domain to be detected. Or, a well mapped semantic domain might have a structure, or generate ideas that feel pregnant, that intuitively seem to have a bearing on other things (Thom, 1990). After which a search for those other things could be initiated. Less likely is the situation where people are confronted with the two domains at the same time, sparking a mapping of one onto the other, and the discovery of insightful analogies.

In this description, too, the starting point keeps receding, and knowledge of one domain seems to imply a simultaneous knowledge of the other. Pure discovery is not possible, as the tool of discovery (the metaphor) already assumes knowledge of what could be discovered. Which, we believe is only another manifestation of the circularity of all discourse, always a product of self-organization, never finding unambiguous ground outside itself (Luhmann, 1989). It is also a reminder that we find ourselves in a world full of other stories, where something unexplored is never entirely undescribed, and where the explorers and their tools are themselves inscribed in a web of stories that generates hints at the further trajectories of explorer and ship (Barthes, 2009; Ricoeur, 2009).

Whereas metaphors can bring realities within the grasp of our thinking by simplification, then building complexity, this does not always work (Figure 3.5b). Not all metaphors are adequate, and some hit the boundaries of their functionality quickly. Simplification can become problematic in several ways. Possibly, the basis for restructuring meaning reveals design flaws to the extent that rebuilding complexity is out of the question: new narratives do not come about, conceptual connections are virtually impossible to forge. Elsewhere, the problem is the mapping of reality itself. The simplification might simply be off the mark, and resist integration with further knowledge because of that reason. As metaphors serve a goal, the distinction between incorrect and inadequate or inappropriate can be subtle (Fernandez, 1972).

> The ideas of development and progress thus hit limits in a world where not all solutions proposed as development worked or were welcomed by the communities where they landed. Both are metaphoric in nature, suggesting a positive movement, growing into something bigger and better, a growing distance from a condition of underdevelopment, which is a state inferior to a future and to other communities that already developed and thus know what development is. In the twentieth century, western nations served themselves of development rhetoric, first to justify colonialism, later to support their interventions in former colonies. Post development thinkers, often people with a first-hand experience of politics in (former) colonies, pointed out the limits of development thinking and the underlying metaphors, which suggested an easy recognition of the right path (forward and up), and a continued dependence on those who knew the path. (Ziai, 2007)

Problematic simplification can thus show itself in hostile reactions, incapacity to connect to audiences, but also through an inability to support narrative development, and further discovery. Not all symptoms need to manifest themselves. A story might take over a community by storm, its central metaphor might be in everyone's mouth yet fade quickly as one finds that what was interesting was mostly the novelty, that not much was explained in the end. Possibly, a recognition follows that what looked interesting was more the difference with a resented story of fading dominance, or the place it came from. An alternative form of fading can come through disappointment in the practical applications of new stories and their metaphors, in terms of technology, or through collective action inspired by them. Inadequacy, however, does not naturally imply rejection, as people and communities have an impressive portfolio of tricks to immunize themselves against disappointment and discovery (Douglas, 1986; Lévi-Strauss, 1974). Old stories can remain in place long after their due date, and novelties can be stubbornly embraced, out of spite against an old order, or because we want to identify with unrealistic aspirations.

The myths of sustainability leadership we discuss in Chapter 5 belong to this category. We speak of myths because they do not adequately explain sustainability, nor leadership, and because their central metaphors fail the test of intellectual or policy relevance. We will engage with them later, and try to explain their popularity and persistence, yet focus our effort now, and throughout this book, on the positive articulation of a more useful perspective on sustainability leadership. Before we grab our tools, the hammers and nails needed for the understanding of sustainability, we leave the terrain of inappropriate metaphors and briefly discuss a series of metaphors which cannot be discarded or ignored when trying to understand sustainability leadership, or to rethink it.

Leadership, Governance and Community

Coevolution Revisited

We spoke of discourse as restless, and as coevolving. Concepts coevolve and discourses coevolve, which means that they shape each other over time, but not all couplings are created equal, meaning that not all stories have the same influence on each other, not all ideas travel together. Stories, in fact, create couplings between ideas that affect their journey, that forges coevolutionary paths (Latour, 1999). What we can call *discursive configurations* are often clusters of stories, that keep each other in place. We know that master narratives can support them, yet other mechanisms might be at work, and a coupling of concepts is one of them. Sometimes, these concepts are metaphoric or derive from latent metaphors (Foucault, 2002a).

Metaphors can create linkages between stories in governance, between levels of governance, between generic and specific stories. Discursive configurations, inside and outside governance, can also come about without the embedding or nesting of narratives. Stories can frame each other, but they can also coevolve in more horizontal relations and the same holds true for concepts (Czarniawska, 2010). All this to say that traveling ideas and stories can relate in various ways, and that, when they do enter a path of mutual influence, a diversity of relations is maintained. At one point, one partner can have a bigger say, yet things can change. Maybe an idea gains currency in the broader culture, in an organizational setting, maybe new stories forge additional connections with ideas and metaphors, thus reshaping a coevolutionary path already embarked upon.

We point this out because the understanding of sustainability leadership hinges crucially on the tracing of coevolutionary paths. Leadership for sustainability is leadership in and through governance, leadership of a community, so ideas of governance and community, of good governance and the good community require our attention. Concepts of leadership are likely shaping and shaped by other ideas, possibly connected through stories about something entirely different (Alvesson & Spicer, 2012). All this, all such couplings and family travels need to be established empirically; they cannot be derived theoretically. How relevant sustainability ideas are versus leadership ideas in their coevolution, and their shaping of stories on sustainability leadership must be determined again in each case. Which form of practical leadership is possible in a given situation, will furthermore depend on the coevolution of institutions and actors, power and knowledge in governance configurations, as established in Chapter 1 (Van Assche et al., 2013).

In other words: which concepts, through which stories, enter the orbit of thinking and organizing regarding sustainability leadership, cannot be predicted. One can safely assume, however, that a few concepts will be relevant. Next chapter will be devoted to sustainability, as stories of sustainability will define both context and goal of sustainability leadership. Now, we sketch the bigger picture of discursive configurations, and consider stories and metaphors of leadership, community and governance.

Thinking and organizing shape each other but cannot be reduced to each other. Translating one to the other is an imperfect affair (Figure 3.6). One mode of organization betrays influences of different ideas, metaphors and stories, while complex organizations and governance systems cannot fully integrate their parts, in institutional and in discursive terms (Hajer, 1995; Van Assche & Gruezmacher, 2025).

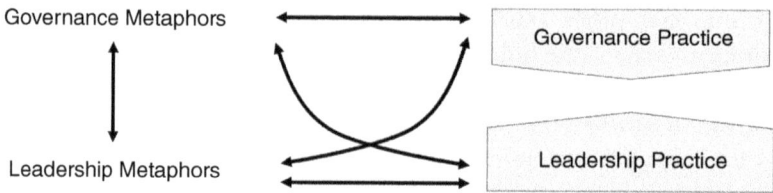

Figure 3.6 Thinking and organizing shape each other but can never be reduced to each other. This is the case because they belong to different domains of human activity, and one cannot be perfectly translated into the other. Different interpretations are always possible, while one form of organizing will always show traces of different ideas, stories, metaphors. Governance metaphors and leadership metaphors can inspire practices of governance and leadership, but they can also shape or contradict each other. Leadership metaphors can directly influence governance practices, while governance metaphors can influence leadership practices. However, the result of this web of relations and interpretations is that leadership practice and governance practice are almost unavoidably in tension.

Conversely, a form of organizing inspires different stories with different observers, introduces new metaphors and associations, into conversations on both thinking and organizing. People looking at anything that is organized come to interpretations that will affect their relation to it. This can happen through a role in the organization, being an active outsider, interacting with it, or as passive outsider still affecting practice – by voting, writing, not buying and so forth. Governance metaphors and leadership metaphors can thus inspire practices of governance and leadership via a diversity of channels. Coexistence of metaphors does not entail cohesion: in the same organization, incoherent leadership ideas might quietly combine with governance stories that do not display much logical fit (Alvesson & Spicer, 2016).

Coevolving metaphors don't always show up together in empirical settings. One cannot infer from coevolution that actual organizational practice takes it cue from it. We need to keep these two points in mind for any discussion of leadership. Leadership metaphors can affect governance practice, governance metaphors can shape leadership practice, but this depends on a variety of factors. Leadership does not necessarily identify with stories about leadership, governance narratives do not necessarily give much thought to leadership, and governance practice can be largely disconnected from both leadership and governance

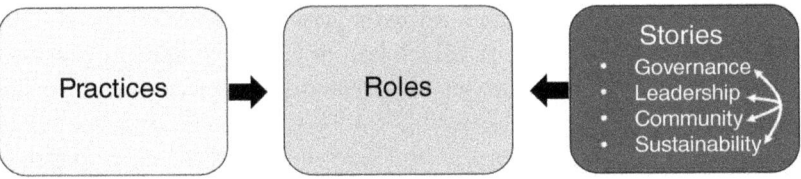

Figure 3.7 Roles arise from narratives that highlight themes like good governance and sustainability. However, what seems desirable in these stories may not always be practical, therefore roles serve as a link between ideas and organization and practice, helping to formalize structures. Roles are thus are key to solving problems and defining the appropriate person for a position, challenges can occur when external narratives shape them rather than internal ones.

narratives (Czarniawska, 2014; Gabriel, 2000) (Figure 3.7) One consequence is that, as we knew, coevolution must be empirically observed, a second one that leadership stories and practices must be related in each case. Third, we can infer that leadership practice and governance practice are almost unavoidably in tension. It is highly unlikely that they stem from narratives that adequately capture the practical traditions and necessities of organizing, and even less likely that these narratives are compatible (March, 2010).

Leadership: Stories and Metaphors

With this big caveat in mind, the warning in the previous paragraphs against seeing tight couplings between ideas and between stories and practices everywhere, we can safely turn to leadership. It is safe to say that speaking about leadership and training for leadership has become an industry in itself. Leadership stories and metaphors have an audience and an influence (Nyberg & Sveningsson, 2014). Stories and metaphors can become influential through key people and organizations embracing them, translating them into action, or by them becoming widely shared. In the case of leadership, its currency is widespread, encompassing elites and large groups aspiring to climb the social ladder (Pfeffer, 2015).

In governance, the influence of neoliberal ideologies and new public management thinking which proposed public sector reform modeled after (often idealized) private sector stories and practices, brought with it not only leadership ideas derived from managerial ideals in the corporate world. It emphasized the importance of leadership itself, as this had been linked firmly in management schools to speed, efficiency and adaptive capacity, which had been traditionally opposed to the slow processes and cumbersome structures of government, in the neoliberal story (Hood & Peters, 2004). A story on governance made an idea of leadership important and vice versa, and the nature of that leadership idea affected leadership styles, functions and roles imagined and implemented (du Gay, 2000; Hood, 2000).

First in private sector, later in the public sector, the leader became a manager and the manager became all-important. New versions of managers emerged, correlated to the belief in continuous reform: interim managers, transition managers, chiefs of restructuring and consultants to whom strategy was outsourced. Management schools promoted the idea of management qualities as leadership qualities that were easily transferable. Managers were supposed to be leaders, and leaders, after the story spread widely, came to look like managers (Mintzberg, 2004). One thing leaders/ managers are supposed to do is to *strategize*, and "big picture stuff" entered the picture of conceptions of both leadership and management. Strategy thinking itself emerged first in military theory, later in political theory, and its jump from business to politics and administration was therefore in a way a jump back. What was new however, is that now also managers of administrative units were expected to strategize, to streamline, while at the same time remaining subjected to bureaucratic realities and political pressures (Mintzberg, 1973).

Meanwhile, business schools competing with each other, proposed new leadership styles and strategy recipes on a regular basis, which provided new opportunities for aspiring leaders to differentiate themselves, for governments and businesses to perform innovation and progress (Parker, 2018). The actual work managers in most governance settings could perform, could not change as much as the fashions in management theory would like, and the requirements of governance, combined with the path and other dependencies to deal with, made for exquisite tensions between expectations and realities of leadership, between story and practice, and between stories of leadership and stories of governance (Pollitt & Bouckaert, 2017).

Mats Alvesson and Andre Spicer, observing leadership ideas and practices, came to a typology of six metaphors of leadership: the leader as gardener, cozy-crafter, saint, cyborg, commander and bully (Alvesson & Spicer, 2010). These metaphors did not derive from management theory, nor directly from stories about leadership circulating more broadly. They were recognized by the authors, in the daily life of organizations, where the self-understanding of managers could differ dramatically from the way their job was perceived. A character considering himself a visionary was appreciated because he "can throw a decent party," an individual priding herself on her empathetic and transformational style might be experienced as a bully. Alvesson's metaphors are therefore not idealized roles, but roles as emerging in practice, out of a host of competing demands, limits on transformation and tensions between stories. Each metaphor leads to other metaphors, and to stories of good leadership, as well as to diverging sets of leadership functions emphasized. It also transpires clearly that each leadership metaphor implies and highlights different relevant coevolutions, different significant relations with other concepts and stories.

If the leader acts as a gardener, and if this metaphor is also on her mind, if it is not a mere accommodation which did not produce much of a story, then this gardener will have a garden, plants, weeds as bad plants, fertilizer. The garden can relate to the larger world in different ways; gardening styles formal and informal, organic or otherwise can be explored. One can recognize forces at work that need to be tamed and others that need to be appreciated and worked with. One can recognize a potential or impose an ideal.

Metaphors of leadership thus help to understand and define roles (hence functions), and, if they take root, they can borrow from or have implications for other notions, such as strategy, system-environment relations, talent, hierarchy and competition. Even concepts such as assets and core business can be redefined through shifting leadership metaphors. A plant might be a weed for one leader; a weed might be an unexpected asset for someone else. It might be good to note that leadership stories have implications for other notions but that, conversely, leadership can be equally defined or redefined by stories about very different subjects. Shifting notions of strategy have implications for leadership, and vice versa (Kornberger, 2012). Which direction prevails hinges on too many factors to summarize, except in the most rudimentary way: *whatever is most important at the moment defines other things*. There is no general rule establishing the dominance of theory versus practice or thinking versus organizing. New and untested ideas can turn out to be a major influence on a wide array of practices, including forms of organizing, and the testing itself can be biased through the same stories (Meyer & Rowan, 1977).

If leaders become more important in a culture, if leadership notions are modeled after ideals of business management, ambitious individuals in the private sector might see their success in business as a clear sign of their leadership qualities. As Nathan Heller, writer for *the New Yorker* (2025) phrases it: "people can acquire a taste for drawing theories of the universe from the growth of their own enterprises." We see here a strong drive to translate theory into practice, success into entitlement, and a reinterpretation of the world (or universe) according to the model of the business enterprise and its leadership roles. Whether this works, depends on more than the business world, yet in a world already simplifying its self-understanding through the prevalence of other business metaphors, it can bring about shifts in political leadership, in thinking and organizing, and rather dramatic shocks in governance.

Governance and Community: Stories and Metaphors

Leadership metaphors can thus fit or inspire leadership styles and actual functioning of leadership, in organizations and communities (Figure 3.8). Similarly, governance metaphors can fit, inspire or reflect actual governance. As with leadership, the governance metaphors and narratives structuring the self-image of a governance system might fit the practice of governance, or less so. New stories might reshape practice, and practice might produce new stories and metaphors, but this does not always enhance the fit between story and practice (Hood, 2000; Power, 2000).

Leadership and governance can match to different degrees, in practice and in stories by insiders or outsiders. The fit is bound to be imperfect, and this is not always a problem. When it becomes a problem, when the always disjointed metaphors of leadership and governance will hit the wall of practice, cannot always be predicted. Insiders might have more information but can also be tied to the stories defining the world they inhabit, and they might be tongue-tied in a more literal sense, as a career might be at stake. Great leaders can turn into jerks easily in storytelling after the storyteller is at a safe distance, maybe after changing jobs.

What leaders do, thus tends to exist in tension with what a governance system might require, as it often misrecognizes the actual

Leadership, Governance and Community

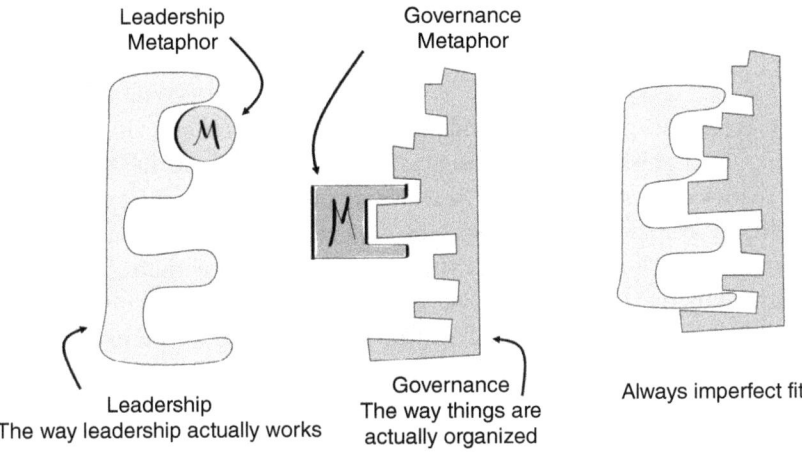

Figure 3.8 Leadership metaphors can fit or inspire leadership styles and actual functioning of leadership, in organizations and in communities. Similarly, governance metaphors can fit, inspire or reflect actual governance in communities. The result is a series of possible fits and nonfits: governance metaphors (and derived narratives) can fit the context of actual governance, or not, and the same applies to leadership. Leadership and governance, structured by more than one metaphor, and more than one narrative, can match to different degrees, but the fit will always be imperfect.

functioning of the system, including the actual flow of decision-making. While this might sound counter-intuitive, we argue that this is mostly the case because of prevalent myths on leadership, systematically overestimating their influence and grip on organizations and larger systems. It might appear as a more natural state of affairs if we accept the mediating role of stories and metaphors in two distinct traditions: those of the persons ascribed as leaders, and those of the collective making the system work. In each tradition, a theory/practice split occurs, an unbridgeable distinction between thinking and organizing.

Political leaders might believe themselves visionaries, heralding a new age by investing heavily in infrastructure projects, while governance might lack the institutional and strategic capacity to implement those projects, to minimize risk and optimize societal benefits. Critical observers might note the role of foreign capital, and the conditions attached to loans and investments. For politicians, administration feels like a stumbling block, to which they respond by continuing the under-investment in governance and edging closer to the foreign partners. Residents, who routinely impute corruption with politicians, and assume incompetence with bureaucrats, see unfinished infrastructure as a symbol of the failure of leadership and governance. (Flyvbjerg et al., 2003)

Gareth Morgan, in his influential 1986 book *Images of organization*, distinguishes eight influential metaphors, which he recognizes in theory and practice: organizations as organisms, brains, machines, political systems, psychic prisons, flux and transformation, and as instruments of domination (Morgan, 1986). More than Alvesson's leadership metaphors, we note that these metaphors easily overlap and combine. More than Alvesson, Morgan tried to be exhaustive, drawing on a wide array of management and organization theory. In our view, the set of metaphors remains rather too much on the side of storytelling in management theory, yet we recognize that all have been influential at some point, either in theory or practice. For us most interesting is that the list already incorporates the idea that boundaries can be transcended. Organizations, processes of community organization we call governance, can be understood in analogy to machines, deploying a metaphor that travelled, as we know, across time and space, between topics and disciplines. They can be psychic prison and instruments of domination (some political systems could be described as such) and they could be understood as political systems.

If organizations can be understood as political systems, political systems can be understood as organizations. Both metaphors have exerted their influence, and an idea of society as a body, of politics as a body politic, can smoothly blend into a corporatist idea of politics, which then translates effortlessly into metaphors of organization (Foucault, 2003b). Boundaries can be blurred further, and not only politics but society itself can then be seen as an organization, as a Swiss watch, where everything must function as clockwork. Individuals and organizations are assigned a place and role, and problems can be diagnosed as issues of dysfunctionality. One can talk politely to the part, replace it, or when respect for the part is too great, adapt the design of the machine, which is an organization, which is society.

Metaphors of governance thus potentially shape metaphors of organization and images of society. Which direction dominates cannot be foreseen. Governance itself appeared on the scene as a concept that was supposed to replace government, with the idea of a pyramid making space for the open table, where governmental and nongovernmental actors find a place (Pierre & Peters, 2020). The shift to governance was supposed to reflect an incipient change in practice, which could be captured in a recipe for participation that could be presented as an ideal for collective decision-making, as a redefinition of the political domain. In reality, the pyramid from theory never existed, and the table was always there, with governmental and other actors always holding sway over the collective.

Using the word "governance," in other words, is not necessary for governance to be there. And if we see collective decision-making as governance, one can trace a variety of stories and metaphors of governance, coevolving with notions of leadership, politics in the narrow sense, strategy, common interests, rights and duties and rules of inclusion. As soon as we think of collective decision-making, and people have thought about this for many centuries, we think of a collective, of decisions, of rules, of patterns of inclusion and exclusion, and of the possibility to move towards a more desirable direction as a community (Aristotle, 2013). The overtly political domain appears as only a part of the configuration of governance, and the boundaries between the political and other forms of organization which contribute to the collective and its decisions, cannot always be drawn (Foucault, 2007).

Distinct models of democracy, in theory and practice, can offer images of governance, and so can other stories about polities and societies. As soon as we have a group organizing itself to take decisions that can bind that group, we can speak of governance (Van Assche & Gruezmacher, 2025). Communities form, and those communities tend to develop discourse regarding themselves and their future and environment, their present and ideal state and ways to maintain or improve an identity. Stories and metaphors of self thus find tight couplings with ideas of relevant environments and of good governance, as well as ideas of belonging and participation (Anderson, 2006; Bevir & Rhodes, 2003). Individuals can be included to different degrees while belonging and participation do not necessarily coincide (Jasanoff, 2011).

If governance is idealized as centralized, with the king as the queen in the beehive, or the pharaoh on top of the pyramid, this describes practice only partially. If, on the contrary, a radical democracy is proclaimed, with total participation by everybody, the practicalities of governance most likely ensure that some decisions are precooked, and that some circles are more influential than others (Loraux, 2019). Governance metaphors in theory and practice need to say something about the distribution of power, so implications for leadership concepts are always nearby. What leadership can do and should do, according to theoretical stories, and stories circulating in practice, cannot be separated from existing and desired governance. Thus, if stories about governance and the reality of governance differ greatly, more space opens up for leadership, either to pursue its own direction, or to fix the gap (Mosse, 2005).

What appears as good leadership can thus stem from governance ideas and from (imperfect) governance practices. Leadership in practice will always be necessary, independently of any discursive construction of leadership, because, in practice, no governance system can do exactly what it pretends to do. Leadership as recognizable discursive position, as formal roles and recognized figures might be necessary for entirely different reasons (Laclau, 2005). This is not an argument against governance, or for weak accountability of leadership, rather an observation that structure and process presuppose each other, while they never match perfectly. Stories of organization, as structure and process, can have a great impact because governance requires both stories and organization and, on the organizational side, both structure and process (Figure 3.9).

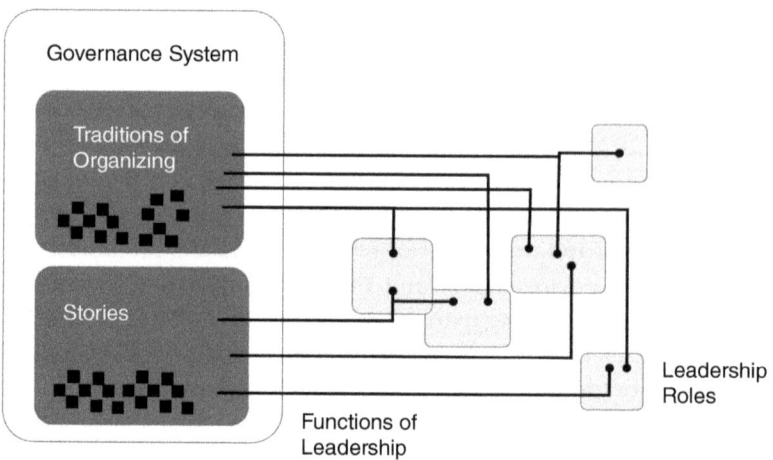

Figure 3.9 Governance encompasses both narratives (stories) and organization, which includes structure and processes. When the narratives about governance and the actual reality of governance diverge significantly, it presents more opportunities for leadership. The established traditions and narratives within the governance system define the functions of leadership, ultimately leading to the structuring of leadership roles.

Reducing the vulnerability of the poor to climate-related events makes sense as a sustainability goal when one believes in climate change, when there are poor and when one believes in the power and authority of governance to do something about this vulnerability. This belief can come in two versions, emphasizing either that governance can meaningfully adapt to climate change, or that governance has a special responsibility towards the poor. The goal can gain importance, when it is silently accepted that a large part of the population will be poor, and leadership embracing it can signify that it identifies with the poor and their concerns, or rather that governance is felt to be failing the poor, and in addressing climate change.

The future and wider environment do not necessarily appear within the sphere of governance, and if so, they are not grasped per se as susceptible to decision-making (Beck, 1992; Latour, 2009). They can appear as context or background, in arguments about other things. Aiming directly at the future, especially the long-term future, or at processes transcending the scale of daily life, is often not evident. Whereas a community might define itself in terms of place and history, that does not guarantee the relevance of those parameters for decision-making, and certainly not that one would imagine changing them, or looking far.

Whether a community considers changing itself and its environment, deliberately, guided by images of environment and future, hinges on the coevolution of discursive and organizational worlds. Stories of leadership, metaphors of governance, organization, of the community itself (clockwork, body or rotten apple?) might have coevolved with versions of an ideal future and a belief that each generation has a duty (to the collective) to bring it closer – as in ancient Greece. Governance tools, policies, laws and plans, to make things happen collectively, to manage risk, to share benefits, to maintain loyalty to the collective while on the road to a better future, might have evolved which support and are supported by those stories and metaphors.

Concluding

Metaphors tend to coevolve, to produce offspring, to travel with stories and produce stories. For the understanding of sustainability leadership, not only metaphors and narratives of leadership are relevant, but given the need to work through governance, understandings of governance. Governance entails a collective, a distribution of power, a web of organizations, and a selection of voices able to speak on a selection of topics, patterns of inclusion and exclusion, hence stories and metaphors on all such topics come within the remit of leadership thinking and practice. Images of organization, stories about the community, concepts of system-environment relations will assert themselves as relevant. Which relations come to the foreground in this process of coevolution has to be ascertained empirically, in each case. Communities, operating on a web of stories and metaphors, supported by an always limited institutional toolbox, cannot always envision themselves in the future, in a wider environment. Leadership is able and willing to produce or alter such vision only under some conditions, conditions again shaped by traditions of thinking and organizing. While prediction remains impossible, observation is in the realm of the possible, however. When neither future, nor environment appear on the radar, when neither routines nor leadership seem to bring it closer, a more precise mapping of metaphors and stories might be in order.

Before we delineate more precisely our perspective on sustainability, and the relevance of narrative and metaphor for its understanding, we derive from the previous paragraphs an idea regarding theory and practice which will inform the following chapters. Metaphor, just as narrative, is useful for us, and we follow Alvesson here, in two ways: to understand practice and to inform and possibly improve practice (Alvesson et al., 2016). If we want to follow his lead, we need to distinguish not two but three things: *stories by outside observers about practice, stories encoded in practice, and the stories circulating in practice.*

Practice can show the traces of metaphors and narratives, becoming reality, however imperfectly, while theory and stories in practice can deploy metaphor directly. Theory can derive from theory and practice. Practice stories can remain close to observation, can use metaphor to understand practice. This can be a newly assembled metaphor, by practitioners, or metaphors and stories borrowed, directly or indirectly, from theory (in management or elsewhere). Practice stories must be distinguished from practice, as stories never capture what actually happens, and self-descriptions, by individuals and organizations require careful distinguishing from their actual functioning and from portrayals of that functioning by others (Luhmann, 2018). Metaphors can play a role in all of them. Any attempt at solving a problem, at transforming an organization or governance system by studying or tinkering with metaphor and narrative, ought to be aware of this diversity of stories and metaphors. Real change might find clues sometimes in practice, elsewhere in theory, or in practice stories, in existing metaphors proving useful or problematic.

If we want to reduce the number of deaths from hazardous chemicals, we need to know about those chemicals, their use and presence in food systems, landscapes, workplaces and ecosystems. Stories about products, about the activities where those products play a role will make a difference, as well as stories about the environments where they show up. Usually, the chemical itself only becomes an object of discourse in a controversy. Sometimes, the compound was consciously promoted as a miracle product to previous generations, now comfortably designated as ignorant, but more commonly, the chemical is hiding in a product, an activity, a place and in stories. Rural landscapes are idyllic, farmers take care of the landscape, are also entrepreneurs in tough markets, thus crop protection cannot be but a good thing, and seems to suggest that benevolent pesticide companies simply support farmers as heroes, protective of our landscapes, their products and our lives. (Brown, 2007)

For the understanding of sustainability, we might want to start by pointing out that it is not a thing but a quality, which means a feature of *something*. Stories about a quality will invoke almost automatically metaphors about the thing imbued with the quality. Stories about improving the quality most likely lead to stories about leadership of the thing imbued with the quality, or the thing that could create the quality somewhere else. As we already established that leadership for sustainability must pass through governance, we know we must speak of governance aiming at a quality of something and usually failing at it. While this starting point appears abundantly vague, it actually offers much to work with, for our analysis of sustainability and sustainability leadership in the following chapters.

References

Ahmed, S. (2014). *Cultural Politics of Emotion*. Edinburgh University Press.
Alvesson, M. (1996). Leadership studies: From procedure and abstraction to reflexivity and situation. *The Leadership Quarterly*, 7(4), 455–485.
Alvesson, M., & Spicer, A. (2010). *Metaphors We Lead By: Understanding Leadership in the Real World*. Routledge.
Alvesson, M., & Spicer, A. (2012). Critical leadership studies: The case for critical performativity. *Human Relations*, 65(3), 367–390.

Alvesson, M., & Spicer, A. (2016). *The Stupidity Paradox: The Power and Pitfalls of Functional Stupidity at Work*. Profile Books.

Alvesson, M., Sveningsson, S., & Blom, M. (2016). *Reflexive Leadership: Organising in an Imperfect World*. SAGE Publications Ltd.

Anderson, B. (American C. of L. S.) (2006). *Imagined Communities: Reflections on the Origin and Spread of Nationalism* (3rd ed., p. 240). Verso.

Aristotle. (2013). *Aristotle's Politics*. University of Chicago Press.

Bakhtin, M., & Iswolsky, H. (2020). Rabelais and his world. In T. Prentki, & N. Abraham (Eds.). *The Applied Theatre Reader* (2nd ed., p. 342). Routledge.

Bal, M., & Marx-MacDonald, S. (2002). *Travelling Concepts in the Humanities: A Rough Guide*. University of Toronto Press.

Barth, F. (1998). *Ethnic Groups and Boundaries: The Social Organization of Culture Difference*. Waveland Press.

Barthes, R. (2006). *Mythologies*. Farrar, Straus and Giroux.

Barthes, R. (2009). *Image-Music-Text* (S. Heath, Trans.). Hill and Wang.

Barthes, R., Howard, R., & Ward, M. (1990). *The Fashion System*. University of California Press.

Baumgartner, F. R., & Jones, B. D. (1993). *Agendas and Instability in American Politics*. University of Chicago Press.

Beck, U. (1992). *Risk Society: Towards a New Modernity*. SAGE Publications Ltd.

Benjamin, W. (1935). The work of art in the age of mechanical reproduction, 1936. In M. Holben Ellis (Ed.). *Historical Perspectives in the Conservation of Works of Art on Paper* (pp. 217–252). New York: Schocken Books.

Bevir, M., & Rhodes, R. A. W. (2003). *Interpreting British Governance*. Psychology Press.

Boulding, K. E. (2011). The economics of the coming spaceship earth. In In H. Jarett (Ed.)*Environmental Quality in a Growing Economy* (pp. 3–14). RFF Press.

Brown, P. (2007). *Toxic Exposures: Contested Illnesses and the Environmental Health Movement*. Columbia University Press.

Charteris-Black, J. (2005). *Politicians and Rhetoric*. Palgrave Macmillan UK.

Czarniawska, B. (2010). The uses of narratology in social and policy studies. *Critical Policy Studies*, 4(1), 58–76.

Czarniawska, B. (2014). *A Theory of Organizing*. Edward Elgar Publishing.

Douglas, M. (1986). *How Institutions Think*. Syracuse University Press.

Dryzek, J. S. (2013). *The Politics of the Earth: Environmental Discourses*. Oxford University Press.

du Gay, P. (2000). *In Praise of Bureaucracy: Weber – Organization – Ethics*. SAGE Publications Ltd.

Eco, U. (1976). *A Theory of Semiotics*. Indiana University Press.
Eco, U. (1986). *Semiotics and the Philosophy of Language*. University of Indiana Press.
Eco, U. (2002). *Art and Beauty in the Middle Ages*. Yale University Press.
Ferguson, J. (1990). *The Anti-politics Machine: "Development", Depoliticization and Bureaucratic Power in Lesotho*. CUP Archive.
Fernandez, J. W. (1972). Persuasions and performances: Of the beast in every body ... and the metaphors of everyman. *Daedalus, 101*(1), 39–60.
Flyvbjerg, B., Bruzelius, N., & Rothengatter, W. (2003). *Megaprojects and Risk: An Anatomy of Ambition*. Cambridge University Press.
Foucault, M. (1971). Orders of discourse. *Social Science Information, 10*(2), 7–30.
Foucault, M. (2002a). *Archaeology of Knowledge* (2nd ed.). Routledge.
Foucault, M. (2002b). *The Order of Things: An Archaeology of the Human Sciences*. Psychology Press.
Foucault, M. (2003a). *Madness and Civilization*. Routledge.
Foucault, M. (2003b). *Society Must Be Defended: Lectures at the College de France, 1975–76*. Allen Lane The Penguin Press.
Foucault, M. (2007). *Security, Territory, Population: Lectures at the College De France, 1977–78*. Palgrave Macmillan UK.
Foucault, M. (2020). *The History of Sexuality: 1*. Penguin Random House UK.
Gabriel, Y. (2000). *Storytelling in Organizations: Facts, Fictions, and Fantasies*. Oxford University Press.
Gibbs, R. W. (1994). *The Poetics of Mind: Figurative Thought, Language, and Understanding*. Cambridge University Press.
Glynos, J., & Howarth, D. (2007). *Logics of Critical Explanation in Social and Political Theory*. Routledge.
Gunderson, E. (Ed.). (2009). *The Cambridge Companion to Ancient Rhetoric*. Cambridge University Press.
Hajer, M. A. (1995). *The Politics of Environmental Discourse: Ecological Modernization and the Policy Process*. Clarendon Press.
Heller, N. (2025, March 3). Will Harvard Bend or Break? *The New Yorker*.
Hesse, M. (2017). Models and analogies. In W. H. Newton-Smith (Ed.). *A Companion to the Philosophy of Science* (pp. 299–307). John Wiley & Sons, Ltd.
Höhler, S. (2015). *Spaceship Earth in the Environmental Age, 1960–1990* (0 ed.). Routledge.
Hood, C. (2000). *The Art of the State: Culture, Rhetoric, and Public Management*. Oxford University Press.
Hood, C., & Peters, G. (2004). The middle aging of new public management: Into the age of paradox? *Journal of Public Administration Research and Theory, 14*(3), 267–282.

Jasanoff, S. (2011). *Designs on Nature: Science and Democracy in Europe and the United States*. Princeton University Press.
Keller, E. F. (2000). *The Century of the Gene*. Harvard University Press.
Kornberger, M. (2012). Governing the city: From planning to urban strategy. *Theory, Culture & Society, 29*(2), 84–106.
Kövecses, Z. (2003). *Metaphor and Emotion: Language, Culture, and Body in Human Feeling*. Cambridge University Press.
Laclau, E. (2005). *On Populist Reason*. Verso.
Lakoff, G. (2014). *The ALL NEW Don't Think of an Elephant!: Know Your Values and Frame the Debate*. Chelsea Green Publishing.
Lakoff, G. (2016). *Moral Politics: How Liberals and Conservatives Think*. University of Chicago Press.
Lakoff, G., & Johnson, M. (2008). *Metaphors We Live By*. University of Chicago Press.
Latour, B. (1987). *Science in Action. How to Follow Scientists and Engineers through Society*. Harvard University Press.
Latour, B. (1999). *Pandora's Hope: Essays on the Reality of Science Studies*. Harvard University Press.
Latour, B. (2009). *Politics of Nature*. Harvard University Press.
Lévi-Strauss, C. (1974). *Savage Mind*. University of Chicago Press.
Loraux, N. (2019). *L'invention d'Athènes: Histoire de l'oraison funèbre dans la »cité classique«*. Walter de Gruyter GmbH & Co KG.
Luhmann, N. (1989). *Ecological Communication*. University of Chicago Press.
Luhmann, N. (1995). *Social Systems*. Stanford University Press Stanford.
Luhmann, N. (2000). *The Reality of the Mass Media*. Stanford University Press.
Luhmann, N. (2018). *Organization and Decision*. Cambridge University Press.
Luhmann, N., Ziegert, K. A., & Kastner, F. (2004). *Law as a Social System*. Oxford University Press.
March, J. G. (2010). *The Ambiguities of Experience*. Cornell University Press.
Meyer, J. W., & Rowan, B. (1977). Institutionalized organizations: Formal structure as myth and ceremony. *American Journal of Sociology, 83*(2), 340–363.
Miller, H. T. (2012). *Governing Narratives: Symbolic Politics and Policy Change*. University of Alabama Press.
Mintzberg, H. (1973). *The Nature of Managerial Work*. Harpercollins College Div.
Mintzberg, H. (2004). Managers not MBSs. *Management Today, 20*(7), 10–13.

Molle, F. (2009). Water, politics and river basin governance: Repoliticizing approaches to river basin management. *Water International*, *34*(1), 62–70.

Morgan, G. (1986). *Images of Organization*. Sage.

Mosse, D. (2005). *Cultivating Development: An Ethnography of Aid Policy and Practice*. Pluto Press.

Mumford, L. (2010). *Technics and Civilization*. University of Chicago Press.

Nyberg, D., & Sveningsson, S. (2014). Paradoxes of authentic leadership: Leader identity struggles. *Leadership*, *10*(4), 437–455.

Ortony, A. (1993). *Metaphor and Thought*. Cambridge University Press.

Parker, M. (2018). *Shut Down the Business School*. University of Chicago Press Economics.

Peters, B. G., & Peters, B. G. (2018). *The Politics of Bureaucracy: An Introduction to Comparative Public Administration* (7th ed.). Routledge.

Pfeffer, J. (2015). *Leadership BS: Fixing Workplaces and Careers One Truth at a Time*. HarperCollins.

Pierre, J., & Peters, B. G. (2020). *Governance, Politics and the State*. Bloomsbury Publishing.

Pollitt, C., & Bouckaert, G. (2017). *Public Management Reform: A Comparative Analysis – Into The Age of Austerity*. Oxford University Press.

Power, M. (2000). The audit society – Second thoughts. *International Journal of Auditing*, *4*(1), 111–119.

Ricoeur, P. (1996). Rhetoric and poetics. In A. Rorty (Ed.), *Essays on Aristotle's Rhetoric* (Vol. 6, p. 324). University of California Press.

Ricoeur, P. (2006). *The Rule of Metaphor: The Creation of Meaning in Language (Repr)*. Routledge.

Ricoeur, P. (2009). *Time and Narrative, Volume 1* (K. McLaughlin & D. Pellauer, Trans.). University of Chicago Press.

Sahlins, M. D. (2009). *Historical Metaphors and Mythical Realities: Structure in the Early History of the Sandwich Islands Kingdom*. University of Michigan Press.

Schön, D. A. (2017). *The Reflective Practitioner: How Professionals Think in Action*. Routledge.

Semino, E. (2008). *Metaphor in Discourse*. Cambridge University Press.

Stone, D. (2012). *Policy Paradox: The Art of Political Decision Making* (3rd ed.). W.W. Norton & Co.

Strathern, M. (1988). *The Gender of the Gift: Problems with Women and Problems with Society in Melanesia*. University of California Press.

Swanson, R. N. (1999). The "mendicant problem" in the later middle ages. *Studies in Church History Subsidia*, *11*, 217–238.

Thom, R. (1990). *Semio Physics: A Sketch*. Addison-Wesley.
Toulmin, S. E. (2003). *The Uses of Argument*. Cambridge University Press.
Van Assche, K., Beunen, R., & Duineveld, M. (2013). *Evolutionary Governance Theory: An Introduction*. Springer.
Van Assche, K., Beunen, R., Duineveld, M., & Gruezmacher, M. (2021). Adaptive methodology. Topic, theory, method and data in ongoing conversation. *International Journal of Social Research Methodology*, 26(1), 1–15.
Van Assche, K., & Gruezmacher, M. (2025). *Psychoanalysis and Governance: Discourse and Decisions, Identities and Futures*. Taylor & Francis.
Van Assche, K., Verschraegen, G., Beunen, R., Gruezmacher, M., & Duineveld, M. (2023). Combining research methods in policy and governance: Taking account of bricolage and discerning limits of modelling and simulation. *Futures, 145*, 103074.
Von Bertalanffy, L. (1967). *Robots, Men, and Minds: Psychology in the Modern World*. G. Braziller.
Ziai, A. (2007). *Exploring Post-development: Theory and Practice, Problems and Perspectives*. Routledge.
Zizek, S. (2009). *The Parallax View*. MIT Press.
Zizek, S. (2019). *The Sublime Object of Ideology*. Verso Books.

4 | *Metaphors and Narratives of Sustainability*

In this chapter, we interrogate the notion of sustainability, and ask ourselves what sustainability could mean, which other concepts or narratives need to be brought into the scope of investigation. We discuss common metaphors and narratives of sustainability and connect them to notions of (good) governance, community and system–environment relations. Sustainability governance, it is argued, requires governance systems equipped with high institutional and adaptive capacity, reflexivity, the possibility to entertain images of the future and devise strategy based on such strategic work. Finally, we remind ourselves of the distinctions made earlier, between stories of sustainability in the community, in theory, and practices of sustainability governance.

Sustainability as an Elusive Goal

Sustainability is a state of something, a feature or set of features of something, where both the qualities and the object to which they are ascribed are tauntingly vague. Which is rather problematic if sustainability is simultaneously presented as something of crucial importance, where a lack constitutes an existential threat (Brown, 2016). What is sustainable is more than our society, and sustainability discourse entailed from the beginning an idea of social-ecological systems, which could be explicitly articulated or not. Sustainability could then be grasped as a relation; a healthy, balanced, or otherwise good and desirable relation that could be projected back and stated as existing in the past, while being threatened now (Van Assche et al., 2019).

Sustainability as a stable state, a state not only desirable but also necessary, representing an older better balance between humans and their environment, benefiting both, is, of course, a fantasy stemming from very real threats (Davidson, 2012; Zizek, 2008). In nature, one can hardly speak of stable equilibria, and if one could recognize something akin to it, there is no logical implication that this would represent an attractive living environment for societies, nor an optimum in terms of biodiversity. Who or what would tell societies how to organize themselves to maintain such imagined balance is not clear at all (Gunder & Hillier, 2009). If it is a matter of deciding what to preserve and protect in society and in nature, what is allowed to change or adapt, the selection cannot be read in the laws of nature, nor in the principles of good governance we agree upon, or the cultural values we cherish (Latour, 1998).

In ancient Greek philosophy, many stories coexisted about our place in the universe, our relation to our social and natural environments. For Plato, nothing observable was real, but reality was a stable order of ideas, while Aristotle saw change in the universe as a universal law, where creatures moved through life as determined by their form, an unfolding of a program that can be identified with their nature. That nature only exists in conjunction with matter, which cannot be organized without form. According to Democritus, the world is a swirl of atoms that stabilizes in patterns we recognize as reality only temporarily, and if we follow Heraclitus' cryptic messaging, stability, unity and harmony in the world are merely self-deceit. What is our philosophy of sustainability?

No state of society, or human–environment relations is ever stable over the long term, so maintaining a stable state is neither possible nor desirable (Luhmann, 1989). Sustainability in a literal sense is an impossibility in other words, an elusive goal that, when it appears more clearly delineated, can easily become problematic and constraining. Metaphors, narratives and fictions help us to grasp what would elude us in a literal sense, yet what can threaten us as a society (Fischer, 2023). Since the early days of the environmental movement, we needed stories and metaphors to understand ourselves in our environment anew, and we argue that an important task for sustainability leadership is to keep the conversation on sustainability open, rather than closing it for the sake of false certainties. Crafting new metaphors and narratives is an essential task for societies that experience very real threats yet are equipped with modes of thinking and organizing that are naturally imperfect.

If we understand sustainability as more than preservation of essential traits and qualities, and remain open to the idea of sustainable development, we easily recognize three distinct versions of the discourse: Sustainability can be the goal of development, it can be a quality of society or ecology unaffected by development, and, third, it could be conceived as a quality of development itself, where certain activities are considered virtuous per se. Narratives, metaphors and policy directions that reflected these types appeared, as well as hybrids between them (Thiele, 2013). As sustainable development took on the mantle of virtue, benefits could be derived from acting sustainably, speaking about sustainability, or performing it. The harder actual improvements are to achieve, the fuzzier the delineation of individual and organizational contributions tends to become, and the more pronounced the incentives for cheating and performing, under names such as greenwashing, greenwishing and ecoscuses (Williams, 2024).

Combating desertification and restoration of degraded lands are credible and laudable goals, which can improve the livelihoods of many. Looking at the narratives where the goal makes most sense, we are asked to assume the desert as an enemy, and degradation as destruction of an asset and an environment. The goal is reasonable if we are not talking about people whose livelihoods depend on drylands and deserts, if we are not dealing with communities adapted to arid environments. Desertification figures as a force to oppose, in a fight, and is expected to sit in a manageable intermediate zone, in between forces beyond our control, and situations where we are clearly the cause of desertification, and no external forces are needed to explain the damage. When we speak of degraded lands, we imply a goal that is out of reach, or a normality that is lost. Who defines goal, normality and degradation is relevant, as degradation stories promoted by governments or international organizations often disregard what people hope to do there, as well as ecological or economic values. (Stafford Smith, 2016)

Narratives assist people and communities in shaping their understanding of problems and solutions regarding human–environment relations, in connecting ideas to action and managing their own emotions in the process (Descola & Palsson, 2003). Spurring people to action might take emotional language, the mobilization of collective affect, but this remains a risky game. Doom and gloom scenarios might inspire inaction rather than anything productive, and traumatizing people easily opens old traumas and social rifts. Guilt can revive a pride long forgotten and trigger a backlash entirely unforeseen. Anxiety can spill over to other subjects and lead to immobility and despair (Latour, 2009; Shellenberger, 2020).

Early evangelists of sustainability were often natural scientists with a modest affinity for storytelling, and less for cultural sensitivities, which did not help. Whereas earlier figures in the environmental movement were often consummate storytellers, focusing on a reintegration of humans in nature, and a reintroduction of nature in communities, later discourse on sustainability tended to revert to mechanistic models of nature and governance (Radomski & Van Assche, 2014; Worster, 1994). When climate change appeared on the horizon as an existential threat, sustainability stories had to become more complicated, yet the preference for quantitative approaches, modeling, mapping and accounting only increased (Hulme, 2009; Jasanoff, 2007).

What tends to be forgotten, at our own peril, in such stories, emotive and quantitative alike, is that we are dealing with stories, moreover stories of a particular kind. They are fictions. Remembering this does not downplay the real threat of deteriorating environments. Rather, the combination of conceptual challenge and physical threat should urge us to consider more carefully what kind of stories we are telling ourselves, and whether the fictions are productive fictions (Hulme, 2012). Productive then means capable of moving societies in a direction that, to our best knowledge, represents a set of social and ecological relations that is not susceptible to immediate collapse, that does not deplete resources before the idea of resource can be redefined and that sustains the reproduction of both social and ecological systems.

Sustainability needs to become a master signifier, to perform the complex coordination tasks expected of the concept. It has to connect to a variety of other concepts, which can happen through roles in a multiplicity of narratives (Gunder, 2019). Those can in turn provide explanation and motivation for action in different governance and community settings. When sustainability narratives are introduced into contexts with minimal expectations of governance and only a loosely defined sense of community, there tends to be a correspondingly weak sense of environmental responsibility (Cook & Swyngedouw, 2012). In such circumstances, it becomes necessary either for these narratives to transform the underlying societal and governance structures, or, alternatively, for them to align with and be supported by other drivers of change operating in parallel. Master signifiers can support each other, even if each finds its anchoring partly in fiction, or, if one prefers, in self-reference.

The master signifier of "sustainability" can suggest agreement on core values, and a range of affinities supporting trust and collaboration. When observed without reference to sustainability discourse, the similarities and the base for collaboration might crumble, as diverging ideas of democracy, common goods, participation and rule of law can radically alter the flavor of interventions on each side. One can argue that "sustainability" takes on overriding importance, and hence excuses the lapse of attention to difference, yet the point is that the blind spots introduced can also obviate the need to look for excuses: "we believe we know each other, while we don't."

Master signifiers support the productive character of sustainability narratives; they can render them recognizable, which immediately generates connections with other ideas, affects and stories. We already know that master signifiers can create stories and vice versa; narratives can reinforce the functioning of master signifiers or bring new ones into existence. Stories can turn rhizomatic when master signifiers appear. Through the connective tissue of metaphors, further connections can be established, amplifying the conceptual and affective reach of sustainability thinking (Davidson, 2025). With that, its potential in governance to connect people can be increased, the options to translate ideas into broadly supported policies. In such community, sustainability thinking could sustain an ongoing conversation in governance on shared problems and desirable communal futures, rather than pursuing an elusive stability through technocratic means.

Narratives and Metaphors of Sustainability

Master signifiers do not exist by themselves, just as metaphors cannot be solitary for long. In the case of sustainability, a series of concepts developed the idea beyond the older typology of social, environmental and economic sustainability. We started to speak of a blue economy, a circular economy, planetary boundaries, ecosystems services, the bioeconomy, transitions, transformations, sustainable innovation and many more. Not all concepts became master signifiers, not all developed beyond circles of academics, bureaucrats, consultants and non-governmental organizations. Some found more resonance in society than others, especially when they found support in stories and values, with already familiar green ideologies, or when they reinforcement appeared through other ascendant master signifiers, such as innovation and inclusivity (Corvellec et al., 2022; Schutter, 2020).

Some stories circled around an affect from which the rest was supposed to flow, meaning other stories, new social identities and loyalties and collective action. Doom and gloom scenarios can radiate their emotive power after much narrative labor, but an already felt sense of bleakness can provide a more immediate narrative inspiration. Other attempts to envelop and develop the empty core of sustainability did not get much further, often restating the categories of earlier stories – people, planet, profit; social and environmental innovation; just transitions (Beckman et al., 2023; Bouzarovski, 2022). Among the most influential operationalizations of sustainability thinking, the Sustainable Development Goals, featuring prominently in this book, aimed to connect a wide variety of stories on social, environmental and economic sustainability, and render them actionable by suggesting they were all sprouting from the fertile master signifier of sustainability, similar and concrete enough to each other to figure as goals in cohesive multi-level governance (Jacob, 2025).

The circular economy metaphor draws attention to the idea that sustainability does not have to detract from economic development, and that new ideas can be rooted in old practices of recycling, repair and good care. Keeping things in use for a longer time, disallowing planned obsolescence, making things easier to repair, working together to fix and learn about fixing things, all find their origin in former phases of capitalism. Such circling back thus forms an affective basis for the discourse, and the circle suggests beyond closure also eternal movement, thus sustainability in a literal sense. One could note the tension between a focus on the economy, on new complex processes of production and recycling, and the quasi-nostalgic hue of much of the rhetoric and many local initiatives. One could question the potentially harmful suggestion that the circle can be squared, that we can keep going forever as long as we follow the circular economy principles, and that economic and social inequalities can be aggravated rather than assuaged if we orient ourselves entirely by the metaphor. (Dermody et al., 2021)

The "development" part of sustainable development moved to the background where resilience metaphors of systems "bouncing back" became prominent, and, in recent years, sustainability could even be equated openly to shrink, in economic discourses of degrowth, and spatial policies of urban shrink and a restructured countryside (Savini, 2025). Different metaphors and narratives of sustainability thus produce quite diverse and divergent rhizomatic connections to other stories, links between disciplines, policy domains, public goods and affects, inspiring hopes for a new technocratic utopia here and elsewhere of an idyllic return to an imaginary past. Each narrative, each metaphor orients us differently, not only in affective and conceptual landscapes, but also towards different policy directions, and, indeed, diverging visions of ideal or suitable governance systems. While most sustainability concepts thus produce ideas of good governance, and demands for governance transformation, what this is supposed to be varies greatly, and looks similar only in the blinding light of the master signifier.

Examining sustainability stories while bracketing their promises, and questioning their shared assumption of systems in equilibrium, makes their dissimilarity glaringly clear, the often-incompatible versions of problems and solution (Worster, 1994). Systems ideas might be prevalent in different stories, but what amounts to a system, a balance, a desirable relation between systems, is much less clear. On the social side of social-ecological systems, there are several elephants in the room, including the issue of democracy and the question of capitalism (Luke, 1997). Which version of democracy is compatible with which version of sustainability, and which manifestation of capitalism, if any? If we speak of just transitions to a sustainable society, who decides this? And which categories would be used primarily to think inclusivity – economic, religious, ethnic, gender, ideological, self-chosen? If we argue that good governance for resilience – as a higher-order sustainability – is adaptive governance, which range of adaptations are we talking about, and do we accept adaptations of our environment to ourselves (Leach et al., 2010)?

Many stories of sustainability, if taken literally, reveal false promises. However, if understood as discursive creations which might enable collective action and solve some of the problems we can relate to sustainability, they can be highly productive fictions (Hulme, 2009; Szerszynski, 2005). Only if we are forced to identify with just one version of sustainability, as an absolute truth guiding us to an undisputable future, are we in trouble. Even the more questionable or limited sustainability narratives can have the virtue, as indicated previously, of making us rethink basic concepts and paradigms in thinking and organizing (Frankel, 2020). Our current version of capitalism, sustainability-induced reflection strongly suggests, is not all that sustainable, whatever version of sustainability we embrace. Democracy is not as unified as often thought, not that powerful in facing environmental challenges and comes with stubborn constraints with regards to long-term policy (Beckert, 2024).

If we broaden our perspective on sustainability transitions, and demand for a socially just transition, this might spark a long-awaited discussion and healthy critique of several sustainability narratives: the stories of techno-utopians, of categorical doomsayers, and the discourse of institutional modernists, ready with blueprints for tinkering or more radical reform. Just transition stories can productively engage communities in discussions about value hierarchies, about the state of democracy, and its potential renovation, on identity politics and patterns and understandings of inclusion and exclusion. They can bridge discussions on environmental quality, economic development, good governance and the good life. In short, they can trigger a revisiting of the key question: what kind of society do we want, in which relation to its natural environment? Next, this can bring up the issue of policy coordination: can we combine policy domains to address social, economic and environmental aspects of this vision? This will only work if no holy cows are spared, if no sacred assumptions are left untouched: are we still starting from an eternal growth model, are we understanding participation in the old way, do we attempt a return to a previous ecological state, which forms of identity politics shape our ideas of (environmental) justice? As soon as formulaic answers start to dominate the discussion, recipes on good governance, inclusion, justice, sustainability, reflexivity is reduced, the visioning becomes self-limiting, and many problems and solutions are not observed anymore. (Rosemberg, 2010)

The governance implications of sustainability stories are not uniform, as some are more compatible with democratic politics than others, or with certain version of democracy. Science acquires a different status in each story. Disciplines bestow prominence upon themselves by promoting one metaphor or narrative (Farley & Smith, 2020). Local knowledge, cultural values and differences are recognized more easily in some narratives than others. Internal diversity in governance is more appreciated under the aegis of one metaphor, while others might be more hopeful about participation as a road to sustainability. Links to other grand narratives can widely differ, with some stories revealing religious overtones. The productivity in terms of new narratives will show a similar variation and will greatly depend on the openness to other truths, either scientific or otherwise (Luke, 1995).

In sustainability narratives, metaphor and narrative relate in myriad manners (Figure 4.1). Metaphors can be explicit or visible in the narrative or rather implicitly present, as assumptions supporting the narrative or certain elements or episodes. A metaphor can be a product of a widely disseminated narrative, as a summary or conclusion that

Narratives and Metaphors of Sustainability 113

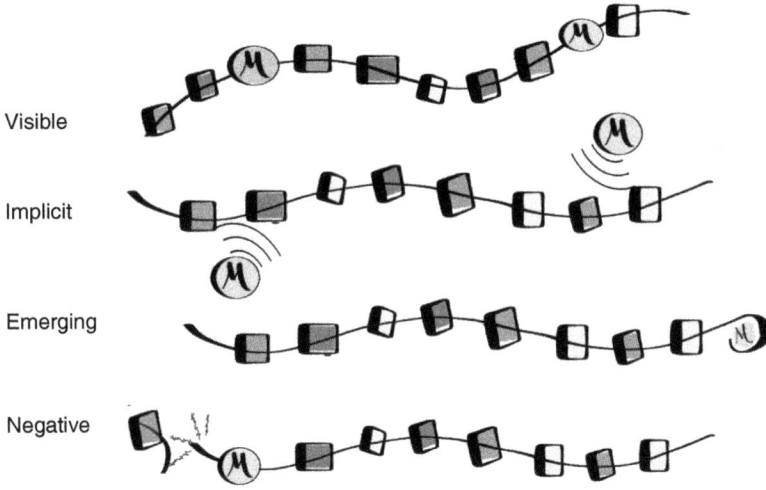

Figure 4.1 Sustainability narratives are often structured, in part, by metaphors, yet the relation between metaphor and narrative can vary. The metaphors can be explicit, or visible, in the narrative; they can be implicitly present, as assumptions underneath the whole narrative, or certain elements. It is also possible that a sustainability narrative produces a narrative, that it emerges as a result, a conclusion, or a summary of the narrative, and then leads its own life, supporting other narratives later on. Less noticeable yet sometimes crucial is the antagonistic role of metaphors in shaping narratives. They can push the narrative in the opposite direction, possibly at multiple points, from a metaphor that is deliberately avoided. This avoidance can be conscious or unconscious. Consequently, narratives can develop through references to negative definitions: "Things aren't like this; we aren't like that."

starts to lead its own life (Bruner, 2009). The metaphor can support narratives only recently encountered, even where the original narrative is entirely forgotten or discredited. Some concepts are metaphorical for outsiders, but do not appear as such for those familiar with them, for people adhering routinely to stories structured by them (Ricoeur, 2006). Metaphors featuring elsewhere can be brought into the orbit; metaphors of sustainability can resonate with current ideas of community, of (good) governance, or economic development, and thus more easily stabilize themselves. Sometimes, the offspring of metaphors can support the parent, and this is easier when the family relation is forgotten, when the nephew appears as a neutral observer confirming the truth of the parent. Self-reference then masks as a new external reference, as when sustainability indicators confirm the success of a solution that starts from (metaphoric) assumptions in the same family as those shaping the problem definition.

Negative Narrative Forces

Metaphors can thus support a sustainability narrative, by figuring within them, existing in their environment, but also as a negative, repulsive force. Stories can develop against the background of disavowed master signifiers, which negatively shape it. Sometimes, the same narrative can be negatively defined in several points by another, invisible, narrative or metaphor, yet this can also be an unconscious process (Bhabha, 2012). Where a detested, anxiety-inducing or otherwise repressed story or metaphor threads the same terrain as a narrative that needs to be constructed, the one deployed could step by step avoid the dreaded one. Where it is not a specific avoidance, it can be generic and less structured one (Foucault, 2002a, 2012b).

We are thus dealing with a negative structuring of stories and metaphors, and this is much more common than usually considered – in management, policy and environmental literatures and beyond. Organizations, societies often subconsciously work around problem definitions and solution directions that are not compatible with their self-image, with proclaimed values (Girard et al., 2003). What is circumvented thus has an influence, as the freedom in choosing or crafting a narrative can be drastically reduced by the presence of such negative attractors. Narratives develop through negative definition: "things are not like this; we are not like that" (Bion, 2023).

Structuring negatives can be located in problems and solutions, as what is to be avoided can be either. If we disavow the existence of poverty in our prosperous country, we can circle around the topic for a long time, keep it out of public discourse. When others or circumstances force us to see poverty, perhaps in forms not expected, one can find excuses in the surprise, in the difference. Alternatively, one can blame the poor, and leave stories about the social order untouched. Or, one can find inspiration in other stories and values, and attempt to help, as an individual, and as a community, looking at the poor as victims of circumstances. This still leaves space to avoid questioning the social order – they had bad luck. Confronting a systemic issue can be daunting because we identify with the system, or because we cannot accept the solution that such problem analysis seems to suggest.

When there is sympathy for individuals experiencing poverty, accompanied by an absence of blame yet a reluctance to invest in mental health services or, more critically, in social housing, some form of disavowal is likely to emerge within the broader narrative. (Butler, 2004)

Reasons to avoid a story can be manifold. The importance and the nature of sustainability as a quality of social-ecological systems, the difficulties signalled above in defining and approaching sustainability, compel us to pay more attention to the phenomenon. We will see later that the implications for sustainability leadership are real enough. For the elucidation of negative structuring of narratives and metaphors we ought to note that stories, with embedded metaphors can be *condensed* into metaphors that can represent a whole cluster of stories, condensations that start to function as master signifiers themselves (Persich et al., 2021). Those signifiers might be consciously acknowledged, or operate subconsciously, through culture and organization. They might already be supported by current governance processes, media narratives and selections of policy tools. We can think of "the left," or "the right" as examples, but also "those days," referring to bad old days when people believed a lot of nonsense.

Speaking of "the west," but also "green dictatorship" or "corrupted democracy," can summarize a set of narratives which then structures thinking and organizing. It might appeal to people worried about the state of the world, who might be nostalgic for less complicated times, when identities were seemingly more stable, and the long term looked less alien and threatening (Bauman, 2013). The synthetic quality of this type of master signifiers can be beneficial, in guiding communities towards a shared future, but they can also negatively structure governance and public discourse in a way that is severely limiting self-definition, hence reinvention and adaptation. Relying on broad concepts such as "democracy," without grasping the contradictions and trade-offs of different models and versions of democracy is already problematic as self-limitation (Sartori, 1987) If, however, we do not even observe an avoided metaphor, the constraint is more severe, and a rational re-evaluation of future options becomes daunting (Fink, 1995).

One reason, beyond intricacy and opacity, is the affective investment in the metaphor summarizing a tangle of stories. Recoiling from the negative structuring power comes instinctively, and what is repulsive is often literally so, viscerally so. This might be the case because of memories, or because of a close identification with groups, ideologies, that polarize themselves against the negative metaphor. One might fear an old or imagined enemy, as in a rivaling power, an alternative ideology, one might hate it for doing bad things to friends or threatening the identity or stability of the world one inhabits. Anxiety can rear its head because the detested master signifier might simultaneously hold an ambivalent attraction, or because it sheds a light on imperfections and incoherence in the narrative fabric one believes in, maybe desperately so (Foucault, 2012a, 2012b).

Accusations of green dictatorship abound in places where the same scrutiny is not accorded to other ideologies. What is done in the name of sustainability, or its coupled master signifiers climate change, biodiversity, organic agriculture, even environment, raises more suspicion and indeed, visceral reactions. What does not feel like a restriction on freedoms, an imposition on the economy, or a threat to democracy in the name of other master signifiers, feels like an existential threat when associated with green devilish discourse. In instances where the association is not immediately evident, yet a comparable affective response arises, it is possible to actively seek out or construct such a connection, and subsequently retroactively posit it as a cause. Signifiers are inscribed in the body, can make us weep or jubilate, and master signifiers can uphold identities both positively and negatively, by maintaining shared values or a common enemy stealing my enjoyment, my access to a world as it should be. (Bell & Ashwood, 2015; Parks & Timmons Roberts, 2006)

Reasons to first construct, then avoid clusters of narratives crystallizing as silent negative master signifiers can be manifold. The issue might be closely associated with lingering self-doubt and internal contradictions, or rather the opposite, with a wounded pride, hurt caused by anyone doubting the realities and ideals fervently embraced. How dare they? The "they" tends to represent a narrative construction reflecting concerns of the community banishing an Other and its stories. That Other might only exist in the social imagination as a necessary counterpoint, and it might be an actual group, which is reinterpreted through the lens of repressed master signifiers (Zizek, 1992)

What strikes a nerve, what must be expertly avoided or cautiously circumvented does not have to be a blatant ideological difference. It might be a problem definition associated with the negative signifier, an idea of the world that would timidly assert itself, not as an ideology, but as an implication of the repressed knot of stories and its versions of problems or solutions. Thinking through those implications does not have to happen, as people often feel where things are going. The master signifiers that guide us, either positively, or as discussed here, negatively, can arouse strong contradictory emotions, confusion and anxiety. All the more reason to suppress the master signifier. What is traumatizing can be the lack of internal cohesion in the stories a community tells itself, but also, in the realm of governance, dashed hopes in schemes that in hindsight look utopian or hair brained (Zizek, 2009).

A chain of associations, conscious and unconscious, can connect a problem definition, a type of solution, a governance reform expected to follow, with a metaphor. A method of analyzing the problem can already associate with competing ideologies, despised enemies, old disappointments or unmanageable uncertainties (Fischer, 2003). Communities may resist solutions reflecting an engineering logic or enhancing the power of engineers and their framing of social issues as technical problems. Implicit machine metaphors, of society, of nature, of the whole social-ecological system, might be sniffed out easily by those with negative experiences with powerful engineers, or a worldview diametrically opposing such metaphors (Scudder, 1981, 2012).

Speaking of marine protected areas can trigger an allergic reaction with fishers, assuming this would undermine their livelihoods, even if such protection would make fisheries around them more sustainable. Environmental impact assessment, as a method, can be felt as an unfair obstacle to the enjoyment of development, even if it can safeguard the development against environmental disasters and costly legal claims. Speaking of vegetables, in the right environment, can raise eyebrows, as real food is meat and vegetarians spell trouble in many ways.

Any master signifier that promises to summarize a complex problem in quantitative terms, preferably in simple indicators, statistics and models, exerts an attraction on those actors in governance who truly believe in conceptual models of objective problem solving. Those who might simply want to do their job, without too many headaches, or prefer not to take too much responsibility, might similarly favor narratives that objectively define, analyze, solve problems, as this reduces the need for actual conversations. Where conversations cannot be avoided, a simplified and rationalized story, the machinic and related metaphors structuring it, gives them strong arguments and little need for further explanation (Porter & Haggerty, 1997).

Many recoil reflexively from the prevalent tendencies to reduce the world to a machine, even when the machine metaphor is not consciously observed. When they detect machinic metaphors in sustainability policy, the discussion is over. Inferences can be made quickly, either from a presence or an absence, from a feeling or an absent feeling: Solutions might not feel right, problem framings might feel off and if there is already a suspicion of prevalent master signifiers in governance, they can be spotted, or imagined, in the blink of an eye (Stone, 2012).

Mutual Metaphor Supports Society

Sustainability narratives can be supported by more than one metaphor. Which is not surprising as sustainability issues can affect potentially anything in society, and as sustainability metaphors can establish a multiplicity of connections to relatives (Figure 4.2). Resistance of the sort discussed in the previous paragraphs can appear more slowly, as new narrative connections indicating affinity with less attractive propositions can appear slowly. When new connections are mushrooming around young discourses, or when they land in a new context, when, for example, communities start to explore sustainability stories and their meaning for governance, they might be welcomed rather warmly. When implementation seems to imply policies that signal proximity to already suspicious ideologies, enthusiasm might cool (Agrawal, 2005).

One effect might be the gradual discoloring of a formerly bright and attractive story; a different response might be cognitive dissonance. Communities and individuals alike might uphold contradictory values, or support some goals only in a general sense, with real-life applications leading to confrontations with competing values, revealed to be dominant. One might be for sustainability, but against any possible manifestation of it, against any policy change that might be an embodiment of the value and goal (Milton, 2002). Of course, this dissonance is also rhetorically used by the proponents of sustainability, hammering any partial disagreement as a rejection of the entire story.

Emerging narrative connections can therefore engender both resistance and support. Mutually reinforcing metaphors can engender community support, by reinforcing reality, naturalizing the contingent, rendering it immune to critique. Such friendship of metaphors, hardening already dominant stories, can have the opposite effect when

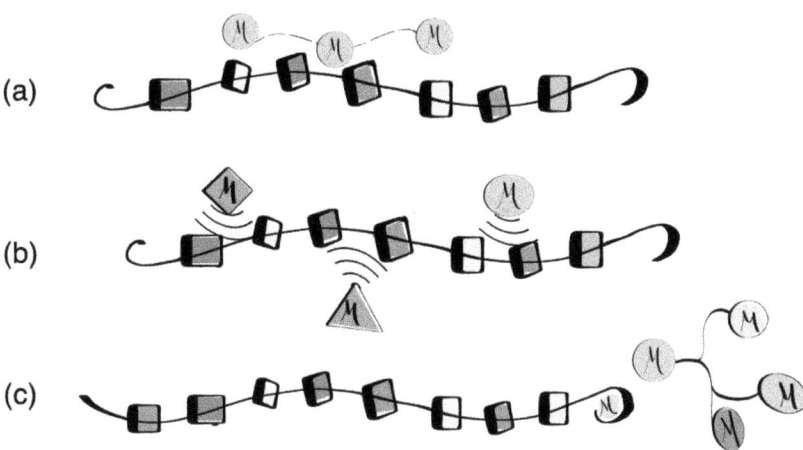

Figure 4.2 Several metaphors can contribute to sustainability narratives. (a) Metaphors can connect to existing ones or produce their offspring within families of metaphors. Such related metaphors can form the foundation of a sustainability narrative. (b) Alternatively, unrelated metaphors can also play a role in structuring the narrative. (c) A third possibility is that a metaphor emerges from a narrative and subsequently develops its own family of metaphors.

outsider positions are still available, and the reinforced reality starts to feel suffocating. In such cases, a discursive configuration is read as a discourse coalition, a group of stories that is supporting not only each other but also a set of actors and power relations (Hajer, 1995). The fact of coalition, and of coupled metaphors, is insufficient to create support. In fact, the more tight-knit a coalition appears, the more appalling it might become, as it leaves less space for partial and personalised agreement with a few of the stories and players, and more opportunity for feelings of exclusion and authoritarianism (Gramsci, 2011).

Technologies might support sustainable agriculture. Precision agriculture, supported by a new combination of technologies, can reduce cost and environmental impact at the same time. Those interested in sustainability might be supportive, as well as the farmers and people in rural areas who see it as a new lease on life for their communities. When governmental actors aggressively promote the new approach, through policies and subsidies, by ignoring alternative forms of agriculture and alternative contributions to sustainability, the greener factions might ask questions. When technology and fertilizer companies start to show up together at gatherings of rural stakeholders, when farmers associations push the new technologies, presenting them as the only viable future, and associated banks require them, farmers feel the new coalition in a different way, and might either feel reassured that, indeed, this is the future, or suffocated and, from now on, highly suspicious of what looked like allies before. (Stock & Gardezi, 2021)

When metaphors already started a family, and when this family is prevalent in a variety of discourses, it is easier to introduce stories to the rest of the family. A sustainability narrative can be underpinned by a family of metaphors, or, if there's a central one, forging a link there with a member of another large family brings that entire group into the picture (Figure 4.3). People will find paths from one relative to another, rhetorical exploration will come easily. Unrelated metaphors, however, can still find a place together in a narrative, and their new proximity might create an affinity that can be exploited later, with implicit analogies proliferating in other policy domains, disciplines or discursive domains. Sustainability discourse holds a great productive potential, as it can come to bear on so many aspects of life and governance (Carolan, 2006).

When stories move between social domains, from science to politics and from public discourse to implementation, they can transform and

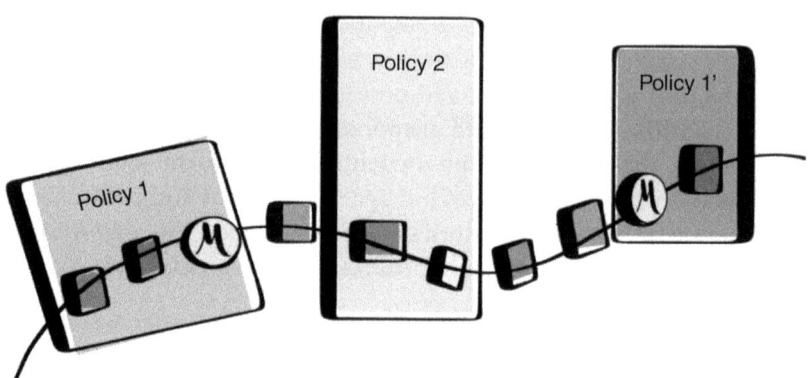

Figure 4.3 One narrative can inspire multiple policies across different policy domains. While different narratives can form the foundation for policy alternatives (e.g., policy 1 and 1') for a single policy topic or goal. For instance, a sustainability narrative can underpin both a water policy and an economic development policy, while a different sustainability narrative can lead to an alternative water policy (e.g., policy 1').

Metaphor Family

Community	Leadership	Adversity	
We will remain afloat	Our leader will keep the boat afloat	Like storms, unavoidable	If we all work together we will keep the boat afloat
			Strategy
We will keep the hive alive	Our leader will ensure the hive survives	Like predators, must be avoided	If we all work together we will keep the hive safe, but some will be sacrificed..

Figure 4.4 Metaphors, when widely used, often give rise to a family of metaphors. Sometimes, a set of metaphors or "offspring" originating from the same family can be employed to comprehend a phenomenon, analyze a problem, or find solutions. For instance, comparing a community to a ship rather than a beehive often leads to related metaphors for leadership, adversity and for ways in which a community can overcome challenges.

find new support. New combinations of metaphors might thus appear by shifting context, or in a path from discourse to policy and implementation (Lipsky, 2010). Science can come in, identity narratives, organizational identities and ideologies that prove to be less cohesive in society than the early storytellers of sustainability might have thought (Jasanoff, 1998). This can come with benefits and appears only as a structural obstacle for those who sell a hard-edged sustainability that demands translation into precisely one form of governance and community. We would argue that awareness of these dynamics can inspire conversations recognizing a greater variety of policy paths (Figure 4.4).

The master signifier of "development" moved between policy domains, aimed to integrate domains, traveled from north to south and back again, and assimilated expertise from a host of disciplines. It somehow harnessed both modernist technocratic and religious values, and, despite attempts by international organizations and governments to unify development discourse, found numerous translations and took on an array of shades. In countries of the global south, increasing agency entailed a proliferation of meanings of "development," of connections to pre-existing stories and metaphors. Ambitions and values could be projected on development policies, projects, agencies, funds, transforming all of them in the process. Some discourses attempted to become hegemonic, but in practice, this hegemony was very partial, and what could sprout as new ideas and practices could either look like a rejuvenation and upscaling of tradition, or a ruthless cutting of roots. (Escobar, 2011)

In academic discourse, sustainability stories found support in systems theories and concepts of social-ecological systems which seemed to promise swift translation of ecological and hydrological concepts to social and economic issues (Holling & Goldberg, 1971). A second promise relates to translation to governance, where more metaphoric concepts from ecology found their way to policy discourse. Resilience traveled to social and policy sciences, and to policy discourse itself. That opened the door to the world of policy and governance for other concepts of a metaphoric nature, such as tipping points and collapse (Milkoreit, 2023; Pierson, 2000). As ecosystems could collapse, in the view of ecologists, with the loss of species diversity, the disruption of ecological processes as a consequence, and as lake systems could suddenly, after gradual changes, tip over to an entirely different chemical, hydrological and ecological state, so societies were imagined to bounce back, collapse, tip over (Scheffer et al., 2012). What this really means, whether these concepts really translate, is very hard to determine, yet if we accept the metaphors, new stories about good governance for sustainability abound. The risks suddenly appear as transparent, and comprehending a desirable system state is rendered less of an effort (Stone, 2012).

Whether one can define an appropriate balance within society and between social and ecological systems, and whether one should speak of a balance at all, is a major question. We can say that the balance and systems metaphors proved highly productive fictions (Hughes et al., 2021; Princen, 2010). They enabled new observations and new conversations on modes of production, policy priorities, and relations to the environment and in many cases promoted long-term perspectives in public discourse and governance where none existed before. At the same time, the prevalence of natural science metaphors in mutual support in sustainability thinking and policy came with trade-offs, as much insight produced in policy-related academia was ignored, and as checks and balances, patterns of inclusion and exclusion moved to the background (Jasanoff, 2011; Leach et al., 2010). Invoking more emergencies, under the climate flag, more metaphors of crisis, did not help to diversify the perspective again, and the careful deliberation of public goods and collective risks remained metaphorically unsupported. If we're under threat of imminent collapse all the time, if we're surrounded by the wreckage of ecosystems, if what's coming is a perfect storm, there's little space to cautiously recalibrate governance in such a way that our response to one problem does not create new ones elsewhere (Chandler, 2014; Hulme, 2009).

The attentive reader maybe raised an eyebrow when we casually called a system a metaphor. "System" is a concept, and thinkers of social-ecological systems might find grounding in a general systems theory that recognizes systems everywhere (Van Assche et al., 2019). Those systems can then be presented as diagrams, where social-ecological systems ideas have proven very fertile, being imagined in myriad ways. The diagrams, or visual representations of what a system or a kind of system is, function certainly as metaphor, as the image is not the system itself, and clearly capture only a selection of traits, even of a very broad system concept, and as such concept can be represented in various other ways (Cetina, 2015; Latour, 1999). As most discourse on sustainability relies on such diagrams, it takes on metaphoric shades immediately. Maybe more fundamentally, one can ask the question whether the "system" idea is not, because its high level of abstraction, a metaphor immediately.

If abstraction is a process of finding essences, if we believe that the world literally consists of systems, then a system is not a metaphor. If, however, we see abstraction as a discursive process where stories emerge that can cover a broad category of phenomena, and where, in discursive production, one can easily go in two directions, from concrete to abstract and from general to specific, then a concept such as "system," can be understood as a metaphor, an image helpful to understand other things (Schon, 2013). Such metaphor can then without much effort connect to other metaphors, of balance or equilibrium, collapse and rebound. Without the systems idea, such operations would be much less persuasive, since not fitting a bigger picture.

Ideas of equilibrium are immediately appealing since they resonate with many other stories, in the western tradition dating back to Greek philosophy and the Christian religion. Themis, the Greek goddess of justice, had scales and Athena, as the goddess of wisdom, always aimed at balanced judgment, and restoring the balance in the world. Crimes were upsetting the balance ordained by the Gods, or, for Christianity, by God. Since the Enlightenment, an imbalance came to represent irrationality, moreover, while a medical perspective on life would similarly reinforce the balance metaphor. A discursive configuration formed, in other words, where the shared metaphor of balance made it easy to project ideals of balancing virtually anywhere, and to see many forms of mobility and dynamism as problems. At the same time, conflict came to symbolize instability, an unfortunate disruption of harmony, and the productive capacity of conflict became almost impossible to observe. (Barthes, 2006; Foucault, 2002b)

Leaving the Greeks aside, a modernist perspective on policy and administration, as a master narrative, seems to revive itself eternally. It smoothly introduces ideas of balanced systems into the realm of balancing interests and decisions (Douglas, 1986; Scott, 1998). Such framing combines the balance metaphor almost imperceptibly with the machine metaphors dominant in modernist narratives of community improvement, so tinkering with the balance is like adjusting a machine, and the concept of system itself takes on machine-like qualities (Capra, 1997). This can happen in public discourse, yet also occurs when sustainability stories translate into policy, or, later, in more detailed or localized policies, if that setting is more thoroughly modernist. An inspiring sustainability vision promoted by politicians sensitive to academic insights and cultural preoccupations might end up as a quantitative improvement of urban greenery, or species counts (Pierre & Peters, 2000).

Even the temporality of systems can enter the machinic world of modernism, as when the cycles recognized through ecological analogies turn into clockwise rhythms, or when the clock is ticking for nature and society, and we just need to intervene quickly and precisely, according to the mechanics of the time bomb. If we combine this with ideas of adaptation suggesting it might be too late for that, we can easily end up with recipes for emergency governance required to break some eggs, images of approaching tipping points and a sense of urgency legitimizing rapid or rash action, or maybe just despondency (Latour, 2015).

What was illustrated by the previous paragraphs was not only the mutual support of metaphors, but also the power of ideology to subsume and connect metaphor. Indeed, modernism might have never died, but the dramatic prospects embodied by sustainability discourse, even if overtly focusing on the positive, brought a revival of ideals of systems engineering which seemed beyond their prime (Latour, 2018). Anxiety about the future and our environment can be a powerful driver of engineering fantasies, of desires for just fixing the problem, desires which can be fulfilled more easily when we see systems as things that can be objectively understood, rebalanced, fixed – as machines (Beck, 1992; Escobar, 2020). Strong desires to deny the problem appeared, to lash out against anxiety-inducing, overpromising and authoritarian academics and bureaucrats (Wynne, 1992). Resistance against the problem – we do not want this to be true – merged with resistance against the proposed solution – "we do not want to be governed like that."

When the enhancement of enabling technologies – particularly information and communications technology – is identified as a sustainable development goal aimed at promoting the empowerment of women, this can be understood, and is often observed, as a strategically appealing simplification of a more complex issue. If we can reduce the ideal balance between women and men to a series of technical problems, where progress can be expressed in numbers, and declared fixed at some point, we do not have to think about that balance. If equal participation in management is the desirable outcome, or equal intake of each gender, similar career patterns, salaries, voice in publications and participatory exercises, comparable roles in organizations, sectors, governmental actors, we say nothing about the process leading to that outcome, and inequalities, exclusions and discouragement there. We can also avoid a consideration of the larger context, both social and economic, the roles, workload, expectations and support there. Quantification of results, and reduction of process to technical problems thus maintain a non-thinking about ever changing roles and identities of genders, in always evolving societies, and a non-reflection about preferable and acceptable relations between the genders. (Enloe, 2004)

To offer a more optimistic example, let us introduce Sigurd Olson. Olson (1899–1982) was a teacher, administrator, canoe guide and conservationist. Based in Ely, Minnesota, for most of his life, he found his true calling in writing. It took him a while to find his stride, but the 1956 publication of *The Singing Wilderness*, a book filled with sharply observed and poetic essays on the nature and landscape around him, made him a celebrity (Backes, 1997). Olson himself found meaning in his, often slow, observation and exploration of this land of lakes, streams and forest, and in writing about it. Those writings created an image not only of a landscape, but of a way of being in the landscape, of relations between nature and culture that could serve as inspiration elsewhere (Van Assche, 2015). He had been a stalwart of the protection movement in his home region, where logging, mining and motorized traffic was kept out of the Boundary Waters Canoe and Wilderness Area (BWCWA). After his rise to fame, he became director of the National Parks Association, and a notable proponent of conservation, but also of environmentally sensitive planning and design, and of lifestyles cognizant of the intricate relations between humans and nature.

Olson thus created stories for himself, to redefine himself, beyond his role as teacher, to find meaning in life, and in sharing these stories through writing. After which they acquired new meanings in politics, and in the life of many readers. He moved through these stages himself yet connected with different people and stories at each stage. Some stories resonated with readers as residents and nature lovers, some as active citizens or politicians, and the master signifier "wilderness" enabled connections, some already codified in his own writings, with a variety of metaphors that proved productive in different spheres of life and society. His trusted paddle became a symbol of adaptation, the slow journey in canoe an analogy for life and a gradual recognition of our dependencies in a web of relations, of "intangible values" revealing themselves bit by bit. A "jumping off point," as starting point for explorations, became a metaphor for a stable and familiar point capable of supporting jumps into the unknown, journeys of self-discovery and reinvention. A "spot of blue," a glimpse of a lake or stream in the distance, morphed into a sign of an alluring goal, but one that could feature only in a green future (Radomski & Van Assche, 2014).

While some of these metaphors have gone by the wayside now (Cronon, 1996), and his reputation as an environmental writer has declined, they did their work. They created an audience, made many look at community and environment anew and paved the way, with other writers, for environmental planning and design, beyond protected areas. "Wilderness" worked as master signifier for a variety of values, for individuals and communities, which could lead to individual and collective action. Wilderness was not untouched, as humans have a place, might even transform it, without its identity and value being lost. It could be experienced far away and close to home, as the wild, if well observed, resides in the cracks of our urban fabric, and the fabric of our cultural discourse (Olson, 2012a).

"One day in the south of England I was walking through a great beech wood on an old estate near Shrivenham. There was a little brook flowing through the woods, and its gurgle as ran through a rocky dell seemed to accentuate my sense of the age of these magnificent trees. I was far from home, as far away from the wilderness of the north as I had ever been. Those great trees were comforting to me, even though I knew that just beyond them was an open countryside. Then suddenly I heard a sound that changed everything: a soft nasal twang from high in the branches, the call of a nuthatch. Instantly, that beech grove was transformed into a stand of tall, stately pines; the brown beech leaves on the ground became a smooth carpet of golden needles (...). The call of the nuthatch had done all that, had given me a vision of the wilderness as vivid as though for the moment I had actually been there." (Olson, 2012b, p. 201)

Narratives and Metaphors of Sustainability Governance

Stories do live eternally. This was true for Olson, and it is true for any other narrative construct. Some master signifiers survive for a long time, others appear unexpectedly, helping us to make sense of new situations. "Innovation" came out of the blue in the 1980s, roughly at the same time as "sustainability"; both addressed different concerns and came with their own temporalities (Barry, 2001). That temporality is one of the features determining the implications for governance: Does this concept imply rapid or slow action, a long-term perspective, regular adaptation of policy, or reform of governance? Does its temporality override others?

The Olson example indicates that temporality here has a second meaning: fitting with the times. Wilderness discourse could unleash its effects in the twentieth century as it coevolved, hence coupled, with other concepts and concerns, as the ruthless exploitation of natural resources and the unstoppable march of industrial expansion were showing their downsides to many, and the earlier ideas of Romanticism (which had opposed industrial development) proved attractive once again (Rigby, 2004). Innovation ideas proved seductive to administrations believing to lag behind but also believing in their own ability to fix the problem. Build more innovation parks, subsidize more tech firms, encourage academics to start companies and all will be well

(Godin, 2015). Techno-utopianism combined, for a long time, with modernist steering philosophies in social democratic countries. That is, until the tech sector redefined itself in ideological terms.

What shapes the effects of a sustainability narrative on governance depends on several features of the narrative and the governance system. Some narratives have discernible implications for governance, others speak directly about ideal forms of governance that would bring about a sustainable society. In other words: Some stories of sustainability *are* stories about governance, while others require a series of translations to see which governance system would bring the goal closer. Sometimes, the idea of a goal appears as clearly defined, and possible to reach, elsewhere, sustainability governance is a *journey*, maybe a very tough and unpredictable one, involving meandering as well as terrifying episodes, like shooting rapids (Olsson et al., 2006; Wals et al., 2009).

Not all sustainability metaphors have strong implications for governance; they might conjure up more readily images of community, or of leadership. Sometimes, problems in governance are highlighted, rather than an ideal model, and wherever cracks in governance are revealed, this creates spaces for leadership. Different perspectives allow for different degrees of contextualization: Do we need to copy a "best practice" solution from a supposedly more sustainable place, or can we rethink sustainability for ourselves, and maybe take a critical look at the best practice? If earth is a spaceship, do we need a captain, or can we muddle through the universe with a variety of political systems?

Coevolving concepts, narratives and metaphors codetermine what happens to stories in governance. And, as we recall, for sustainability governance, we can identify community, (good) governance, system–environment relations and leadership as noteworthy candidates for relevant coevolutions. We need to pay close attention to prevalent stories about community (hence inclusion, identity, history), governance (hence democracy, efficiency, legitimacy, checks and balances, corruption), leadership (thus strategy, routines, institutions, power) and environments (therefore resources, threats, balance).

If we live in an Italian rural town with Etruscan roots, surrounded by vineyards dating back to Roman times, in a townscape of mostly medieval origin, and we identify more than anything with the town, its history, its sometimes bitter rivalries that were always cast aside when envious neighbors attacked, then sustainability will look more than anything like continuing traditions. It will mean that fractious and seemingly never-ending meetings of the town council, with shifting coalitions between leading families and factions, between old and older money, are considered good governance(Ingold, 2000). It might also mean that newcomers have a hard time, and find themselves in a precarious position, even when they are contributing to the maintenance of tradition, and of the scenery that forms a backdrop for daily life, a backdrop imagined as eternal. When European funds for sustainable development arrive at the doorstep, they will be diverted for projects that benefit the local elite, as they see themselves as the guarantors of sustainability, and probably for heritage preservation, as this keeps the narrative intact, and possibly pockets lined.

The sustainability story itself might have something to say about the other concepts. Possibly, stories on good governance (or others) are already implied in the version of problem, solution, goal, context marking the sustainability story. In other cases, sustainability has initially few assumptions on governance, but the discourse develops its own perspective and from there asks for reform – as happened the resilience literature, where governance recipes gradually asserted themselves. We would like to add a distinction here, between *response and narrative of response*. Climate change denial can be a response to climate change, yet not every denial leads to stories of denial. The stories have distinct consequences for governance. When stories focus on a problem, versus a solution, this can have different implications for governance, where the effect hinges on associated stories of problems and solutions. A solution might not transpire from the story, yet appear to be available in governance, which makes the story likely more attractive for that community (Ricoeur, 2009). Responses might more easily be formulated and appear in narrative form, which makes them available to deliberation and transformation (Jones & McBeth, 2010).

Ideas of sustainability can thus trigger responses that circumvent narrative, yet narrative answers offer more opportunities for guided self-transformation. Prevalent notions of community, systems relations, governance and leadership might welcome sustainability stories, and provide answers, or such notions might be encoded in the sustainability story itself. Alternatively, the actors who promote a version of sustainability might craft their versions of sustainability governance, leadership, of a sustainable community, adapted to their circumstances.

If a sustainability narrative lands in a territory that does not really considers itself a community, and does not accept technocratic governance, chances are that whatever version of sustainability is promoted will not gain much traction (Dryzek, 1997). In theory, this collection of individuals might still agree on a version of sustainability and a set of policy tools to make it a reality, but without a notion of a shared identity, collective goals are much harder to define and pursue. If the community is there, but defines itself through an opposition to environmentalism, or a pursuit of short-term profit or welfare maximization, sustainability will sound alien.

Stories about the community and how it should be governed tend to be closely coupled. A view on what the real community is tends to imply stories on the good community, and on the way that community should be governed (Anderson, 2006; Foucault, 2003). If a community is seen as a collection of individuals marked by individual rights and preferences, or a set of organizations, or rather a collective sharing a past, or (as with communism) a future, this means something for the forms of participation and representation envisioned, for the relation between individual, organization, local community and higher-level governance (Held, 1996). And it means something for the articulation of collective futures and the observation of different environments. Stories of democracy as good governance can focus on very diverse spatial scales, modes of representation and participation, distributions of power between politics and administration, between center and the regions and so forth (Bevir, 2011). Which reflects ideas on the nature of the community: Is the community a nation, a nation state, or rather a village? Do we start from shared traditions or cultural similarity or rather from administrative units where fairness and diversity take central place (Luhmann, 1995)?

These tightly coupled stories of community and good governance might be the most significant environment for sustainability stories to land, as they define a set of master signifiers and narratives that can open or close the doors for stories that can be perceived as green, utopian and authoritarian or rather as responsible, caring, a matter of self-preservation (Jasanoff, 2016). If political parties are at the center of the local version of democracy, sustainability stories must connect to the discourse of those parties, which can differ in terms of master narratives of governance, community and environment. If administrative actors de facto determine most policy, it is worth studying what those actors think, even if one disagrees with their position of power (Fischer & Gottweis, 2012).

Where politics is village politics first and foremost, where regional governance took the form of competition between villages, and national politicians are perceived as representatives (possibly members) of leading companies and families in the capital, good governance is open participation in village politics and respect for the autonomy of the village. A reduction of national power is seen as desirable. The community is the village, and sustainability means a thriving village in an environment that can support it. Convincing locals of a national sustainability strategy, and its implications in terms taxes, paperwork, environmental and land use regulation, is therefore not so much a matter of translating the sustainability narrative, but of rendering relevant a shared national interest, and, who knows, identity.

How governance systems observe their environment correlates with this coupling of governance and community ideas. If community is primarily the local community, then stories about other scales, and policies requiring observation of systems change over large areas, might be a hard sell. When a nation state operates on the assumption that individuals and organizations must lobby and compete for influence on the writing of law and policy, observations which could underpin a sustainability strategy probably do not take place. And where the environment is mostly a space for the extraction of resources by private actors, rebalancing the relation between social and ecological system escapes the imagination of the governance system (Moser, 2010). When, moreover, governance is the governance of a divided polity, with factions opposing each other in principle, a sustainability story entering the arena through one of the factions will most likely perish (Hoffman, 2015).

Leadership appears on the horizon in several ways. Stories of sustainability can require a certain form of leadership, or, stories on governance and community might have produced a leadership that selects and molds sustainability stories in governance and community. Significantly, existing leadership might be able to see the limits of current governance in grasping the importance of sustainability and help to make things happen despite those imperfections. Fourth, leadership could craft a new sustainability narrative, a creative contextualization that might finally enable the community to embark on a sustainability journey. Or, where rhetoric of sustainability remains out of the question, it can deploy different stories to achieve similar goals. Finally, it might open up the conversation about the long term and the environment, where such conversation did not exist.

When discussing the discursive coevolutions that shape the reception or crafting of sustainability stories, we have to keep in mind that sustainability discourse not only reflects ideas, but can also *create* new ideals for society, a new ideology, innovative understandings of relating to our environment (Jasanoff, 2004). We cannot assume that this is possible for all circumstances, however; the rhetorical effect of the same story, as we know, can vary dramatically. What might provide openings for sustainability stories are other signifiers already circulating, as potential starting points for sustainability discourse or goals (Figure 4.5a). Sustainability might be present under other names, or

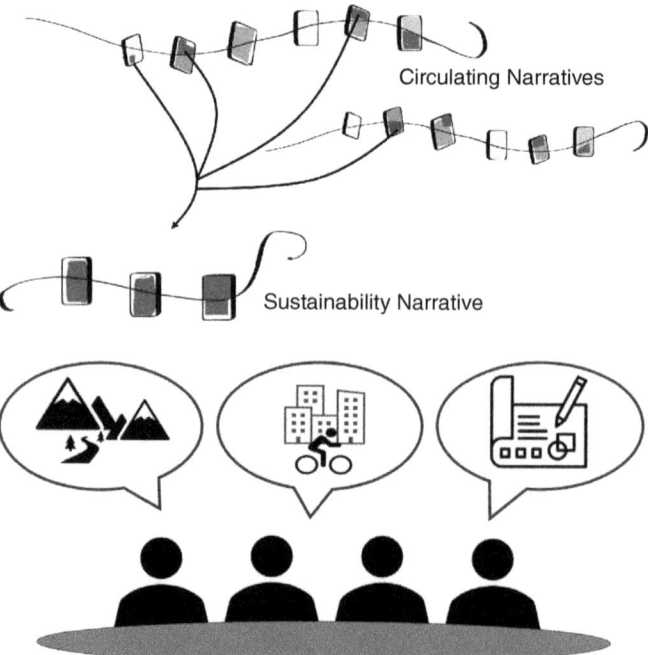

Figure 4.5 (a) Opportunities for sustainability narratives may arise from existing signifiers that are already circulating, serving as potential starting points for discussions or objectives related to sustainability. Sustainability may be known by different names, or current narratives can be easily reinterpreted within the context of sustainability. (b) Different sustainability narratives can coexist in governance, each highlighting and drawing on different systems relations.

existing stories can be reinterpreted easily under the signifier of sustainability. In a twenty-first century context, different narratives of sustainability likely coexist already, in the community and in governance, even if they do not translate into policy yet (Figure 4.5b).

A Normative Stance on Sustainability Governance

Not all narratives are created equal. Sustainability discourse, however, has to rely on narratives, metaphors and master signifiers to unfold itself, and come within grasp of policy and community (Gunder & Hillier, 2009). A wide variety of stories converged on problems in social-ecological systems relations, however imperfectly we could comprehend those relations. Experiences in different parts of the world, observed from different angles, through the lens of myriad narratives, pointed at similar problems.

Whether we believe in the systemic character of social-ecological systems or not, whether we think that systems have to be balanced and whether societies can collapse in ways similar to ecosystems, stories and metaphors help us to grasp effects of society on our environment and impacts of a deteriorating ecology on our social and political systems. If sustainability narratives are productive by creating support for concerted action, for more systematic observation of processes long ignored, of patterns long dismissed, they are productive (Bulkeley & Betsill, 2005). If, on the other hand, stories of sustainability increase rigidities in governance, reduce diversity in perspectives and critical discussion of explanations and policy options, they become harmful (Hulme, 2009). We can locate ourselves in the tradition of American pragmatism (Dewey, 2012), as stories, for us, can be supported if they work, and in the case of sustainability, their validity is of crucial importance, since the sustainability rhetoric aims to refocus our attention on the survival of societies and ecosystems – they need to work, even if we cannot be sure if they are true.

What good sustainability governance would look like can therefore not be summarized that easily, since the issues of sustainability are not the same everywhere, and as the cost of certain policies or reforms to pursue partial goals might be outweighed by damaged done to other infrastructures, institutions and values (Goldman, 2005; Van Assche et al., 2024). Moreover, what can be achieved in one place might be beyond reach elsewhere, and what first appears as a reasonable reform to address contextualized sustainability issues, might not be feasible because of insurmountable resistance, or, in other terms, dependencies in governance evolution (Van Assche et al., 2013). Whether communities are willing to sacrifice other goals and goods, whether they are willing to bet on an enlightened green dictatorship, and whether that benevolent authoritarianism would be sustainable itself, can only be decided by communities themselves. The broad question is: Would we like to survive? Even if the answer is rather obvious, many policy directions offered under the flag of sustainability overpromise and undercontextualize.

We do believe it is possible to take a normative stance on good governance for sustainability. In most cases, it will be costly and require reform (Chaffin et al., 2016). Our story on good governance integrating sustainability as a key concern in community development requires communities to *envision and deliberate the long term*. If governance sites and arenas do not offer opportunities to consider the implications of current practices, and envision alternatives, this is a problem. Governance, second, needs to build up *strategic capacity*, meaning that visions for the future can be coupled to policy tools, and that the strategy itself can function as an institution, as a device of coordination. Strategic capacity entails *institutional capacity*, the capacity to coordinate, and it counts on expanded *observational capacity*. Sustainability issues place high demands on observation, both on the interface between social and ecological systems, the impacts in two directions, and on self-observation or reflexivity (Folke et al., 2005; Mitchell, 2013).

Reflexivity is essential, since the shifts in policy, and likely governance reform on the road to sustainability, however defined, are more plausible when supported by a deep understanding of actual system functioning, and of the dependencies constraining a particular governance path (Jasanoff, 2004). Understanding system function, actual power relations, narrative knots and patterns of inclusion and exclusion, grasping the real, is of the essence when aiming to navigate the waters of sustainability reform. Similarly, observation of system–environment interactions, whether one places trust in equilibrium models or not, comes at a premium, if reform wants to be inspired by dangers that are actually dangers for the community.

Observational capacity, institutional capacity and strategic capacity thus produce adaptive capacity, a feature of governance systems which cannot be measured but assessed regularly. Systems cannot adapt to any change imaginable, and adaptation to a particular change renders adaptation to a correlated and particular set of other challenges difficult. Trade-offs are contextual, and adaptation is always adaptation to an array or range of conditions, with escalating trade-offs beyond that range (Van Assche et al., 2024). Whether societies will accept some trade-offs, not other, cannot be predicted or decided by outsiders.

Long-term perspectives, strategy, self-reflection and careful scrutiny of relevant environments thus represent our basic recipe for good sustainability governance. These conditions can be met under different ecological and economic conditions, and in different versions of democracy, or other types of polity. They can appear under most master signifiers of community, governance and environment and materialize under different styles of leadership. The conditions are necessary but not sufficient for embarking on a sustainability journey. Stories about environments, and about desirable relations with them must be crafted contextually, fit into local discursive and institutional configurations. Leadership moves governance towards the basic conditions sketched, or beyond. Where governance seems to be in good shape, but sustainability does not seem close, leadership will be called upon to get things moving, or to overcome imperfections.

If we want to abolish fisheries subsidies that contribute to overcapacity and overfishing, all features of good sustainability governance must be in place, if the prohibition wants to gain support and if adaptations and alternatives need to be ready to go. Governance systems must be able to consider the effects of current fisheries on the ecosystem, and of subsidies on fisheries. System-environment interactions are to be observed carefully, and reflexivity is of the essence to understand how governance functions in the social-ecological system, and where support and resistance can be expected. Long-term perspectives need to find a place in governance, and their construction and assessment must include effects of fisheries and subsidies, as well as adaptations of fisheries and alternatives to fisheries. Both the visioning effort, and the subsequent work entails institutional and strategic capacity. In short: abolishing subsidies of this sort, while maintaining stability, requires both an understanding of the subsidy problem and a capacity to formulate new futures for the community, as, in many cases, dropping fisheries support without offering or rethinking anything is a death sentence for fishing communities.

Concluding

Sustainability narratives and sustainability governance ought to be crafted to fit the situation in the triple context of governance, community and ecology. What it should do and can do might differ significantly. What the community expects it to do and enables it in practice might vary. Its activities will hinge on the actual gaps and imperfections in the system, and on the governance functions that already support sustainability policy or transformation. Contradictory emotions, incoherent discourse must be diagnosed, passivity overcome, reasons to deceive detected.

What we are left with is not just a tangle of stories, but a situation where conditions for good sustainability governance can be outlined, and where sustainability stories will always be stories but still amenable to critical assessment. Stories must serve a double pragmatic goal, that is, mobilizing the community to reflect, and supporting the governance system to transform itself, to meet the conditions of good sustainability governance and give them shape contextually. Further, stories of sustainability might never touch the untouchable, be able to precisely define what sustainability objectively is, but they can be wrong, nevertheless. They can misrecognize or ignore social and ecological impacts and relations, misread collective sentiment, and fail to protect the balancing act between interests and ideas that governance always is.

This is the context for sustainability leadership to analyze, navigate, mobilize and transform. In Chapters 6 and 7, we further develop our perspective on sustainability leadership, linking back to the ideas on leadership introduced in Chapter 1 and leaning on the perspective on narrative and metaphor presented in Chapters 2 and 3. We reflect on the leadership functions and roles more likely to be relevant under common conditions of governance limitations and sustainability problems. In this, we return to the importance of coevolution, between system and environment, institutional and discursive configurations in governance, and between stories and metaphors of sustainability and other powerful master narratives and signifiers in the community. Now, however, we devote Chapter 5 to common misconceptions on sustainability leadership, which we can describe as myths. Not all stories are created equal, indeed and many communities have followed the path of false promises and alluring simplicity towards a state one cannot describe as sustainable in any sense.

References

Agrawal, A. (2005). *Environmentality: Technologies of Government and Political Subjects*. Duke University Press.

Anderson, B. (American C. of L. S.) (2006). *Imagined Communities: Reflections on the Origin and Spread of Nationalism* (3rd ed., p. 240). Verso Books.

Backes, D. (1997). *Wilderness Within: The Life of Sigurd F. Olson*. University of Minnesota Press.

Barry, A. (2001). *Political Machines: Governing a Technological Society*. A&C Black.

Barthes, R. (2006). *Mythologies*. Farrar, Straus and Giroux.

Bauman, Z. (2013). *Liquid Modernity*. John Wiley & Sons.

Beck, U. (1992). *Risk Society: Towards a New Modernity*. SAGE Publications.

Beckert, J. (2024). *How We Sold Our Future: The Failure to Fight Climate Change*. John Wiley & Sons.

Beckman, C. M., Rosen, J., Estrada-Miller, J., & Painter, G. (2023). The social innovation trap: Critical insights into an emerging field. *Academy of Management Annals*, 17(2), 684–709.

Bell, M. M., & Ashwood, L. L. (2015). *An Invitation to Environmental Sociology*. SAGE Publications.

Bevir, M. (2011). Governance and governmentality after neoliberalism. *Policy & Politics*, 39(4), 457–471.

Bhabha, H. K. (2012). *The Location of Culture*. Routledge.

Bion, W. (2023). *Learning From Experience*. Routledge.

Bouzarovski, S. (2022). Just transitions: A political ecology critique. *Antipode*, 54(4), 1003–1020.

Brown, T. (2016). Sustainability as empty signifier: Its rise, fall, and radical potential. *Antipode*, 48(1), 115–133.

Bruner, J. S. (2009). *Actual Minds, Possible Worlds*. Harvard University Press.

Bulkeley, H., & Betsill, M. (2005). Rethinking sustainable cities: Multilevel governance and the "urban" politics of climate change. *Environmental Politics*, 14(1), 42–63.

Butler, J. (2004). *Precarious Life: The Powers of Mourning and Violence*. Verso Books.

Capra, F. (1997). *The Web of Life: A New Scientific Understanding of Living Systems*. Knopf Doubleday Publishing Group.

Carolan, M. S. (2006). Do you see what I see? Examining the epistemic barriers to sustainable agriculture. *Rural Sociology*, 71(2), 232–260. https://doi.org/10.1526/003601106777789756

Cetina, K. K. (2015). Metaphors in the scientific laboratory: Why are they there and what do they do? In Z. Radman (Ed.), *From a Metaphorical Point of View: A Multidisciplinary Approach to the Cognitive Content of Metaphor* (pp. 329–350). De Gruyter. www.degruyterbrill.com/document/doi/10.1515/9783110867831-016/pdf?licenseType=restricted

Chaffin, B. C., Garmestani, A. S., Gunderson, L. H., Benson, M. H., Angeler, D. G., Arnold, C. A. (Tony), Cosens, B., Craig, R. K., Ruhl, J. B., & Allen, C. R. (2016). Transformative Environmental Governance. *Annual Review of Environment and Resources*, 41(2016), 399–423.

Chandler, D. (2014). *Resilience: The Governance of Complexity*. Routledge.

Cook, I. R., & Swyngedouw, E. (2012). Cities, social cohesion and the environment: Towards a future research agenda. *Urban Studies*, 49(9), 1959–1979.

Corvellec, H., Stowell, A. F., & Johansson, N. (2022). Critiques of the circular economy. *Journal of Industrial Ecology*, 26(2), 421–432.

Cronon, W. (Ed.). (1996). *Uncommon Ground: Toward Reinventing Nature*. W. W. Norton & Company.

Davidson, D. (2025). *Feeling Climate Change: How Emotions Govern Our Responses to the Climate Emergency*. Routledge, Taylor & Francis Group.

Davidson, M. (2012). Sustainable city as fantasy. *Human Geography*, 5(2), 14–25.

Dermody, J., Koenig-Lewis, N., Zhao, A. L., & Hanmer-Lloyd, S. (2021). Critiquing a Utopian idea of sustainable consumption: A post-capitalism perspective. *Journal of Macromarketing*, 41(4), 626–645.

Descola, P., & Palsson, G. (2003). *Nature and Society: Anthropological Perspectives*. Routledge.

Dewey, J. (2012). *The Public and Its Problems: An Essay in Political Inquiry* (M. L. Rogers, Ed.). Penn State Press.

Douglas, M. (1986). *How Institutions Think*. Syracuse University Press.

Dryzek, J. S. (1997). *The Politics of the Earth: Environmental Discourses*. Oxford University Press.

Enloe, C. (2004). *The Curious Feminist: Searching for Women in a New Age of Empire*. University of California Press.

Escobar, A. (2011). *Encountering Development: The Making and Unmaking of the Third World*. Princeton University Press.

Escobar, A. (2020). *Pluriversal Politics: The Real and the Possible*. Duke University Press.

Farley, H. M., & Smith, Z. A. (2020). *Sustainability: If It's Everything, Is It Nothing?* (2nd ed.). Routledge.

Fink, B. (1995). *The Lacanian Subject: Between Language and Jouissance*. Princeton University Press.

Fischer, D. (2023). *Narrating Sustainability through Storytelling* (S. Fücker & H. Selm, Eds., 1st ed.). Routledge.

Fischer, F. (2003). *Reframing Public Policy: Discursive Politics and Deliberative Practices*. Oxford University Press.

Fischer, F., & Gottweis, H. (2012). *The Argumentative Turn Revisited: Public Policy as Communicative Practice*. Duke University Press.

Folke, C., Hahn, T., Olsson, P., & Norberg, J. (2005). Adaptive governance of social-ecological systems. *Annual Review of Environment and Resources*, *30*(1), 441–473.

Foucault, M. (2002a). *Archaeology of Knowledge* (2nd ed.). Routledge.

Foucault, M. (2002b). *The Order of Things: An Archaeology of the Human Sciences*. Psychology Press.

Foucault, M. (2003). *Society Must be Defended: Lectures at the College de France, 1975–76*. Allen Lane The Penguin Press.

Foucault, M. (2012a). *Discipline and Punish: The Birth of the Prison*. Knopf Doubleday Publishing Group.

Foucault, M. (2012b). *The History of Sexuality: An Introduction*. Vintage.

Frankel, B. (2020). *Fictions of Sustainability: The Politics of Growth and Post Capitalist Futures*. Greenmeadows.

Girard, R., Oughourlian, J.-M., & Lefort, G. (2003). *Things Hidden Since the Foundation of the World*. A&C Black.

Godin, B. (2015). *Innovation Contested: The Idea of Innovation Over the Centuries*. Routledge.

Goldman, M. (2005). *Imperial Nature: The World Bank and Struggles for Social Justice in the Age of Globalization*. Yale University Press.

Gramsci, A. (2011). *Prison Notebooks Volume 2*. Columbia University Press.

Gunder, M. (2019). Visionary idealism in environmental planning. In S. Davoudi, R. Cowell, I. White, & H. Blanco (Eds.), *The Routledge Companion to Environmental Planning* (pp. 43–51). Routledge.

Gunder, M., & Hillier, J. (2009). *Planning in Ten Words or Less: A Lacanian Entanglement with Spatial Planning*. Ashgate Publishing, Ltd.

Hajer, M. A. (1995). *The Politics of Environmental Discourse: Ecological Modernization and the Policy Process*. Clarendon Press.

Held, D. (1996). *Models of Democracy*. Stanford University Press.

Hoffman, A. J. (2015). *How Culture Shapes the Climate Change Debate*. Stanford University Press.

Holling, C. S., & Goldberg, M. A. (1971). Ecology and planning. *Journal of the American Institute of Planners*, *37*(4), 221–230.

Hughes, I., Byrne, E., Mullally, G., & Sage, C. (2021). *Metaphor, Sustainability, Transformation: Transdisciplinary Perspectives*. Routledge.

Hulme, M. (2009). *Why We Disagree about Climate Change: Understanding Controversy, Inaction and Opportunity*. Cambridge University Press.

Hulme, M. (2012). "Telling a different tale": Literary, historical and meteorological readings of a Norfolk heatwave. *Climatic Change, 113*(1), 5–21.

Ingold, T. (2000). *The Perception of the Environment: Essays on Livelihood, Dwelling and Skill*. Psychology Press.

Jacob, J. (2025). A background history of the sustainable development goals. *Sustainable Development, 33*(3), 3747–3759.

Jasanoff, S. (1998). *The Fifth Branch: Science Advisers as Policymakers*. Harvard University Press.

Jasanoff, S. (2004). Ordering knowledge, ordering society. In S. Jasanoff (Ed.). *States of Knowledge* (pp. 13–45). Routledge.

Jasanoff, S. (2007). Technologies of humility. *Nature, 450*(7166), 33–33.

Jasanoff, S. (2011). *Designs on Nature: Science and Democracy in Europe and the United States*. Princeton University Press.

Jasanoff, S. (2016). *The Ethics of Invention: Technology and the Human Future*. W. W. Norton & Company.

Jones, M. D., & McBeth, M. K. (2010). A narrative policy framework: Clear enough to be wrong?: Jones/McBeth: A narrative policy framework. *Policy Studies Journal, 38*(2), 329–353.

Latour, B. (1998). To modernise or ecologise? That is the question. In N. Castree, & B. Braun (Eds.). *Remaking Reality* (pp. 221–242). Routledge.

Latour, B. (1999). *Pandora's Hope: Essays on the Reality of Science Studies*. Harvard University Press.

Latour, B. (2009). *Politics of Nature*. Harvard University Press.

Latour, B. (2015). Waiting for Gaia: Composing the common world through arts and politics. In A. Yaneva, & A. Zaera-Polo (Ed.). *What Is Cosmopolitical Design? Design, Nature and the Built Environment* (pp. 21–32). Routledge.

Latour, B. (2018). *Down to Earth: Politics in the New Climatic Regime*. John Wiley & Sons.

Leach, M., Stirling, A. C., & Scoones, I. (2010). *Dynamic Sustainabilities: Technology, Environment, Social Justice*. Taylor & Francis.

Lipsky, M. (2010). *Street-Level Bureaucracy, 30th Anniversary Edition: Dilemmas of the Individual in Public Service*. Russell Sage Foundation.

Luhmann, N. (1989). *Ecological Communication*. University of Chicago Press.

Luhmann, N. (1995). *Social Systems*. Stanford, CA: Stanford University Press.

Luke, T. W. (1995). Sustainable development as a power/knowledge system: The problem of "governmentality." In F. Fischer & M. Black (Eds.), *Greening Environmental Policy: The Politics of a Sustainable Future* (pp. 21–32). Palgrave Macmillan US.

Luke, T. W. (1997). *Ecocritique: Contesting the Politics of Nature, Economy, and Culture*. University of Minnesota Press.

Milkoreit, M. (2023). Social tipping points everywhere? – Patterns and risks of overuse. *WIREs Climate Change, 14*(2), e813.

Milton, K. (2002). *Environmentalism and Cultural Theory: Exploring the Role of Anthropology in Environmental Discourse*. Routledge.

Mitchell, T. (2013). *Carbon Democracy: Political Power in the Age of Oil*. Verso Books.

Moser, S. C. (2010). Communicating climate change: History, challenges, process and future directions. *WIREs Climate Change, 1*(1), 31–53.

Olson, S. F. (2012a). *Reflections from the North Country*. Knopf Doubleday Publishing Group.

Olson, S. F. (2012b). *Singing Wilderness*. Knopf Doubleday Publishing Group.

Olsson, P., Gunderson, L. H., Carpenter, S. R., Ryan, P., Lebel, L., Folke, C., & Holling, C. S. (2006). Shooting the rapids: Navigating transitions to adaptive governance of social-ecological systems. *Ecology and Society, 11*(1). www.jstor.org/stable/26267806.

Parks, B. C., & Timmons Roberts, J. (2006). Globalization, vulnerability to climate change, and perceived injustice. *Society & Natural Resources, 19*(4), 337–355.

Persich, M. R., Steinemann, B., Fetterman, A. K., & Robinson, M. D. (2021). Drawn to the light: Predicting religiosity using "God is light" metaphor. *Psychology of Religion and Spirituality, 13*(4), 390–400.

Pierre, J., & Peters, G. B. (2000). *Governance, Politics and the State*. Basingstoke: Palgrave Macmillan.

Pierson, P. (2000). Increasing returns, path dependence, and the study of politics. *American Political Science Review, 94*(02), 251–267.

Porter, T. M., & Haggerty, K. D. (1997). Trust in numbers: The pursuit of objectivity in science & public life. *Canadian Journal of Sociology, 22*(2), 279. Canadian Business & Current Affairs Database; International Bibliography of the Social Sciences (IBSS); Sociological Abstracts.

Princen, T. (2010). Speaking of sustainability: The potential of metaphor. *Sustainability: Science, Practice, & Policy, 6*(2), 60–65.

Radomski, P. J., & Van Assche, K. (2014). *Lakeshore Living: Designing Lake Places and Communities in the Footprints of Environmental Writers*. MSU Press.

Ricoeur, P. (2006). *The Rule of Metaphor: The Creation of Meaning in Language (Repr)*. Routledge.

Ricoeur, P. (2009). *Time and Narrative, Volume 1* (K. McLaughlin & D. Pellauer, Trans.). University of Chicago Press.

Rigby, C. E. (2004). *Topographies of the Sacred: The Poetics of Place in European Romanticism.* University of Virginia Press.

Rosemberg, A. (2010). Building a just transition: The linkages between climate change and employment. *International Journal of Labour Research,* 2(2), 125–161. ABI/INFORM Collection; ProQuest One Business.

Sartori, G. (1987). *The Theory of Democracy Revisited.* Chatham House Publishers.

Savini, F. (2025). Strategic planning for degrowth: What, who, how. *Planning Theory,* 24(2), 141–162.

Scheffer, M., Carpenter, S. R., Lenton, T. M., Bascompte, J., Brock, W., Dakos, V., van de Koppel, J., van de Leemput, I. A., Levin, S. A., van Nes, E. H., Pascual, M., & Vandermeer, J. (2012). Anticipating critical transitions. *Science,* 338(6105), 344–348.

Schon, D. A. (Ed.). (2013). *Displacement of Concepts.* Routledge.

Schutter, M. S. (2020). Ecosystem Services and the Blue Economy: Navigating Power and Values [Ph.D., Lancaster University (United Kingdom)]. In PQDT – Global (2461031914). ProQuest Dissertations & Theses Global.

Scott, J. C. (1998). *Seeing like a state: How certain schemes to improve the human condition have failed.* Yale University Press.

Scudder, T. (1981). What it means to be dammed: The anthropology of large-scale development projects in the tropics and subtropics. *Engineering and Science,* 44(4), 9–15.

Scudder, T. (2012). *The Future of Large Dams: Dealing with Social, Environmental, Institutional and Political Costs.* Routledge.

Shellenberger, M. (2020). *Apocalypse Never: Why Environmental Alarmism Hurts Us All* (1st ed.). HarperCollins Publishers.

Stafford Smith, M. (2016). Desertification: Reflections on the mirage. In R. Behnke & M. Mortimore (Eds.), *The End of Desertification?: Disputing Environmental Change in the Drylands* (pp. 539–560). Springer.

Stock, R., & Gardezi, M. (2021). Make bloom and let wither: Biopolitics of precision agriculture at the dawn of surveillance capitalism. *Geoforum,* 122, 193–203.

Stone, D. (2012). *Policy Paradox: The Art of Political Decision Making* (3rd ed.). W.W. Norton & Company.

Szerszynski, B. (2005). *Nature, Technology, and the Sacred.* Blackwell Publishing.

Thiele, L. P. (2013). *Sustainability.* John Wiley & Sons.

Van Assche, K. (2015). Semiotics of silent lakes. Sigurd Olson and the interlacing of writing, policy and planning. *Journal of Environmental Policy & Planning,* 17(2), 262–276.

Van Assche, K., Beunen, R., & Duineveld, M. (2013). *Evolutionary Governance Theory: An Introduction.* Springer.

Van Assche, K., Beunen, R., & Gruezmacher, M. (2024). *Strategy for Sustainability Transitions: Governance, Community and Environment*. Edward Elgar Publishing.
Van Assche, K., Verschraegen, G., Valentinov, V., & Gruezmacher, M. (2019). The social, the ecological, and the adaptive. Von Bertalanffy's general systems theory and the adaptive governance of social-ecological systems. *Systems Research and Behavioral Science*, 36(3), 308–321.
Wals, A. E. J., van der Hoeven, E. M. M. M., & Blanken, H. (2009). *The Acoustics of Social Learning: Designing learning processes that contribute to a more sustainable world*. Wageningen Academic Publishers.
Williams, J. (2024). Greenwashing: Appearance, illusion and the future of "green" capitalism. *Geography Compass*, 18(1), e12736.
Worster, D. (1994). *Nature's Economy: A History of Ecological Ideas*. Cambridge University Press.
Wynne, B. (1992). Misunderstood misunderstanding: Social identities and public uptake of science. *Public Understanding of Science*, 1(3), 281–304.
Zizek, S. (1992). *Looking Awry: An Introduction to Jacques Lacan through Popular Culture*. MIT Press.
Zizek, S. (2008). Nature and its discontents. *SubStance*, 37(3), 37–72.
Zizek, S. (2009). *In Defense of Lost Causes*. Verso Books.

5 | Five Myths of Sustainability Leadership

In this chapter, we discuss five common misunderstandings about sustainability leadership – we speak of myths – that muddle the discourse and stand in the way of understanding and application. As myths to dissect, we consider the idea that sustainability leadership is all about money, that it is about perfect institutions and that expertise is the key. The idea that morality is fundamental, as well as the narrative that prioritizes innovation, are dismissed as myths as well. We look at the implications for leadership functions and roles to emerge in those myths, and try to discern, positively, what we can learn from the myths about the realities of sustainability leadership.

Introduction

Sustainability leadership requires thinking and organizing. As the previous chapters demonstrated, what sustainability leadership means and can achieve hinges on stories about sustainability, leadership, governance and community, and it depends on traditions of organizing, which we summarized under the terms of governance path and governance configuration. We reminded ourselves that sustainability goals can be approached and sustainability journeys navigated without explicit rhetoric of sustainability, and we noticed that, from the multiplicity of sustainability stories, a few shared characteristics emerged which are the foundation of our normative idea of sustainability governance, summarized near the end of Chapter 4. Metaphors structure the mythologies to different degrees, and each associates with a different set of coevolving stories.

What sustainability leadership is and what it can and should be can be understood through a metaphorical lens. Roles of the leader can appear as new guiding metaphors, or the options for leadership can become visible as the result of dominant metaphors of governance (Alvesson & Spicer, 2010). Leadership metaphors, as others, do not

Introduction

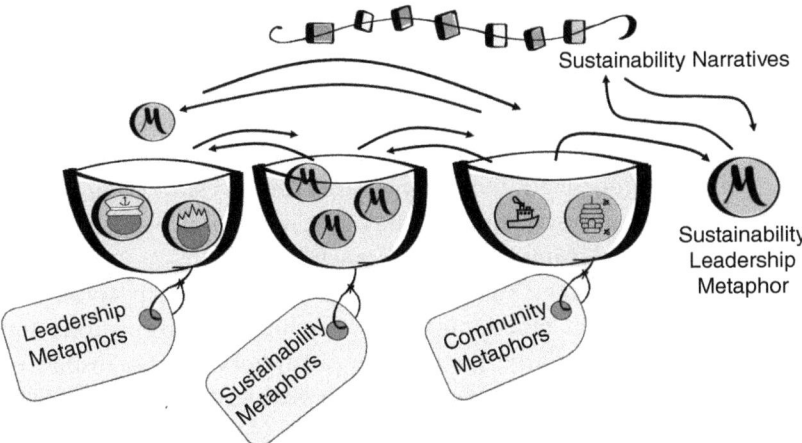

Figure 5.1 Sustainability leadership, as understood through a metaphorical lens, encompasses various interpretations of what it is, what it can be, or should be. These metaphors are not isolated entities but are often interconnected in chains of associations between other metaphors (and narratives) of communities, of sustainability and of leadership. The concept of leadership has gained prominence in recent decades, leading to a broader understanding of various phenomena as requiring leadership. Consequently, leadership metaphors have become increasingly influential in comprehending and organizing these phenomena.

exist in isolation, being formed in a chain of associations between other metaphors and narratives, of leadership itself, of community, governance, sustainability (Mintzberg, 1989) (Figure 5.1). Sustainability leadership can be understood through stories on human–nature relations, elsewhere it appears as a product of good governance narratives. What it can achieve sometimes hinges on cracks in the fabric of governance, in other cases on traces of older stories in the structure and process of governance.

Leadership itself has gained currency in recent decades, and more and more is expected of it (Bass, 1998). More phenomena are thus looked at as requiring leadership, and where it does not work, prominent leadership stories will see the solution as better leadership, new forms of leadership – rather than other things (Pfeffer, 2015). Which then means that leadership metaphors and their associations, become more important in thinking and organizing. Those metaphors can be old ones, or the ones in fashion at the moment and enjoying wide circulation. They can also be new, as new forms of leadership, real or imagined, desired or existing, might coin new metaphors. These can be negative as much as positive: new and desirable roles for the leader can be grasped through contrast with old ones, or with emerging problematic ones. *Tech bros* are new yet problematic outside tech – they do capture the imagination of many. Analyzing the staggering success of the high-tech industry under a single metaphor of new leadership is problematic but alluring (Vinsel & Russell, 2020).

Metaphors of leadership can fit or inspire leadership styles and roles, and the actual functioning of leadership, in organizations and in communities. Similarly, governance metaphors can fit, inspire or reflect actual governance in communities (we refer to Figure 3.6). The result is a series of possible fits and nonfits. Governance metaphors and their narratives can work in the context of one governance configuration, or not, and the same applies to leadership. Leadership and governance, each structured by more than one metaphor and narrative, can match to different degrees but the fit will always be imperfect (see also the introductory passages on leadership in Chapter 1).

In other words, leadership is always imagined in ways, even by leadership itself, that do not exactly match the way governance works and, interestingly, the way governance is imagined (see earlier). While the way governance is imagined does not accurately reflect the way it works, de facto creating roles for leadership beyond what was imagined (Senge, 2006). Narratives concerning governance may describe leadership in various roles, some of which involve actions that extend beyond routine practices and encompass several of the leadership functions outlined in Chapter 1. However, such narratives do not necessarily imply that the envisioned roles or actions correspond to the actual options or constraints faced by leadership in practice (Hood & Peters, 2004). What remains, for us, is the idea that leadership options are determined by the traditions of stories and of organizing, coevolving and distinct. Second, the idea that leadership is not what is understood as leadership in the self-description of governance systems, but rather in compensating for the imperfections of routines, and, in doing so, navigating the complexities of power relations, incoherent stories and institutions and lacking certainties.

Sustainability leadership must manage more complexity, and overcome more obstacles, as it likely embarks on a governance transformation, toward some form of what we called good sustainability governance (Adams, 2013). It might have to introduce long-term perspectives, first developing such perspective for itself, then cultivating more sustained reflection in the system, supported by organizations and institutions. Leadership may be required to navigate backlash originating from sustainability advocates themselves, particularly when such advocates operate from a position of absolute certainty (Brand, 2010). This form of advocacy can generate further opposition due to its misalignment with principles of effective governance and with community narratives that leadership cannot reasonably overlook (Stephenson, 2023).

The mythologies dissected in the following paragraphs fail to meet several criteria. Not criteria of truth primarily, but criteria of functionality. They do not reflect how narratives work, nor how institutions work; they cannot be compatible with democratic and other ideals espoused by the communities they land in. Thus, they cannot deliver, they can do damage, and they cannot be productive fictions. That is, they cannot operate as recipes for success in sustainability leadership and do not represent the nature of such leadership. However, in particular cases, the approach encapsulated in a particular myth might work, as what might be missing in a community, or what might get it out of a rut, might be what one of the mythologies would emphasize. We must be cautious with generalizing, just as the CEO of a successful company should be cautious with generalizing his success to a theory of the universe. A second risk related to generalization lies in attributing value to leadership ideals developed in other contexts when applying them to sustainability leadership in governance. This is problematic, as sustainability governance extends beyond the pursuit of shareholder value and is required to fulfill distinct and context-specific conditions (Lapuente et al., 2020).

Myth: Expertise Is Key in Sustainability Leadership

Sustainability leadership is not only a matter of knowledge. Certain narratives of sustainability and governance can however feed into this idea. Most commonly, we find stories of modernist origin, understanding governance and perhaps the whole social-ecological system as a machine, a machine that requires tinkering (Latour, 2004). The assumption can be that we only need new policies, inspired by better and more expertise, or that we need to rebuild governance, with

Figure 5.2 Leaders who are considered experts often perceive governance and perhaps the entire social-ecological system as a machine that requires the intervention of an expert to "tinker" and "fix" it.

the help of governance expertise, so we can formulate better policies afterward (Fischer, 2003). The superiority of social-democratic polities, mobilizing more powerful administrative systems, filled to the brim with expertise, is often taken for granted. One can also recognize versions where private-sector expertise, either in management (for reform), or on subjects related to sustainability (assuming private innovation power) would make the difference (Hart, 2005; Munslow & Ekoko, 1995; Rashed & Shah, 2021) (Figure 5.2).

Different types of expertise can be foregrounded in versions of the myth, a different balance between local knowledge and expert knowledge. The function of leadership can then be seen as reinforcing governance with new or existing expertise, or as transforming governance. Transforming governance itself requires expertise, and this can be in the domain of politics, of administrative reform, or of subject knowledge associated with sustainability, knowledge which, so to speak, needs to burst the seams of the governance system, requires and guides its transformation (Biermann et al., 2012).

What leadership should do in this perspective can thus still differ widely, and the kind of expertise expected from leadership itself can vary. Building new expertise into an already expert-driven system is a different challenge from building such system, and it still differs from what is needed in terms of knowledge and skills to shift from one sort of dominant knowledge to another one, or from one model of knowledge integration to something new (Graham, 1993). Assigning roles to local knowledges is both cognitively demanding and politically tricky, as this decision is relevant both for the perspectives entering the system, and for the support and legitimacy of what is decided (Berkes, 2017).

For similar reasons, dislodging one type of experts from long-held positions of power, or questioning stories in society about their prominence, is not an easy matter (Hall, 1993). Which knowledge is needed to bracket the prominence of another one cannot be determined in general terms. Possibly, local knowledge or other expert perspectives produce alternative narratives which are persuasive enough by themselves, for the community and for actors in governance. Where this is not the case, or where old experts still do not budge, the art of politics and administrative reform comes in its own (Wilson, 2019). Insider knowledge on self-transformation, shifting power relations and potential discursive coalitions becomes valuable and leadership must play a role, as it has been proven that the procedures reproduce unwanted hierarchies in expertise.

If we understand the goal of sustainability leadership as transforming governance to transform society, it transpires that neither subject knowledge nor managerial expertise is enough, though. The key to sustainability leadership cannot be found in knowledge, neither in the community nor in the governance system itself. Certainly, sustainability, however understood, will require expertise in governance and community, but sustainability leadership will have to be persuasive to transform society, and that persuasion needs to take into account what looks real, what feels important, what appears as in character with the community (March & Weil, 2009).

In other words, affect, shared values and narratives of identity, origin and reality can easily override whatever fact is presented, inside and outside the governance system. Insider/outsider dynamics can undermine any sustainability policy and leadership will have to navigate this distinction and sometimes locate itself on two sides, requiring skilful risk management (Jasanoff, 2007; Mitchell, 2002). Expertise can enter the equation in a different form: Dissemination of expertise through stories, developing awareness in the community, through stories of sustainability problems and acceptable directions to solve them (Wals et al., 2009).

Once people are used to experts, and have access to the prestige of their expertise, their view might be less contested. Soviet hierarchies of expertise were rigid, with engineers at the top, yet people were given routes of advancement through education, and study was presented by Lenin as the road to communism (Fitzpatrick, 1992). Rural areas were devoted to large-scale farming, and governed by agricultural and civil engineers, in the management of mega-enterprises that also functioned as local government. Sustainability issues, if observed, are reduced to engineering problems of the types recognized in their speciality, and environmental pollution or degradation in many forms did not appear on the radar. Protected areas for scientific study were in existence in the early Soviet years, but an environmental movement, instigated by natural scientists took off in the 1960s, and in the late Soviet years, civil society organizations mushroomed to mitigate the effect of often ruthless Soviet industrialization and resource extraction. (Weiner, 1999; Westerman, 2012)

Complaints about lack of awareness and environmental education feature commonly in narratives about difficulties in sustainability transitions. "The people do not understand the experts" leaders backing up the experts would say. We would argue that the issue is more that those experts are not understanding society, nor processes of social change and governance transformation (Birkeland et al., 2018; Duxbury et al., 2018). This is not the expert's fault, but rather that of leadership for not choosing different combinations and roles of expertise in governance or choosing not to reframe the key insights into stories that might make sense for the community, and that might guide transformation (Van Assche et al., 2024). Selecting and discussing insights, deciding what should be key for new stories, and carefully weighing whether linking to existing stories, or trying to persuade people of new stories, is part and parcel of governance, not science.

Picking experts is an exercise not decided by experts and lending a listening ear to some experts and not others cannot follow an expert prescription (Pielke, 2007). Where experts, in already modernist administrations, feverishly argue for the superiority and necessity of their kind of expertise, this must be recognized by leadership as damaging and countered (Jasanoff, 1987), only after carefully listening and weighing their arguments. Disseminating knowledge, similarly, cannot be left entirely to experts. Experts can speak freely, and be engaged as they like, yet governance has to take its own role seriously, and articulate stories that fit a localized vision of sustainability problems and solutions (Corner & Clarke, 2016). Those narratives will always foreground a selection of facts shaped through a selection of expert discourses, while the stories will produce new facts that can orient the community towards more sustainable futures.

Hence, in stories enshrining expertise as the key to sustainability leadership, those leaders can perform different roles. As noted, they can be subject experts themselves, or generalists capable of digesting a wide array of information; they can be experts in listening to the subject specialists. Alternatively, they can be specialists in reform towards sustainability governance. The leadership functions highlighted by this myth vary even more widely, yet emphasize either the superior cognitive skills of leadership, or their subservience to the real experts, who need to save us. Experts figure as heroes and saviours, as cyborgs uniquely capable of guiding us (Alvesson & Spicer, 2010). They can be formal leaders themselves, or formal leadership can rubberstamp what they proposed. When the expert-centered stories recognize the existence of competing expert perspectives, which have to be interpreted and balanced, a more significant place for leadership can be delineated (Brand & Karvonen, 2007).

If the tech bros consider themselves a cognitive elite, which deserves political power, as they and only they know the future, and if they are given that power, the knowledge hierarchies in governance will be rattled, and machinic metaphors will be given free reign. Imagining a diversity of futures, and endowing governance with the power to pursue them, becomes less likely.

Linking to the conditions of good sustainability governance outlined earlier, we can say that the myth of expertise can instill long-term perspectives in governance yet risks doing so in a limited and rigid range. The problem is that local perspectives, which might reflect local values and master narratives, but also local interpretations of the environment that could serve as corrective, are not entertained. In addition, where experts dominate, this tends to be one expert group, with claims to truth that are questionable from other expert positions and claims to power that undermine a deliberation of more than one problem definition, and more than one solution. If this expertise is allowed to dominate a transformation of governance, and its assumptions are more deeply entrenched in decision-making, rigidity increases and even where institutional capacity is augmented, adaptive capacity is reduced. This is the case because of cognitive and institutional reasons, since policy integration will favor the dominant experts to frame general policy directions, and because what is observed in the system–environment interactions will be limited.

Myth: Money Is Key in Sustainability Leadership

Niccolo Machiavelli reminded us centuries ago that money does not win wars (Machiavelli, 2009). Good soldiers win wars, and good leaders make soldiers better. A common assumption, especially in less prosperous regions, is that sustainability policy is a luxury, or a matter of extra expenses, a matter of doing more things. Where resources are scarce, and where ideology instills strong feelings about small government, about a limited number of services as core functions, this belief can be a hard nut to crack for those aiming at more sustainable development paths (Beckerman, 2002) (Figure 5.3).

Ideologically inspired rhetoric of governmental wastefulness, narratives of unlimited natural resources, resilient environments, technical solutions in the future can be used and abused in politics, can harden the public idea that focusing on sustainability now is spending more and spending unnecessarily (Eckersley, 2004). Why pay attention to our environment if it is a landscape of resources, and if there are no indications of natural limits? Or, if there are, we can move to the next resource, while the damage to the landscape can be ignored because we don't live there. Mythologies of individual resilience, of rugged survivalism in tough landscapes can inspire actual resilience, but also ruthless disregard of environmental damage, and dismissal of sustainability initiatives as catering to leftist urban elites (Nixon, 2011).

Figure 5.3 The notion that procuring financial resources is the defining characteristic of sustainability leadership is misleading.

Under such conditions, what we call concentration problems can mark governance, a simplification of governance, where a small set of actors and institutions dominate, and residents identify with narratives about community and environment that render it difficult to envision and organize alternative futures. Under concentration problems, observing system-environment relations is rudimentary, and usually focused on few activities relevant for the identity story. Let's say we are here to dig for gold. The river is not an ecosystem but a source of water to sift through sediment, so no harm in damming it, moving it, cutting off wetlands, polluting groundwater we don't see or use anyway. Limits to observation combine with limits to self-observation, as a simple identity narrative does not encourage reflexivity. (Van Assche et al., 2023)

If the environment is seen as a treasure trove of resources, or if government is seen as an obstacle to self-expression, two common metaphors, sustainability appears as a nonissue. Those who speak of it are a hindrance, and those who argue for strategy and planning, sustainable or not, appear in the enemy camp. An aversion to environmental discourse often blends with a distaste for stories about planning, and collaboration towards shared futures, and where this happens, sustainability appears as a nuisance, or, minimally, as a waste (Bell & Hindmoor, 2009; Wynne, 1992).

Also under different master narratives, or ideological conditions, translation of sustainability into extra costs can occur. And leadership can refrain from taking action because of this costly story. Even where many share a belief in the need for more sustainable communities, and where the functions of governance are more broadly defined, sustainability initiatives are often translated intuitively into extra costs. Widely diverging ideologies assume that more expensive policies and interventions are expected or that profitable activities must cease. Ideology might not see sustainability as a core concern, or refuse a questioning of everything already in place, of any task already carried out. An intuitive hesitation about the difficulty, hence cost, of sustainability policy might also stem from a lack of curiosity about system-environment interactions, in turn inspired by other stories, and, possibly related, it can stem from a feeling of urgency about other tasks, a feeling that renders any discussion about reshuffling priorities unlikely (Giddens, 2009; Young, 2010).

Several mechanisms might be at work, under different master narratives, hindering new concerns on the agenda, making them look as luxuries. One would be the black-boxing of everything that already happens, hence not only rendering the current system immune to critique, but also to observation. Reflexivity is dramatically reduced, and, with that, adaptive capacity. If we do not know what happens exactly, if we refuse to look at the fine mechanics of governance, because we believe it's as good as it gets, because we leave it to the few experts in governance, or maybe since we see major headaches on the horizon if we try to tinker, then deliberate forms of adaption are not to be expected (Kingdon, 2011; Latour, 2012). Refocusing on system–environment relations is not in the cards and crafting new stories about the future which might entail reform, will not be encouraged.

If we understand our governance as handed down, in poor shape, and of little value, and we leave its daily operations to a small and underpaid group of civil servants and an informal business circle at the Leopards Club, and if any civil servant showing too much ambition is judiciously cut to size, the idea that governance can do more has few chances to assert itself. Local ideas of sustainability are limited to an extension of the present, and dreams of development might be a bit more of the same. We find a double problem here, as sustainability problems and solutions are not in the picture, and as little insight exists in the functioning of governance, its potential paths of reform, and its potential to achieve more. Which means that the actual cost of sustainability strategy is not known, the losses because of poor governance in the present, while the need to do and spend more is not understood. Leadership for sustainability is not likely to emerge, as there is no feeling that a problem needs to be solved, a goal to be reached.

Perhaps black-boxing is not an issue, but current configurations of governance are left in place because they represent a fragile compromise between interests, maybe between different narratives of what good governance and the real community is. If so, adding tasks to governance is sensitive, and looking far into the future a political risk. Organizational identities might wish to protect their idea of important work. A compartmentalized administration can have such effect, even if no specialized department is opposed to sustainability policy (Back et al., 2002).

A different factor causing governance to see sustainability initiatives as extra cost, and therefore leadership as the work of finding money, is institutionalized blindness for externalities and long-term costs of current policies and activities (Boulding, 2011). Those can be the activities of businesses but also of citizens and public actors.

We find here the effects of limited observation of system–environment relations, rudimentary self-observation and lacking spaces to craft long-term perspectives. If all such features are missing, damage to the environment might not appear on the radar, economic costs will not be calculated, while the benefits or even ultimate frugality of alternative forms of organization remain out of sight.

Nonaction can be costly in reality, and additional action might save money or bring in revenue yet acknowledging this is a different matter altogether (Stern & Stiglitz, 2023). If ideology allows, polluters can be taxed. If environments are preserved, tourism development could become realistic, new residents might be attracted and housing prices might be supported. If resources are not rapidly extracted, a slower speed might support a population for the longer run and enable the community to develop added-value processing or place branding strategies (Daly, 1993; Markey et al., 2010). The myth of money as the key to sustainability leadership, highlighting the leadership function of finding resources, easily blinds leaders to the possibilities to save and make money thanks to sustainability strategy. When governance reform is out of the question, those savings and revenues are harder to calculate and promote to the community. If leaders can create narratives that reveal alternative futures, in a different relation to the environment, and convince actors that these futures are not impoverished, yet require reform, opinions might shift. For that to happen, the myth of missing resources and luxury sustainability must be weakened already.

The myth of money as the key to sustainability leadership does not adhere to one ideology, and the reasons for its embrace are quite diverse. It can be used to avoid any thinking or action about sustainability, to prevent even the formation of sustainability leadership and the articulation of strategy. When ideology is not inimical to sustainability per se, the myth can, positively, encourage an entrepreneurial attitude towards sustainability leadership, and the leader can then appear as dealmaker, hustler, charmer, evangelist, yet always looking for resources (Senge et al., 2010). Fundraising, grant-writing, networking, innovating, looking for efficiencies, dreaming up self-financing environmental ventures, attracting residents and interesting investors in new activities, to support the green extras, are all part of the repertoire of leadership under such mythology (Westley et al., 2009). As with the myth of expertise, one can discern a kernel of truth, and under some conditions it can work. However, as with the previous myth, it cannot be generalized and comes with serious risks that require assessment.

If we believe that, for our region, big infrastructure projects are the gateway to sustainable development, and financing is the issue, this might be reasonable or unreasonable. What constitutes a separate risk is the lure of the big project, as a symbol of ambition and change, as a metaphor for the clear and unified engineering solution. In other words, even if a new bridge or dam is a good idea, thinking in terms of bridges and dams as the sole path to sustainability, succumbing to the lure of engineering magic, is a problem in itself. It makes it harder to re-evaluate system-environment relations, to maintain reflexivity and adaptive capacity. While sustainability leadership that embraces novel and entrepreneurial approaches may be essential for advancing initiatives, it becomes problematic if it represents the sole form of leadership pursuing that objective. (Escobar, 2011)

Returning to our normative stance on good sustainability governance, we can say that adaptive capacity is on the one hand encouraged through entrepreneurship, on the other hand limited, in most practical cases, by a reluctance to rethink policy priorities and governance structures. Long-term perspectives can be cultivated by leadership itself, but when they are not present in governance more broadly, introducing them is a tall order under this mythology. This renders long-term perspectives more fragile, less easily institutionalized, and less subjected to democratic controls and deliberation. Institutional capacity might be reinforced, yet in constrained paths, such as adding activities after securing new funding or conserving existing resources. This strengthening is only possible if leadership has enough freedom to reform governance effectively. If their hands are tied, and if the prevailing mindset acts as a defense against sustainability thinking or a barrier to change, the consequences can be more harmful. Conversely, if the community is generally cautious, resource-conscious and not well-versed in sustainability efforts and governance reform, and if leadership enjoys trust, they might be able to persuade others that creatively seeking resources can align with careful reform to envision more stable futures. What happens to self-observation and observation of system–environment relations under the spell of this myth, will depend again on the underlying ideology, trust in leadership, in the desirability and possibility of change and capacities of leadership.

Myth: Perfect Institutions Are the Key to Sustainability Leadership

A third myth, less prevalent possibly in public discourse, but common in the academic literature, is that sustainability would be an effect of perfect institutions. We can design governance as a clockwork, with bespoke patterns of inclusion, organizational structures and procedures, producing the best possible decisions, which would then naturally lead to a sustainable society (Folke et al., 2005; Gupta et al., 2010; Ostrom, 1990; Pahl-Wostl, 2017). In a different version of the myth, a more explicit sustainability vision could be helpful yet would only be effective if produced by a perfect system of institutions (Biermann et al., 2010; Boström et al., 2018; Pelling, 2010). Imperfection is unsustainable, as it would entail limiting observation, misunderstanding risk and trade-offs. Leadership could play a role on the stage of already amazing institutions, and if the stage isn't there, it ought to be constructed (Figure 5.4)

Sustainable development discourses show several versions of the myth. Rule of law, good governance, property rights are all considered, in different corners, the key to stable societies capable of caring for people and planet (Van Assche & Hornidge, 2015). Each version is a universe in itself, with many proliferating varieties hoping to be the only story in town. Believing that perfect decisions also generate sustainability, and that such decisions have to emanate from a perfect system of institutions tends to link to the idea that perfection has one form, a form that is knowable and susceptible to engineering, or institutional design (Grindle, 2017; Taylor, 2011).

Figure 5.4 Pursuing institutional perfection may inadvertently create avenues for grievance.

A simple, classic American version of this myth would be not to make sustainability too important yet see it as an effect of a well-functioning democracy, defined by voting, and a set of economic parameters to be respected (Dryzek, 2000; Held, 2009). Often, a concept of rule of law is added, as its absence would produce instability. What rule of law could mean, however, is not self-evident, and its many apostles produce as many versions (Tamanaha, 2004). Under social-democratic master narratives, rule of law can be maximalist and many public goods can be understood as rights, with rule of law making sure those benefits accrue to all. Where voting is deemed an insufficient marker of democracy, often after histories of corrupt governance and failed development policies, participation moved to the foreground as a hallmark of a well-functioning democracy and "good governance" (Poto & Fornabaio, 2017).

Beyond macroeconomic indicators and a form of rule of law, academics, policy advisors and NGOs in the 1990s proposed ideas of good governance as additional conditions for the development of or transition to democracy and capitalism (Khan, 2013). Good governance was supposed to be inclusive, participatory, sustainable, free from corruption and grounded in the rule of law. However, articulating a clear and consistent framework for recognizing and achieving these principles proved challenging. As with the concept of the rule of law, the confidence of its advocates was often at odds with the diversity of their interpretations – an issue that also plagues notions of participation and inclusivity (Meyer et al., 2018). In practice, each democracy is unique and this is expressed in, among other things, the balance between participation and representation, and the patterns of inclusion and exclusion, of voices and perspectives (Grindle, 2004; Jabri & O'Gorman, 1999).

If we realize that good governance cannot be defined that easily, but that corruption and bribery are more obvious obstacles to sustainable development, we still need to define those vices. Machiavelli, in the sixteenth century, would have recognized the problem, and declared multiple times that the danger of corruption is always present, that factional and individual interest have the tendency to obscure the public interest (Machiavelli, 2012). He, and we, would also note that corruption takes many forms, most of which remain in the dark. Further, that formal institutions tend towards imperfection and that what looks like corruption might be a way to make things work (Rose-Ackerman, 2013). Leadership cannot start from the assumption that all corruption must be weeded out before anything becomes possible, or, that its pernicious character is always self-evident. A more common problem arises when external actors such as international organizations and foreign NGO's, promote anticorruption measures, without paying much attention to local traditions, informality and necessity. Anticorruption rhetoric then easily gets recuperated by those who want to assert themselves as leadership locally and might cause as many problems as it solves. (Bukovansky, 2006)

Older versions of modernist development, dominated by economic or engineering perspectives, might have claimed that the policy, the plan, the strategy could embody objectivity, certainty and, indeed, perfection. If we as experts come up with a plan, and other experts implement it, the result will be the best achievable under the conditions and will represent "development" or "progress" (Ferguson, 1994). More recent versions can be detected under the flag of sustainable development, where engineering projects are supposed to bring prosperity and additional engineering interventions make it sustainable (J. D. Sachs, 2015). While the versions of perfect institutions in the previous paragraphs have the benefit of recognizing the importance of the context in which projects land, they succumb to the same modernist fallacy of formulaic striving for perfection (Steffek & Wegmann, 2021). The fallacy is a double one, since perfect institutions do not exist and as formulaic approaches to institutional design miss the specificity of community and environment.

Modernism thus again appears as the culprit; the machinic thinking of subject experts, dominant in the first myth, is now replaced by a similarly machinic metaphor, not of ecological but of institutional environments (March & Olsen, 1989). Tinkering with institutions can happen on the basis of blueprints for perfection, and those designs will bring about the best possible decisions (Bevir & Rhodes, 2010). If people are aware of environmental risks, they and their representatives will take the best possible decisions, minimizing risk and maximizing economic opportunity, or, in more humanistic versions, human well-being. Ecological modernization appeared on the scene in the 1980s, emphasizing institutional tinkering and technological solutions to environmental problems, a recognition of a special category of issues, related to sustainability, but grounded in the same narrative schemes (Heiskala, 2011). Expert myths and myths of perfect institution reinforce each other.

The rise of indicators in sustainability governance represents a similar mix of myths. One can recognize the modernist assumptions of indicators expressing realities objectively, and of sustainability existing in one knowable ideal state of the social-ecological system (Saltelli et al., 2020). We can know and measure objectively, monitor system and environment, experiment with policy options and pick the best one. Perversely, the best institutional design starts to look as one capable of using indicators and generating a state of affairs with good scores on all of them (Merry, 2016). Here, the idea of a perfect balance between system and environment, and the idea of perfection in institutional design reinforce each other, although in the recognition that a search process might be involved: We can slowly figure out what the best institutional configuration is, as indicators will reveal it (Underdal, 2010).

As with large infrastructural projects, the problem with indicators is not that they are despicable per se. In fact, as is the case for such projects, they can unlock untapped potential. With large projects, key is to identify objects that indeed, function as a key, a missing piece in a puzzle that is mostly there. Or, to stretch the metaphor, one is looking for an infrastructural object can be the centerpiece of a new puzzle. For indicators, the potential for development is one step removed; what can be unlocked is the capacity of governance to achieve more, to support sustainable development. As with infrastructure projects, the problem is that they can become a goal in themselves, and that they render it harder to think outside indicators, to envision the complexity of both problems and solutions. That projects and indicators can be used for purposes contrary to sustainability thinking is not an argument against them. An issue, though, is that the practice of reducing governance to the monitoring of indicators, tends to vindicate ways of thinking that support the master narratives of new public management, which is inherently represents obstacles to reimagining governance. (Collier, 2008; Osborne & Gaebler, 1992)

The literature on resilience assembled its own institutional toolkit, and, although its perspective is steeped in ecological thinking, it espoused a version of institutional modernism, of idealizing institutional design that is ambitious. It is, in fact, so ambitious that, in assembling features of good governance derived from various policy literatures, it mixed metaphors to a degree that they cannot reflect a really existing polity (Rosenzweig et al., 2014). By which we refer to the long list of features of good governance for resilience that routinely appear in the resilience literature, but which derive from different stories about the good community, the real community, useful knowledge in governance, power relations, about adaptation, the selection of actors and experts, the possibilities and limits of steering (O'Brien, 2021; Rose et al., 2025). If we emphasize local governance and local knowledge, if the community is the village, and local knowledge is deemed to be valuable ecological knowledge which leads to stable environments, then higher-level experts, their policies and plans, the interest of larger communities, the possibilities of adapting environments, all remain out of sight (Richards, 2023).

Not only do we ignore the numerous observations that locals make mistakes and can undermine sustainability policies benefiting themselves and their compatriots, but we also ignore the basic fact that not everything can be combined in an institutional design (Crewe & Harrison, 2002). Just as not all narratives blend well, as metaphors can clash, one cannot impose a machinic idea of nature on a community and then claim that their truly local perspective will naturally fix the machine (Wynne, 1992). Adaptive capacity at a local level might be there, but not of a sort that respects what ecologists find valuable, and it might entail adapting the environment more than the lifestyles, consumption patterns or institutions of the human community (Fairhead & Leach, 1996).

Resilience thinking did coin the valuable concept of adaptive capacity, a feature of institutional design that enables, also in our view, good sustainability governance. If however the idea of adaptive capacity is interpreted under the narrative of perfect institutions, it starts to look like a feature of governance one can easily recognize and one that can be optimized in an objective manner. Most such modernist versions of adaptive capacity, recognize the real issue of increasing uncertainty and fluctuations in environmental conditions but unfortunately throw in a third assumption. We refer to the idea that adaptive capacity can be engineered as a systemic skill to adapt to anything. In reality, no governance systems can cope with every imaginable internal and external shock and contingency (Ribot, 2011). One cannot represent adaptive capacity on one dimension, as more or less of something, and hope that optimization could produce perfection. Adaptation to one thing can require the introduction of rigidity and blindness with regards to other risks (Pelling et al., 2015). Introducing flexibility in governance, to enhance adaptive capacity, comes with its own risks, as some stabilizing and guiding institutions require stability, no, anchoring (Jessop, 2015; Walker & Cooper, 2011). What functions as an anchor, cannot be decided by experts.

Summer floods have bothered a small town in the foothills of the Himalayas for centuries, and they seem to get worse. The town is crossed by two small rivers, which can suddenly swell in the rainy season. Development near the rivers has exacerbated the situation, as well as deforestation higher up. Consultants supported by World Bank suggested to increase resilience, by constructing steel bridges across the streams (the old ones collapsed with tragic consequences), reforestation where possible, and restoring the natural floodplain vegetation near the river. Problem is that neither financing nor local support are abundant. Borrowing means dependence on a foreign government and forcing relocation out of the floodplain is bound to trigger backlash, especially since capacity is missing to manage it. Thus, the destabilizing effect of rigid resilience definitions easily swamps the resilience goal. Adaptive capacity, as a key to resilience, probably needs to find a local version, in a transformation of institutions, building on existing ones, which can then guide interventions in the landscape.

Throughout this book, we argue that the imperfection of institutions, of governance systems as such, makes leadership essential, to deal with shocks, to guide the transformation of governance systems, to help communities and their governance systems to recognize new problems and new solutions, to stretch their time horizons in new narratives of sustainability. Institutional capacity and adaptive capacity (as features of institutional design) are key to sustainable development, yet agency cannot be reduced to following stipulated procedures. It requires insight into the imperfection of the system of formal institutions, recognizing when and how to change institutions, or simply their interpretation and implementation. Which entails navigation of the landscape of informal institutions. Citizens, actors in governance and leadership can partake in such broader version of agency, yet leadership is part of the picture. It is precisely because of the forms of agency associated with leadership that flexible adaptation can appear; the impossibility of perfect institutions can thus be interpreted as the possibility of sustainability leadership.

Further reconnecting to our normative stance on good sustainability governance, we can say that the precepts we formulated, conditions for good governance, are not presented as sufficient conditions, and next that our view on good sustainability governance does not amount to one institutional design, nor a choice of ideology. All the qualities mentioned can appear under different forms of democracy or nondemocracy, under the aegis of diverging master narratives. In the mythology of perfect institutions, the good governance features we identified do appear when sustainability is explicitly acknowledged as a goal and a value. Where the focus is on perfect institutions, not on perfection for sustainability, the interest in observation, adaptation and the long term disappears. What remains an Achilles heel in all versions is the drive for perfection itself. In the environmentally sensitive versions, an emphasis on flexibility, an often-minimal interest in the social and the tendency to mix incompatible governance models and principles speak of an overriding and sincere desire to solve ecological problems, yet a desire that can be blinding for the complexities of social-ecological problems.

Myth: Morality Is the Key to Sustainability Leadership

Leadership, in much of modern management theory, and popular culture, has circled in its imagery around hero figures, and, in the world of environmentalism and sustainability leadership, the figures of prophets and saviors (Maniates, 2001). Rousing people towards a common goal they already felt to be important or kicking them a conscience, would be suitable tasks for a sustainability leader in this myth. Yet, we know that leaders as individuals are insufficient to cope with the complexity of sustainability transformations, and it is well understood that people aren't thrilled when addressed as morally deficient and environmentally guilty at the same time (Latour, 2004, 2012) (Figure 5.5).

Morality of the leader and morality of the community are two different things, and a third version of the story would emphasize the high moral standards of the governance system, setting an example. If the

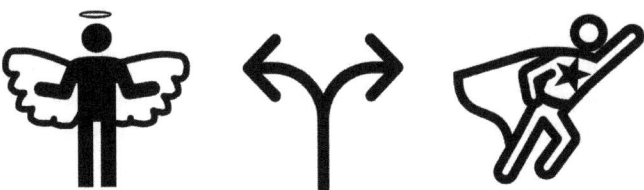

Figure 5.5 Sustainability leadership, as a moral compass, is likely to encounter intricate and complex paths.

leader as an individual is supposed to embody qualities not achievable by others yet inspiring them to follow, alter their mindset and behavior, we can still go in different directions. Leaders can lead by moral example, or they can mostly tell stories emphasizing our responsibility to take care of the earth, do the right thing, give space in our heart to the more-than-human. Ideally, stories and actions align, at least in public perception, and, hopefully, the example gains traction. One can infer, from cases where it does not work, that both the image of the leader and the ethics implied need to connect to circulating narratives of leadership and the good (Kahan et al., 2012; Merchant, 2012). No perfect fit is required, values can diverge from the ones guiding good behavior, as ambivalence might have crept in over time, as seeing or hearing something different might make one aware of issues with current norms (Hulme, 2009; Plumwood, 2006).

Affect thus plays a central role, feelings that something isn't right or that an alternative provided by leadership is the right thing to do. Desire will be at play, as one might hope that the world could be better, and this hope could be aroused by leader figures. Ethical systems might consider themselves universal, yet what constitutes the good, and which precepts ought to be followed, is framed by culture and ideology, hence by narrative (Callison, 2014). Whether one looks for a leader to sacrifice herself for the greater good and wake us up in this manner, or someone to point out that the good is in valuing connections in larger systems, in caring for other humans and other creatures, stories about the good, the social, the caring and the strong are never far away (Rose, 2004). Desire, too, springs from experience, example and story, as we craft stories to know our own desire; narrative fragments, hence culture are deployed as materials in an ever-shifting bricolage.

An appeal to morality might represent a hope to transcend culture, relativity, story, by talking or acting in reference to the Absolute, but there is no escape from narrative. New prophets might find it hard to attract believers, and prophets with less laudable motives might have an easier job, by connecting intuitively, perhaps shamelessly, to dominant stories and metaphors, by addressing collective desires, acknowledged and otherwise. If people believe in Jesus, the Buddha and Zarathustra, then combining them into one narrative where I play a key role, would embody the perfect religion, right? This, at least, seems to be what Mani, Persian prophet from the 3rd century AD seems to have thought. (Tardieu, 2008).

A leader figure can attempt to transcend the context of leadership stories and values, by referring to absolute leadership qualities. A community can project those values on a leader. A desire for the Absolute, for absolute certainty, maybe for not reflecting on the imperfections of this world can translate into a call for guidance and leadership. This should be taken seriously and might be productive in sustainability terms – leaders can assist in overcoming our own moral limitations and take care of problems, all too easy to ignore (Taylor, 2009). If however, leaders forget entirely they are dealing with humans, and if every injunction appeals to the Absolute, critical deliberation finds no place.

An escape from narrative, into an ethics of absolute responsibility and care for the environment, or a duty of self-preservation, can be confined to general principles, without indicating precise adaptations, policy directions or ideology. In such scenario, stories can proliferate on a stable basis, an unquestioned ethic of sustainability (Macy & Johnstone, 2012). Leadership of an enlightened sort might introduce us to such ethics, or remind us of it, if we already know the principles in a different form, through other stories (Berry, 2000). Confusingly, ideologies might also invoke the Absolute, and those appeals are certainly interpreted through a partisan lens. Thus, when ideology enshrines an environmental ethic, ideological opponents cannot be blamed for questioning the universality of the ethic (Zizek, 2009).

St Francis, in the 13th century, traveled widely to preach his principles, and to gain followers for his new monastic order. He saw the hand of God in nature, in all of its creatures and their interdependence. In the 20th century, he was therefore officially declared the patron saint of ecology. Saint Francis did not expect everybody to emulate his radically low impact lifestyle. He did not expect others to behave as saintly as he did, yet called upon everybody to respect all life, and to praise God and all his good works in this world (Sorrell, 1988). Preaching to a flock of little birds in a tree, he reminded them of their moral duty, to sing and praise the lord in their own way.

If morality is restricted to leader figures, or leadership circles in governance, it reduces the responsibility of the masses. This is risky, in terms of actual behavior, and sustainability effects, but comes with advantages. A religious leader sacrificed herself for humanity, going beyond her duty, to show us the nature and the limits of our moral obligations (White & Jha, 2023). Within communities, priests and other spiritual leaders help us to be moral, by offering us models, but also by reminding us of our duties, so we don't have to remind ourselves of them, and by observing moral ambivalences we prefer not to notice (Gardiner, 2011). Governance then appears as a protection of individuals and communities against themselves, and institutions, laws but also policies, plans, rules in general, help us to deal with our contradictions and weaknesses.

Psychoanalysis helps us to see why people identify with leader figures, why they ignore them, and why they can be resented, especially when bringing up ideas and feelings not readily admitted to. Both blind following and resentment can be problematic for sustainability transformations, while embodying an exemplar, sincerely, remains a real possibility. Leaders might indeed offer models for identification, with the individual leader, or with the group represented, sometimes created, by the leader (Zizek, 2014, 2019).

Leaders can draw upon unacknowledged resentment or give form to such sentiment through stories that articulate emotions otherwise diffuse or unexpressed, engaging in a process of emotional framing of public perception and discourse. Anxieties might translate into stories, figures, metaphors constructed or capture by leaders, stories of enmity and aggression, but also of hope and connection. Hopes and fears can be projected on leaders, in a transference that can be productive or destructive. Leaders often encourage such transference, as it means they can mean many things to many people (Laclau, 2005). What feels good or bad about a leader, what gives them more or less power of example and imbues their decisions with the power to create compliance, often involves transference.

Leaning on morality does not always work. It might be felt as distasteful, out of place, infantilizing. Stories of doom and gloom, to inspire long-awaited environmental action, might simply leave an impression of doom and gloom, might trigger unconscious associations with latent fears, undermine scarce social trust. A reasonable and feasible sustainability strategy might then feel as entirely utopian.

Moralizing environmental rhetoric can mobilize, if people already feel guilty about environmental conditions. Where people feel that those lecturing them are a bit too smug, too eager in taking up the mantle of moral superiority, and when they feel that aspects of their identity are misrecognized, that their roles and values are vilified, resentment can brew. When farmers are villains, and not given realistic alternatives, when butchers are branded killers, and oil workers simply need to wake up from their moral slumber, they, and others observing their treatment, are not likely to respond well. If some farmers, butchers and oil workers do feel a degree of responsibility, but are obliged to agree with a whole ideology, and all its positions, they have no viable ways to shift identifications. (Latour, 2017)

Linking to our normative stance on good governance for sustainability, the myth that the key to sustainability leadership is morality, is therefore a myth with a kernel of truth. Morality must be considered, as simply assuming people will do the right thing, will act sustainable and accept more sustainable policies because they know what is good, is a risky proposition. Hammering on a universal green ethics or painting an alluring picture of simple rules solving all problems, and ensuring a return to a harmonious world, however, is both ineffective and irresponsible. If morality appears as absolute truth and the future of the planet, then disagreement looks like heresy, and those branded as heretics might not be open to reasonable discussion when they come to power later. Adaptive capacity is an issue in this myth. System-environment interactions might become observable in detail, in a governance system structured by an environmental ethics, yet a risk asserts itself when self-observation in the system is shaped by the parable – we are ok because we are doing the right thing, and we know what that is. If so, the quality of environmental observation can hardly be ascertained (Beck, 1992).

Myth: Innovation Is the Key to Sustainability Leadership

Stories about leadership have a cultural background, and innovation represents a curious case indeed. Private sector innovation has been the model for public sector innovation for several generations, and public sector reform has been understood as modelling the private sector (Czarniawska, 2010). This increased the narrative role of leadership, and supported innovation outside community governance, that is, in the private sector and at universities and institutes. In its most rudimentary version, the innovation narrative celebrates what is new and different, especially so if the new is technological in nature, is rather obviously new, and seems to have the potential to cause change beyond its immediate context. One can see traces of enlightenment thinking, ideals of progress, driven by scientific and technological

Figure 5.6 Focusing solely on innovation for sustainability leadership may miss the target and overlook essential aspects.

discovery. One can notice an antiestablishment streak, where the lone innovator, the hero of the future, does thing better than whoever knew better before, and the glamour of innovation narratives owes much to the upsetting of an established order (Latour, 2012) (Figure 5.6).

As innovation gained cultural and political currency, everything became innovation, every problem awaited an innovative solution, though resistance against the dominance of tech and disruption in policy agendas led to a productive resistance. The concept of social innovation was born, with an emphasis not on technology and profits, but on social benefits and self-organization by citizens (Osburg & Schmidpeter, 2013). Hero figures were not prominent, but creative collectives who could, through creativity, collaboration and experiment, foster inclusive and, indeed, sustainable communities, without relying entirely on governmental or business initiatives. Ideally, governmental actors could learn from social innovation and policies; governance configurations could be transformed by engaging respectfully with a pallet of social innovation and reflecting on what could be upscaled (Loorbach et al., 2020; Westley et al., 2009).

Steward Brand (1938-) is a figure not easy to capture by single labels. Most famous for his "Whole Earth Catalog," a series of oversized books (1968–72) explaining how to fix machines yourself, how to build things, where to find a mountain bike (a novelty), an aroma therapist, or the best compost for organic gardening, Brand was an inspiration for Steve Jobs and many tech innovators and a sustainability pioneer. He imagined cyberspace as a fourth dimension, where new encounters could be empowering, new communities could be created. Stretching dimensions was part of the game, as he and other Californians eagerly experimented with various substances to expand the imagination. Opening the mind can align green and technological futures more easily. (Markoff, 2022)

If innovation stories shame governmental actors because their supposed slowness and lack of creative thinking, continuous reform and glamorization of leadership can be expected. Administrative managers hope to play the role of policy entrepreneur, and share the room with politicians, industry lobbyists and civil society actors, to influence the agenda of higher-level decision-makers, persuade each other and push for new policies that could break the status quo on an important topic (Kingdon, 2011; Moore, 1997). Internal tensions, in such practice, can arise between on the one hand established roles and rules structuring governance, and on the other hand the expectations to innovate, to disrupt, to be entrepreneurial (as a condition for innovation). Policy entrepreneurs can undermine checks and balances, and, maybe inadvertently, reduce space for social innovation, while technical innovation can increase or reduce the affordances of policy entrepreneurs (Fischer, 2003; Wagenaar, 2014).

The narrative of innovation overlooks the discursive, economic and governance dynamics which led to the centrality of innovation concepts (Latour, 2012; Stone, 2012). It multiplies blind spots in terms of common goods, shared values and long-term futures. Nevertheless, innovation and the innovator did appear on the scene of sustainability discourse, in a variety of manifestations. The unbridled belief in new technologies to solve environmental problems, even climate change, revealed itself in such figures as the geoengineer, while neoliberal ideas such as carbon pricing were applauded in some circles as examples of innovation and policy entrepreneurship. Social innovation entered the orbit of sustainability discourse in a few ways, via small-scale experiments in communal organic gardening or greening the neighborhood, over sustainable neighborhood initiatives to social mobilization addressing regional water issues. A perception of inadequate government policies for sustainability and a feeling that government left many local issues unaddressed thus combine into an argument for social innovation – we cannot leave it to them (Scoones et al., 2015; Temper, 2015; Wood & Baker, 2019).

Social innovation for health is not new, as communities for centuries had to fend for themselves. Specialized professions might have existed, but their capacity was limited. Even in welfare states, such as in 1970s Quebec, public health systems were imperfect, so initiatives such as the Pointe-Saint-Charles community clinic proved a helpful addition. Many in the working-class neighborhood did not have access to affordable healthcare, and a group of activist students at McGill University, with the support of a number of professors, took the initiative in 1967 for a health clinic, where locals could see a doctor for 50 cents. The students worked together, from the start with locals, and by 1970, the community was fully in charge. Programming expanded, and the centre transformed into a community services hub, a model moreover, for a new provincial network of similar centres (CLSC), established a few years later. (Triollet & Bernier, 2016)

As innovation ideas entered sustainability thinking, sustainability gained more than a foothold in innovation discourse. Early academic stories of innovation might have seen innovation as a goal and a good in itself, or, as a driver of economic growth, in line with the desires of policy makers, yet influential innovation narratives shifted tack rather dramatically by envisioning the overarching goal of innovation a transition to sustainability (Elzen et al., 2004; Loorbach, 2007; Markard et al., 2012). Earlier version of socio-technical transition thinking envisioned collaboration between industry, government and university to accelerate innovation and amplify its effects, but the new story recognized social innovation as a pillar of sustainability transitions (Avelino & Rotmans, 2009; Kohler, 2019).

A risk of innovation narratives in sustainability thinking is that what stabilizes the social system is structurally under appreciated. Self-observation is restricted immediately by a focus on either problem solving or finding problems to deploy new tools. Observation of system-environment relations is constrained for the same reasons. Strategy looks unimportant or reduced to innovation strategy, and other tools of governance are undervalued. The goal of such strategy, sustainability, also looks less relevant in an innovation perspective as ideas of balance and stability, the understanding of feedback loops, fast and slow cycles, and, in governance, ideas of coevolution and dependencies, barely register.

In innovation stories that explicitly aim to be sustainability stories, the situation is of course a bit different, yet the same insensitivities can trip up strategies. What sustainability would mean, even for an innovator trying to achieve sustainability, is muddled at the most elementary level, since the cult of change and disruption gives no indication whatsoever about environmental or societal values, regarding desirable relations between social and ecological systems.

Many relations can appear as feasible and desirable, and social and ecological transformation might be presented as key to a future balancing of systems where unforeseen benefits of innovation will accrue untested or unknown technologies are supposed to restore a balance that is not conceptualized (Orr, 2011; W. Sachs, 2015).

A cult of change easily blinds to the messianic character of innovation thinking and the enormous risks of blind spots it embodies. At the same time, a drive for innovation, as a systematic questioning of received wisdom and inherited modes of organization, as a creative enterprise that can be collective as well as individual, can contribute to problem solving in social, economic and ecological arenas. Governance can greatly benefit from innovation thinking, therefore, but governance itself cannot be taken over by it, and sustainability leadership ought to weigh risks and benefits of the discourse.

In the Sahel region of Africa, the area between the Sahara Desert and the savannah, desertification has been a problem hard to ignore. For decades, the Sahara has been gaining ground, but as this military metaphor suggests, western narratives of the desert as a foe crept into the reasoning of many. In 2007, the African Union and the UN embarked on a project to reclaim 100 million hectares of degraded land, the "Great Green Wall" initiative. Tree planting, aided by the latest scientific insights in forestry, was supposed to halt the desert, and bring back the good old days. Western and indeed colonial ideas of productivism and healthy ecosystems and communities shaped the policy, so the good old days were dramatically misremembered. Seminomadic lifestyles were interpreted as pitiful, arid ecosystems as degraded. As trees need soil improvement and water, many healthy ecosystems were disturbed, giving rise to now nearly irreversible desertification; water resources carefully calibrated towards other uses were wasted, and livelihoods depending on different landscapes, crumbled. An unfortunate combination of a colonially colored messiah complex, modernist love of large technical projects and the traditional blind spots of innovation discourse, can account for the disaster. (Cropper, 2024; Turner et al., 2021)

Concluding: The Utility of Myths

None of the myths encountered can be dismissed as nonsense. All of them have something to say about sustainability leadership. They all contain a kernel of truth. They could all guide sustainability policy in certain cases and under certain conditions. Yet none of them can be generalized and presented as a panacea for the ills of our times. They come with risks that are not observed when staying within the perspective of the story, and with affinities for particular contexts that are not understood when seen as a universal recipe.

Each mythology has preferential links to some ideas of sustainability and sustainability governance, stories of leadership and community, and none of them naturally produces the conditions for good sustainability governance. We know that sustainability leadership will have to fit the context of sustainability problems facing a community, the cultural context, that it must resonate with stories on leadership, community and others that together frame what sustainability leadership could be. It must work in the context of governance, where coevolutions created limits to steering. A fourth necessary adaptation of sustainability leadership to context stems from the cracks in governance, from that what requires more than procedures, that what does not work without a nudge or a shove. Those cracks are unique as well and help to further specify leadership.

Combining elements of stories, including myths, is not out of the question. A locally persuasive perspective on sustainability might be the result. If we cannot trust the myths to tell us everything, we cannot afford to reject them either. In Chapter 6, we bring together several storylines into a perspective on sustainability leadership that does not aspire to be a bigger and better myth, but rather a way to contextualize such leadership for a community. We do delineate roles and metaphors that might prove themselves worthy when things got rough, when people are so shaken up that community survival is in question.

References

Adams, C. (2013). The role of leadership and governance in transformational change towards sustainability. *Global Responsibility*, 9(9), 9–12.

Alvesson, M., & Spicer, A. (2010). *Metaphors We Lead By: Understanding Leadership in the Real World*. Routledge.

Avelino, F., & Rotmans, J. (2009). Power in transition: An interdisciplinary framework to study power in relation to structural change. *European Journal of Social Theory*, 12(4), 543–569.

Back, L., Keith, M., Khan, A., Shukra, K., & Solomos, J. (2002). New labour's white heart: Politics, multiculturalism and the return of assimilation. *The Political Quarterly*, 73(4), 445–454.

Bass, B. M. (1998). *Transformational Leadership: Industrial, Military, and Educational Impact*. Lawrence Erlbaum Associates.

Beck, U. (1992). *Risk Society: Towards a New Modernity*. SAGE.
Beckerman, W. (2002). "Sustainable development": Is it a useful concept? *Environmental Values*, 3(3), 191–209. https://doi.org/10.3197/096327194776679700
Bell, S., & Hindmoor, A. (2009). *Rethinking Governance: The Centrality of the State in Modern Society*. Cambridge University Press.
Berkes, F. (2017). Environmental governance for the Anthropocene? Social-ecological systems, Resilience, and Collaborative Learning. *Sustainability*, 9(7), Article 1232.
Berry, T. (2000). *The Great Work: Our Way into the Future*. Crown.
Bevir, M., & Rhodes, R. A. W. (2010). *The State as Cultural Practice*. OUP Oxford.
Biermann, F., Abbott, K., Andresen, S., Bäckstrand, K., Bernstein, S., Betsill, M. M., Bulkeley, H., Cashore, B., Clapp, J., Folke, C., Gupta, A., Gupta, J., Haas, P. M., Jordan, A., Kanie, N., Kluvánková-Oravská, T., Lebel, L., Liverman, D., Meadowcroft, J., ... Zondervan, R. (2012). Transforming governance and institutions for global sustainability: Key insights from the Earth System Governance Project. *Current Opinion in Environmental Sustainability*, 4(1), 51–60.
Biermann, F., Betsill, M. M., Vieira, S. C., Gupta, J., Kanie, N., Lebel, L., Liverman, D., Schroeder, H., Siebenhüner, B., Yanda, P. Z., & Zondervan, R. (2010). Navigating the Anthropocene: The Earth System Governance Project strategy paper. *Current Opinion in Environmental Sustainability*, 2(3), 202–208.
Birkeland, I., Burton, R., Parra, C., & Siivonen, K. (2018). *Cultural Sustainability and the Nature-Culture Interface: Livelihoods, Policies, and Methodologies*. Routledge.
Boström, M., Andersson, E., Berg, M., Gustafsson, K., Gustavsson, E., Hysing, E., Lidskog, R., Löfmarck, E., Ojala, M., Olsson, J., Singleton, B. E., Svenberg, S., Uggla, Y., & Öhman, J. (2018). Conditions for transformative learning for sustainable development: A theoretical review and approach. *Sustainability*, 10(12), 1–21. November, Article 12.
Boulding, K. E. (2011). The economics of the coming Spaceship Earth. In *Environmental Quality in a Growing Economy*. RFF Press.
Brand, R., & and Karvonen, A. (2007). The ecosystem of expertise: Complementary knowledges for sustainable development. *Sustainability: Science, Practice and Policy*, 3(1), 21–31.
Brand, S. (2010). *Whole Earth Discipline: Why Dense Cities, Nuclear Power, Transgenic Crops, Restored Wildlands, and Geoengineering Are Necessary*. Penguin.
Bukovansky, M. (2006). The hollowness of anti-corruption discourse. *Review of International Political Economy*, 13(2), 181–209.

Callison, C. (2014). *How Climate Change Comes to Matter: The Communal Life of Facts*. Duke University Press.

Collier, P. (2008). *The Bottom Billion: Why the Poorest Countries are Failing and What Can Be Done About It*. OUP Oxford.

Corner, A., & Clarke, J. (2016). *Talking Climate: From Research to Practice in Public Engagement*. Springer.

Crewe, E., & Harrison, E. (2002). *Whose development? An ethnography of aid (3. impr)*. Zed Books.

Cropper, J. (2024). 'Growing a world wonder': The great green wall and the history of environmental decline in the Sahel, 1450–2022. *Environment and History*, *30*(2), 291–313.

Czarniawska, B. (2010). Translation impossible? Accounting for a city project. *Accounting, Auditing & Accountability Journal*, *23*(3), 420–437.

Daly, H. E. (1993). Steady-state economics: A new paradigm. *New Literary History*, *24*(4), 811–816.

Dryzek, J. (2000). *Deliberative Democracy and Beyond*. Oxford University Press.

Duxbury, N., Garrett-Petts, W. F., & Longley, A. (2018). *Artistic Approaches to Cultural Mapping: Activating Imaginaries and Means of Knowing*. Routledge.

Eckersley, R. (2004). *The Green State: Rethinking Democracy and Sovereignty*. MIT Press.

Elzen, B., Geels, F. W., & Green, K. (2004). *System Innovation and the Transition to Sustainability: Theory, Evidence and Policy*. Edward Elgar Publishing.

Escobar, A. (2011). *Encountering Development: The Making and Unmaking of the Third World*. Princeton University Press.

Fairhead, J., & Leach, M. (1996). *Misreading the African Landscape: Society and Ecology in a Forest-Savanna Mosaic*. Cambridge University Press.

Ferguson, J. (1994). *Anti-Politics Machine: Development, Depoliticization, and Bureaucratic Power in Lesotho*. U of Minnesota Press.

Fischer, F. (2003). *Reframing Public Policy: Discursive Politics and Deliberative Practices*. Oxford University Press.

Fitzpatrick, S. (1992). *The Cultural Front: Power and Culture in Revolutionary Russia*. Cornell University Press.

Folke, C., Hahn, T., Olsson, P., & Norberg, J. (2005). Adaptative governance of social-ecological systems. *Annual Review of Environment and Resources*, *30*(1), 441–473.

Gardiner, S. M. (2011). *A Perfect Moral Storm: The Ethical Tragedy of Climate Change*. Oxford University Press.

Giddens, A. (2009). *Politics of Climate Change*. Polity.

Graham, L. R. (1993). *Science in Russia and the Soviet Union: A Short History*. Cambridge University Press.

Grindle, M. S. (2004). Good enough governance: Poverty reduction and reform in developing countries. *Governance, 17*(4), 525–548.

Grindle, M. S. (Ed.). (2017). *Politics and Policy Implementation in the Third World*. Princeton University Press.

Gupta, J., Termeer, C., Klostermann, J., Meijerink, S., van den Brink, M., Jong, P., Nooteboom, S., & Bergsma, E. (2010). The Adaptive Capacity Wheel: A method to assess the inherent characteristics of institutions to enable the adaptive capacity of society. *Environmental Science & Policy, 13*(6), 459–471.

Hall, P. A. (1993). Policy paradigms, social learning, and the state: The case of economic policymaking in Britain. *Comparative Politics, 25*(3), 275–296.

Hart, S. L. (2005). *Capitalism at the Crossroads: The Unlimited Business Opportunities in Solving the World's Most Difficult Problems*. Pearson Education.

Heiskala, R. (2011). From modernity through postmodernity to reflexive modernization. Did we learn anything? *International Review of Sociology, 21*(1), 3–19.

Held, D. (2009). Restructuring global governance: Cosmopolitanism, democracy and the Global Order. *Millennium, 37*(3), 535–547.

Hood, C., & Peters, G. (2004). The middle aging of new public management: Into the age of paradox? *Journal of Public Administration Research and Theory, 14*(3), 267–282.

Hulme, M. (2009). *Why We Disagree about Climate Change: Understanding Controversy, Inaction and Opportunity*. Cambridge University Press.

Jabri, V., & O'Gorman, E. (1999). *Women, Culture, and International Relations*. Lynne Rienner Publishers.

Jasanoff, S. (1987). Contested boundaries in policy-relevant science. *Social Studies of Science, 17*(2), 195–230.

Jasanoff, S. (2007). Technologies of humility. *Nature, 450*(7166), 33–33.

Jessop, B. (2015). *The State: Past, Present, Future*. John Wiley & Sons.

Kahan, D. M., Peters, E., Wittlin, M., Slovic, P., Ouellette, L. L., Braman, D., & Mandel, G. (2012). The polarizing impact of science literacy and numeracy on perceived climate change risks. *Nature Climate Change, 2*(10), 732–735.

Khan, M. H. (2013). Governance and development: The perspective of growth-enhancing governance. In A. Ohno & I. Ohno (Eds.). *Eastern and Western Ideas for African Growth: Diversity and Complementarity in Development Aid* (pp. 86–117). Routledge.

Kingdon, J. W. (2011). *Agendas, Alternatives, and Public Policies*. Longman.

Kohler, M. (2019). Language education policy in Indonesia: A struggle for unity in diversity. In S. Evans & T. He (Eds.). *The Routledge International Handbook of Language Education Policy in Asia* (pp. 155–168). Routledge.

Laclau, E. (2005). *On Populist Reason*. Verso.

Lapuente, V., Suzuki, K., & Van De Walle, S. (2020). Goats or wolves? Private sector managers in the public sector. *Governance, 33*(3), 599–619.

Latour, B. (2004). *Politics of Nature: How to Bring the Sciences into Democracy*. Harvard University Press.

Latour, B. (2012). *We Have Never Been Modern*. Harvard University Press.

Latour, B. (2017). *Facing Gaia: Eight Lectures on the New Climatic Regime*. John Wiley & Sons.

Loorbach, D. (2007). Governance for sustainability. *Sustainability: Science, Policy & Practice, 3*(2), 1–4.

Loorbach, D., Wittmayer, J., Avelino, F., von Wirth, T., & Frantzeskaki, N. (2020). Transformative innovation and translocal diffusion. *Environmental Innovation and Societal Transitions, 35*, 251–260.

Machiavelli, N. (2009). *Art of War*. University of Chicago Press.

Machiavelli, N. (2012). *Discourses on the First Decade of Titus Levius*. Hardpress Publishing.

Macy, J., & Johnstone, C. (2012). *Active Hope: How to Face the Mess We're in Without Going Crazy*. New World Library.

Maniates, M. F. (2001). Individualization: Plant a tree, buy a bike, save the world? *Global Environmental Politics, 1*(3), 31–52.

March, J. G., & Weil, T. (2009). *On Leadership*. John Wiley & Sons.

March, J., & Olsen, J. (1989). *Rediscovering Institutions: The Organizational Basis of Politics*. Free Press.

Markard, J., Raven, R., & Truffer, B. (2012). Sustainability transitions: An emerging field of research and its prospects. *Research Policy, 41*(6), 955–967.

Markey, S., Connelly, S., & Roseland, M. (2010). 'Back of the envelope': Pragmatic planning for sustainable rural community development. *Planning Practice & Research, 25*(1), 1–23.

Markoff, J. (2022). *Whole Earth: The Many Lives of Stewart Brand*. Penguin Publishing Group.

Merchant, C. (2012). *Radical Ecology: The Search for a Livable World*. Routledge.

Merry, S. E. (2016). *The Seductions of Quantification: Measuring Human Rights, Gender Violence, and Sex Trafficking*. University of Chicago Press.

Meyer, S. T., Ptacnik, R., Hillebrand, H., Bessler, H., Buchmann, N., Ebeling, A., Eisenhauer, N., Engels, C., Fischer, M., Halle, S., Klein, A.-M., Oelmann, Y., Roscher, C., Rottstock, T., Scherber, C., Scheu, S.,

Schmid, B., Schulze, E.-D., Temperton, V. M., ... Weisser, W. W. (2018). Biodiversity–multifunctionality relationships depend on identity and number of measured functions. *Nature Ecology & Evolution*, 2(1), 44–49.

Mintzberg, H. (1989). *Mintzberg on Management: Inside Our Strange World of Organizations*. Simon and Schuster.

Mitchell, T. (2002). *Rule of Experts: Egypt, Techno-Politics, Modernity*. University of California Press.

Moore, M. H. (1997). *Creating Public Value: Strategic Management in Government*. Harvard University Press.

Munslow, B., & Ekoko, F. E. (1995). Is democracy necessary for sustainable development? *Democratization*, 2(2), 158–178.

Nixon, R. (2011). *Slow Violence and the Environmentalism of the Poor*. Harvard University Press.

O'Brien, K. (2021). Reflecting on the Anthropocene: The call for deeper transformations. *Ambio*, 50(10), 1793–1797.

Orr, D. W. (2011). *Hope Is an Imperative: The Essential David Orr*. Island Press.

Osborne, D., & Gaebler, T. (1992). Reinventing government: How the entrepreneurial spirit is transforming the public sector. Reading, MA: Addison-Wesley Public. A. W. Patrick Book.

Osburg, T. H., & Schmidpeter, R. (2013). *Social Innovation: Solutions for a Sustainable Future*. Springer Berlin Heidelberg.

Ostrom, E. (1990). Analyzing long-enduring, self-organized, and self-govern CPRs. In *Governing the Commons: The Evolution of Institutions for Collective Action* (pp. 58–102). Chapter, Cambridge: Cambridge University Press.

Pahl-Wostl, C. (2017). An evolutionary perspective on water governance: From understanding to transformation. *Water Resources Management*, 31(10), 2917–2932.

Pelling, M. (2010). *Adaptation to Climate Change: From Resilience to Transformation*. Routledge. https://doi.org/10.4324/9780203889046

Pelling, M., O'Brien, K., & Matyas, D. (2015). Adaptation and transformation. *Climatic Change*, 133(1), 113–127.

Pfeffer, J. (2015). *Leadership BS: Fixing Workplaces and Careers One Truth at a Time*. HarperCollins.

Pielke, P. (2007). *The Honest Broker: Making Sense of Science in Policy and Politics*. Cambridge University Press.

Plumwood, V. (2006). The concept of a cultural landscape: Nature, culture and agency in the land. *Ethics and the Environment*, 11(2), 115–150.

Poto, M. P., & Fornabaio, L. (2017). Participation as the essence of Good Governance: Some general reflections and a case study on the Arctic Council. *Arctic Review on Law and Politics*, 8, 139–159.

Rashed, A. H., & Shah, A. (2021). The role of private sector in the implementation of sustainable development goals. *Environment, Development and Sustainability, 23*(3), 2931–2948.

Ribot, J. (2011). Vulnerability before adaptation: Toward transformative climate action. *Global Environmental Change, 21*(4), 1160–1162.

Richards, P. (2023). *Indigenous Agricultural Revolution: Ecology and Food Production in West Africa*. Taylor & Francis.

Rose, D. B. (2004). *Reports from a Wild Country: Ethics for Decolonisation*. UNSW Press.

Rose, M., Newig, J., & Jager, N. W. (2025). Does participatory governance help address long-term environmental problems? Conceptualization and evidence from 23 democracies. *Policy Studies, 0*(0), 1–25.

Rose-Ackerman, S. (2013). *Corruption: A Study in Political Economy*. Academic Press.

Rosenzweig, C., Horton, R. M., Bader, D. A., Brown, M. E., DeYoung, R., Dominguez, O., Fellows, M., Friedl, L., Graham, W., Hall, C., Higuchi, S., Iraci, L., Jedlovec, G., Kaye, J., Loewenstein, M., Mace, T., Milesi, C., Patzert, W., Stackhouse, P. W., & Toufectis, K. (2014). Enhancing climate resilience at NASA centers: A collaboration between science and stewardship. *Bulletin of the American Meteorological Society, 95*(9), 1351–1363.

Sachs, J. D. (2015). *The Age of Sustainable Development*. Columbia University Press.

Sachs, W. (2015). *Planet Dialectics: Explorations in Environment and Development*. Zed Books Ltd.

Saltelli, A., Benini, L., Funtowicz, S., Giampietro, M., Kaiser, M., Reinert, E., & van der Sluijs, J. P. (2020). The technique is never neutral. How methodological choices condition the generation of narratives for sustainability. *Environmental Science & Policy, 106*, 87–98.

Scoones, I., Leach, M., & Newell, P. (Eds.). (2015). *The Politics of Green Transformations*. Taylor & Francis.

Senge, P. M. (2006). *The Fifth Discipline: The Art and Practice of the Learning Organization*. Doubleday/Currency.

Senge, P. M., Smith, B., Kruschwitz, N., Laur, J., & Schley, S. (2010). *The Necessary Revolution: Working Together to Create a Sustainable World*. Crown.

Sorrell, R. D. (1988). *St. Francis of Assisi and Nature: Tradition and Innovation in Western Christian Attitudes toward the Environment*. Oxford University Press.

Steffek, J., & Wegmann, P. (2021). The standardization of "Good Governance" in the Age of Reflexive Modernity. *Global Studies Quarterly, 1*(4), ksab029.

Stephenson, J. (2023). *Culture and Sustainability: Exploring Stability and Transformation with the Cultures Framework*. Springer Nature.

Stern, N., & Stiglitz, J. E. (2023). Climate change and growth. *Industrial and Corporate Change, 32*(2), 277–303. https://doi.org/10.1093/icc/dtad008

Stone, D. (2012). Transfer and translation of policy. *Policy Studies, 33*(6), 483–499.

Tamanaha, B. Z. (2004). *On the Rule of Law: History, Politics, Theory*. Cambridge University Press.

Tardieu, M. (2008). *Manichaeism*. University of Illinois Press.

Taylor, B. (2009). *Dark Green Religion: Nature Spirituality and the Planetary Future*. University of California Press.

Taylor, B. D. (2011). *State Building in Putin's Russia: Policing and Coercion after Communism*. Cambridge University Press.

Temper, L., del Bene, D., & Martinez-Alier, J. (2015). Mapping the frontiers and front lines of global environmental justice: The EJAtlas. *Journal of Political Ecology, 22*(1). https://doi.org/10.2458/v22i1.21108

Triollet, K., & Bernier, J. (2016). Appropriation citoyenne de l'aménagement urbain à Pointe-Saint-Charles, Montréal. *Les Politiques Sociales, 12*(1), 89–102.

Turner, M. D., Carney, T., Lawler, L., Reynolds, J., Kelly, L., Teague, M. S., & Brottem, L. (2021). Environmental rehabilitation and the vulnerability of the poor: The case of the Great Green Wall. *Land Use Policy, 111*, 105750.

Underdal, A. (2010). Complexity and challenges of long-term environmental governance. *Global Environmental Change, 20*(3), 386–393.

Van Assche, K., Beunen, R., & Gruezmacher, M. (2024). *Strategy for Sustainability Transitions: Governance, Community and Environment*. Edward Elgar Publishing.

Van Assche, K., Gruezmacher, M., Marais, L., & Perez-Sindin, X. (2023). *Resource Communities: Past Legacies and Future Pathways*. Taylor & Francis.

Van Assche, K., & Hornidge, A.-K. (2015). *Rural development; Knowledge and expertise in governance*. Wageningen Academic.

Vinsel, L., & Russell, A. L. (2020). *The Innovation Delusion: How Our Obsession with the New Has Disrupted the Work That Matters Most*. Crown Currency.

Wagenaar, H. (2014). *Meaning in Action: Interpretation and Dialogue in Policy Analysis*. Routledge.

Walker, J., & Cooper, M. (2011). Genealogies of resilience: From systems ecology to the political economy of crisis adaptation. *Security Dialogue, 42*(2), 143–160.

Wals, A. E. J., van der Hoeven, E. M. M. M., & Blanken, H. (2009). *The Acoustics of Social Learning: Designing learning processes that contribute to a more sustainable world*. Wageningen Academic Publishers.

Weiner, D. R. (1999). *A Little Corner of Freedom: Russian Nature Protection from Stalin to Gorbachev*. University of California Press.

Westerman, F. (2012). *Engineers of the Soul: The Grandiose Propaganda of Stalin's Russia*. Abrams.

Westley, F., Zimmerman, B., & Patton, M. (2009). *Getting to Maybe: How the World Is Changed*. Random House of Canada.

White, S. C., & Jha, S. (2023). Exploring the relational in relational well-being. *Social Sciences*, *12*(11), 600. Article 11. https://doi.org/10.3390/socsci12110600

Wilson, J. Q. (2019). *Bureaucracy: What Government Agencies Do and Why They Do It*. Basic Books.

Wood, G., & Baker, K. (2019). *The Palgrave Handbook of Managing Fossil Fuels and Energy Transitions*. Springer Nature.

Wynne, B. (1992). Misunderstood misunderstanding: Social identities and public uptake of science. *Public Understanding of Science*, *1*(3), 281–304.

Young, O. R. (2010). Institutional dynamics: Resilience, vulnerability and adaptation in environmental and resource regimes. *Global Environmental Change*, *20*(3), 378–385.

Zizek, S. (2009). *First as Tragedy, Then as Farce*. Verso Books.

Zizek, S. (2014). *Welcome to the Desert of the Real: Five Essays on September 11 and Related Dates*. Verso Books.

Zizek, S. (2019). *The Sublime Object of Ideology*. Verso Books.

6 | *Leadership for Sustainability*

What can leadership for sustainability mean? Sustainability leadership is a creature of governance and establishing conditions for good sustainability governance enhances its chances to survive and thrive. Against this background, we consider which roles and functions of leadership might prove more helpful when building sustainable communities, and, while eschewing formulaic recipes or heroic figures, we come to delineate four roles which can be taken up, in distributive leadership, under conditions where sustainability asserts itself as an urgent policy priority. We provide suggestions for both the analysis and crafting of leadership narratives, in the knowledge that both are highly dependent on the context of the community, its problems and the coevolutions in its governance system.

Leadership Roles and Sustainability Governance

Sustainability leadership is making sure that governance systems achieve or maintain the features of good sustainability governance, which we outlined before. Second, if these features can already be recognized, leadership needs to ensure that the governance process functions effectively, meaning it needs to articulate a desirable and realistic vision of sustainability and guide the community toward that goal (Figure 6.1a). In the first endeavor, the key leadership role, in metaphoric terms, is one of a *builder*. Such a builder will have to be knowledgeable about governance and sensitive to local stories, which means that she must be a persuasive *storyteller*, and an *expert* in the functioning and transformation of governance. In the second situation, where conditions for good sustainability governance seem to be in place already, what might be appropriate is sometimes a *mechanic*, someone who understands the details of governance, and can get things unstuck, or paper over some cracks. Since the

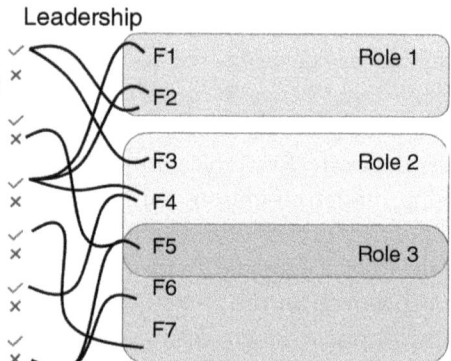

Figure 6.1 (a) Sustainability leadership is making sure that governance systems achieve or maintain the features of good sustainability governance. When rigidities in governance are increased, diversity of perspectives and critical deliberation are reduced, we cannot speak of good sustainability governance and (b) good sustainability governance traits may either be present or absent in the current system. In either case, specific leadership functions will necessarily be defined and linked to corresponding roles. It is important to note that these functions may be shared or overlap between different roles.

structural features of good sustainability governance do not lightly translate into good governance processes, a labor of specification and contextualization is implied, where maybe a mechanic could suffice, but where a *visionary* might shine (Figure 6.1b). Let us look now at each of the conditions of good sustainability governance and consider in more detail which leadership roles might be helpful to create and safeguard them.

Observation of System–Environment Interactions

What kind of leadership might be involved in improved observation of system–environment interactions? If we word it like this, an all-knowing *cyborg* might be the figure. However, if we look at it as being aware, as a society, of the effects we have on our environment, and, conversely, of the impact of changing environments on us, we can broaden the idea of the leader. One can either increase the observational capacity of governance itself, or welcome observations made by others. Those could be experts in a field related to ecology or society, and they could be locals who are aware of changes but found no way or reason to bring it up in public (Berkes, 2017). Such locals might tell stories that differ from what subject experts and bureaucrats tell, so a role as *translator* might be appropriate (Agrawal, 2005).

Bringing in observations is often a matter of eliciting them and trying to come to a synthesis. We would go one step further and note that enhancing and diversifying observations, as well as improving the quality and interpretation of those observations, can take place within the community just as much as in governance. This requires leadership that fosters opportunities, sites and arenas where diverse voices can be heard, by supporting local media, social learning in a vibrant civil society and public discourse in different forms (Dryzek, 2013). If we give hunters a chance to be heard, opportunities for mutual learning might arise; welcoming farmers in an environmental committee can create a welcome opportunity for them to get upset with journalists and trigger an overdue public discussion.

Within governance, a diversity of perspectives on community and environment can be cultivated and recognized. If observational infrastructures are missing, a role as *builder* might focus on increasing expertise, increasing it in a systematic manner, bringing it together in an environment where learning, rather than competition, is valued. Truly diverse perspectives ought to be encouraged, and where conflict erupts, a role of *broker* or again *translator* can be more valuable than a *peace builder*, as, in sustainability issues, it is often in disagreement that problems can be delineated more clearly (Stirling, 2010). Which observations are missing, cannot be recognized outside context and will be defined by the nature of the problem and the character of governance. The builder can be a builder of roles devoted to the gathering of information and elicitation of voices (Fischer, 2009).

Robert Angus Smith discovered acid rain in 1852, and coined the term in 1872, based on research in the vicinity of Scottish factories. Before any policies changed, more work of discovery had to occur, especially in the 1960s and 70s, indicating that dramatic effects of industrial and other pollution could be felt at a great distance and that forests and wetlands around the world were under threat. Sweden took an early initiative to ban sulphuric oils, air pollution policies proliferated in the 1970s, and in 1979 the United Nations (UNECE) enacted a policy on transboundary air pollution, which smoothened international collaboration in the 1980s. American, Canadian and European governments, as well as a young yet assertive European Union (then European Economic Community) all helped to raise the profile of the issue. Svante Oden, a Swedish scientist with connections in politics and administration, wrote in 1967 a deliberately provocative newspaper article, and contributed to reports for government soon after; Swedish politicians picked up the issue, brought it to the attention of the international community, to little avail. Only after warning about the widening effects implied after a nuclear disaster, did opinions start to move. (Reed, 2016)

Self-Observation

Improving observation only works on the basis of self-observation, just as self-awareness only comes about on the back of a deepening awareness of the world. In complex governance systems, individuals and specialized organizations typically concentrate on their immediate responsibilities and local environments. Reflection on the underlying rationale for and effects of their actions – how these actions relate to broader contextual dynamics, contribute to overarching objectives, or signal more systemic transformations – is often overlooked or not systematically considered. This is what organization theorist Mats Alvesson calls functional stupidity (Alvesson & Spicer, 2016) and leadership in all matters sustainable could very well require the role of *stupidity foe*. Making people, organizations think about their work, its assumptions and implications, can contribute greatly to the quality of self-observation of governance systems (Shiva, 2018).

Shallow self-observation and functional stupidity are often the product of organizational cultures and obtuse leadership yet sometimes appear because of a perceived need to fit the brand, or to stick to a specialized perspective. The sustainability leader as stupidity foe, as hero of reflexivity, thus must address such issues. Here, again, distributed leadership is the key, as individual leaders cannot carry this burden alone. Leadership of this sort likely entails confrontation with other leaders, at the risk of antagonizing them. Reflexivity is essential not only to the quality of environmental observation, for the recognition of problems but also for the delineation of possible solutions. Which means that, for the understanding of real, versus imagined, policy options, one needs to grasp very clearly how governance works, as opposed to how it is supposed to work, or how it says it works (Beck et al., 1994). Instinctively leaning on the same people producing more plans, will never reveal that the people or the type of instrument might be the problem. A deep familiarity with the functioning of governance can help leaders to, on the one hand, correct reflexivity and recognize more appropriate policy solutions, and, on the other hand, encourage reflexivity in a more systemic manner. To explain that stupidity is in the room, and to move from individual reflexivity to systemic reflexivity, translators and brokers might again be required, while sites for more systematic reflection and comparison might be constructed, in a process where builders cannot be missed.

Institutional Capacity

Reflexivity contributes to institutional capacity simply by knowing what the actual capacity is. Governance systems and communities alike are usually wrong in assessing what governance can do (Luhmann, 1990). Sustainability concerns can tax a governance system easily beyond its capacity to organize itself and its environment, beyond what it believes it can and should do. Indeed, systems tend to overestimate and underestimate their own capacity at the same time, which is a different way of saying that they do not have a clear understanding of what they can achieve. More difficult is the self-assessment of their potential to transform: Can we, from the current state, develop the capacity to address new problems of this sort (Luhmann, 1989)?

Leadership aiming to develop institutional capacity, once shortcomings are diagnosed, can face several obstacles, which correlate with different leadership roles. If what is missing can materialize by harnessing expertise and resources, the leader as *builder* can have a free hand. If, on the other hand, what is holding back the development of institutional capacity are master narratives imposing limited or misdirected capacity on governance, a role as *storyteller* is more of the moment (Ganz, 2009a). If what is in the way are entrenched interests and power relations, a *Machiavellian* character might be required, less picky about the methods to clear the road of obstacles, willing to do whatever it takes. Leadership might come to realize that what is at stake is power itself. People might cling to ideas at all cost, and the question then arises what cost one is willing to pay to remedy this situation. People cling to power, and to any story that justifies that power. If sustainability arguments do not hold much weight for such comrades or coteries, one might be confronted with the Machiavellian question: How far are we willing to go to break up the coteries and convert the comrades in the name of a common good (Welzer, 2017)?

In spring 1972, Sicco Mansholt, European commissioner for agriculture, and known as one of the proponents of the "green revolution," which promoted mechanization and upscaling of agriculture to boost economic development and reduce hunger, wrote a letter to his superior. We do not know the answer provided by Franco Maria Malfatti, commission president at the time. The letter had no real effect on European policy and paid little attention to implementation difficulties. It represented a real crisis of faith for the old school modernist, caused, in part, by an early version of the report by the Club of Rome he saw, a document ringing the alarm bell about limits to growth, overpopulation, collapsing ecosystems and resource depletion. Responding creatively to the message of Dennis Meadows and his MIT colleagues, Mansholt proposed nothing less than an overthrow of the existing social, political and economic order. Neither capitalism nor socialism would be able to do what was necessary, which included a drastic reduction of consumption, a focus on longevity and recycling of consumer goods, draconic interventions in family planning, economic protectionism at EU level and central economic planning. While he was not a sage, and alienated the whole political spectrum, limiting his influence, he was a visionary, as that one letter summarizes problems and solutions unveiling themselves in a slow struggle over decades. (Lorenzini, 2022; Merriënboer, 2014)

Adaptive Capacity

What a system might achieve in the given circumstances, takes art and wisdom to assess, hence a figure of the *sage*. A *sage* might also show up to consider the adaptive capacity of a system. Adaptive capacity is impossible to quantify, as it must be tailored to circumstances and limited to a pallet of possible states of the environment. If institutional capacity can be summarized as the power to organize *things*, adaptive capacity is the ability to adapt, per definition, to things *in an environment*. It is hence more specified than institutional capacity, yet its specificity is difficult to establish (Leichenko & O'Brien, 2008). One reason is the opaque set of coevolutions that shaped the system of governance. Over time structures and processes appeared, actors and institutions, stories and expertise that are a product of the environment, and a result of constrained self-reproduction.

Redesigning governance to enhance adaptive capacity is possible, and in our sustainability perspective often necessary, but if we understand this as a technical operation allowing for an approximation of an ideal, we are blinding ourselves to the reality of coevolution and risk reducing the actual adaptive capacity. We learned that adaptive capacity cannot be equated to flexibility. Maximizing flexibility comes at great risk since stabilizing functions are vital to governance and its survival. One form of flexibility might reduce risk in accommodating more versions of one type of event, yet likely increases risk for a variability somewhere else in the environment. Habitually locating adaptive capacity in governance design creates new rigidities, diverts attention from flexible *thinking*, from organizational cultures that allow for critical debate and, if necessary, overriding and canceling of procedure, rather than wayfinding in a bureaucratic labyrinth (Berkes et al., 2002).

A sage and a builder therefore might have to get along in leadership for adaptive capacity. A few other roles enter the scene of the drama of adaptive capacity, as the tight coupling with an environment renders knowledge of that environment essential. Assessing adaptive capacity and the need for greater or different adaptive capacity involves expertise and actually transforming that capacity most likely benefits from translators and storytellers. As tinkering with adaptive capacity likely implies governance reform, and confrontations with entrenched interests, the Machiavellian might be invited again (Bevir, 2013).

Long-Term Perspectives

Master narratives denying the importance or even possibility of envisioning the long term are a common issue. Ideologies might emphasize the futility of such effort, as the world is too complex or God's will unknowable. All such constraints are highly damaging to any efforts to articulate sustainability policy. Leadership that finds itself in this situation must deliberate carefully, calibrate tactics and strategy, ethics and effectivity and consider the roles we deemed pertinent when building institutional capacity. The stories told to persuade communities of the value of long-term perspectives, the tools deployed to remove obstacles, can vary widely.

Connecting to values dearly held, emphasizing long-term threats to what seems so stable and natural, might gain traction in a community unwilling to look ahead (Leiserowitz, 2006). The role of *visionary* might work but holds great risks if the risk communicated is not felt viscerally by the community, if trust in leadership is not deep, and if those preaching the importance of the long term do not hold power and prestige (Dobson, 2007). Becoming an institution builder, to give a place to the articulation of long-term perspectives in governance is nearly impossible if master narratives glorify the present or the present organization, anchoring it in nature, identity or the past, and it is not much easier when collective futures or influencing them is dismissed.

Thus, the storyteller takes center stage, in positive and negative versions: New stories can be told, old ones dismantled, silenced or dismissed (Latour, 2017). The stories can be self-invented or found; they can find their first cues in collective desires and beliefs, in other stories more warmly embraced, or, conversely, by forging new observations into a narrative form. In such case, observations of diverse sorts must find a place in the story, and translation occurred before storytelling. A Machiavellian streak is not out of place, as new discourse coalitions might have to be brokered, new voices brought into the fray and old ones associated with anything that can be portrayed as problematic.

Strategic Capacity

While a leader, and a leadership group interested in sustainability should always be open to play the role of *strategist*, encouraging systemic strategic capacity is a different matter altogether, and could lead to almost any of the roles distinguished previously. Strategic capacity is the ability for communities, through governance, to entertain alternative versions of the future, articulate one that can function as guidance, and connect policy tools old and new to a narrative that can then start to function as master narrative, and as tool of coordination, as institution itself (Van Assche et al., 2024).

Sustainability thinking almost always stretches strategic capacity, even where communities believe they have it all covered. Countries, regions and towns with elaborate systems of spatial and environmental planning polities guiding themselves through comprehensive economic development schemes, nations proud of social welfare systems will still be tested in their ability to comprehend and coordinate (Jasanoff, 2004). Sustainability issues, if taken seriously, do not manifest themselves solely within the conceptual and organizational boundaries of complex administrations and they tend to transcend the capacities of those administrations. As we know, if the boundaries are taken too seriously, much of what could constitute sustainability problems and promises will not be observed. Traditions of steering are typically geared toward topics dear to a community, and amenable to steering, while what sustainability might demand can be a relaxation of steering on such topic, while a cherished domain of freedom or benign neglect might require intense scrutiny and micro management.

Assessing and enhancing the strategic capacity of a community and its governance system is an effort where the distributed character of leadership comes into its own most marvelously. Gifted individual leaders might strategize by themselves, with great success, and bring communities closer to a sustainable state, but chances are small that the result simultaneously enhanced the collective capacity to strategize. Likely, a Machiavellian leadership, envisioning the common good of sustainability sidelined enough opponents, and sidestepped enough checks and balances to reduce the strategic capacity of the collective (Arendt, 2019). If this is the case, if there is insufficient public *and* elite support for a strategy spearheaded by leadership, the maneuvering by leaders to get it through comes with the unwelcome consequence that next time, governance is unable to strategize. What leadership can only hope for, then, is that good intentions and the common good are broadly recognized, or that the resulting situation, maybe through storytelling, maybe through continuous mobilization of expertise or simply by silence, becomes naturalized (Luhmann, 2017). Chapter 7 is devoted entirely to the topic of strategy for sustainability and we will continue the discussion on leadership roles and functions for strategy there.

Leadership Functions and Sustainability

In Chapter 1, we spoke of leadership functions, which could feature in several leadership roles, and we looked at leadership as that what goes beyond existing procedures and routines, that what is needed

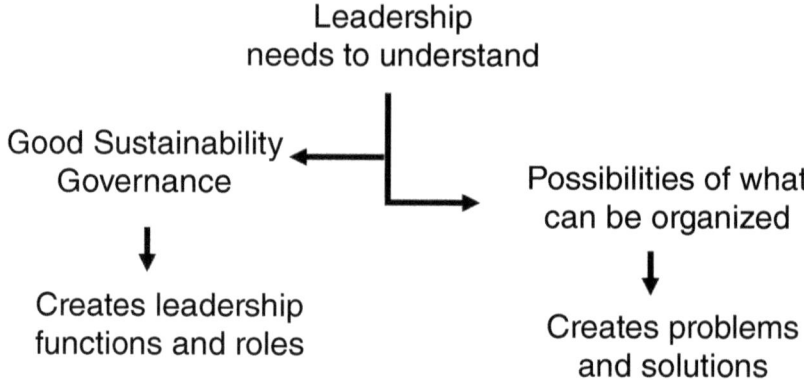

Figure 6.2 Effective sustainability governance requires specific leadership roles. Leaders must understand both the existing traits of good sustainability governance and those that are lacking. This will determine the leadership functions and roles that need to be created. Recognizing what can and cannot be organized will help identify the problems, issues and opportunities that leadership will encounter.

to make things work, by either improving institutions or to compel them into action. This, we said, could involve activities, or functions such as the creative search for resources, taking initiative and reshuffling power relations. Finding, crafting and telling stories, sometimes with the aim of building long-term perspectives and strategies, belong to the core repertoire of leadership. In pursuing strategy and solving problems, combining tactics and strategy, identifying new policy tools or creative uses of old ones can render a solution or goal realistic. Returning to good sustainability governance and its features, we can now refine our investigation of sustainability leadership in those terms (Figure 6.2). We remind ourselves that leadership roles are bundles of functions, with overlap between roles through shared functions, and certain roles dominated by one function (Figure 6.3). Under dire circumstances, we will see, specific functions can be foregrounded more easily, defining roles that become key to addressing such circumstances. Functions of leadership and the actions they require to ensure good sustainability governance are harnessed and maintained are listed below. We must leave space for functions that might emerge out of problems and governance features, the list will change as conditions change.

Leadership Functions and Sustainability 191

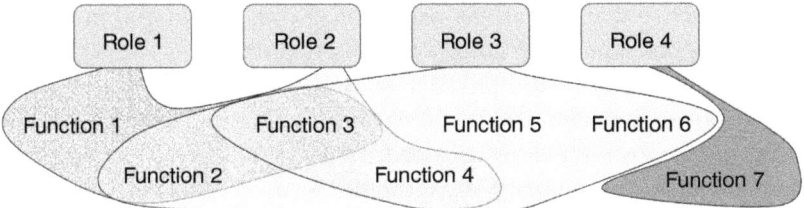

Figure 6.3 Leadership roles bundle a set of functions. It is possible to observe overlap among roles due to shared functions. Additionally, certain roles are predominantly characterized by a single dominant function.

- Functions of leadership
  - Finding resources
  - Bringing in ideas
  - Forging coalitions
  - Telling stories
  - Crafting new policy tools
  - Devising new uses of old tools
  - Establishing external relationships
  - Building institutions
  - Strategizing
- Actions involved
  - Linking short and long term
  - Linking governance and community
  - Assessing risk
  - Connecting formal and informal institutions
  - Balancing rigidity and flexibility
  - Balancing slow and fast changes
  - Assessing fit of old and new
  - Access to internal and external perspectives
  - …
  - …

Observation of System–Environment Interactions

Where a storyteller is needed, telling stories (a function) is of course a core requirement. Before a good story can be told, much needs to be in place. As noted, crafting a story about the environment, and about the need and the manner to improve systemic observation of system–environment relations will entail translation of and brokering between stories and their human characters (Luhmann, 1989). We can add that leadership will need to avail itself of observations and interpretations of environmental interactions that are different, that it will need to learn more than others about outside perspectives and hence re-relate inside and outside (Gaventa & Cornwall, 2015). New observations enable new stories, but stories are often required to gather those observations, and doing so systematically, can involve storytelling, building, brokering within governance. Where reform is needed to diversify observation, more actors will have to be persuaded. If a meteorological service or an environmental protection agency does not exist, bringing it into existence will necessitate leadership to form broader coalitions, possibly to deploy Machiavellian schemes, likely to court audiences outside governance. Once such infrastructures are in place, new stories about the environment are on the horizon, and further observational improvement of systems relations.

A cyborg is a dangerous creature and must be assigned a carefully delineated task. Other leadership roles and functions are more important to enhance observation or draw better conclusions from it. For this feature of good governance, the navigation of risk and opportunity, hence the interpretation of risk, deserves priority. Strategy embodies risk navigation most clearly maybe, but navigation cannot wait until then. When arguing for sharper and more coordinated environmental observation, for monitoring and assessment in the technical sense and inclusion of more varied perspectives, a prior assessment needs to be in place. Systems cannot observe everything, cannot worry all the time and need to discern what can be normalized or adapted to easily (Seidl, 2016). Therefore, a selection of observations that indicate a real threat, one where answers are not immediately available, and where more observation over the longer term is needed, is essential. Leadership can assert itself in the interpretation of existing observations, and the improvement of observational infrastructures, where recognizing risk and telling stories about it, is helpful throughout, and where reinforced infrastructure and sharpened interpretation can feed off each other (Schön, 2017).

Brokering and translation can then signify the assemblage of new environmental stories that find resonance, but it can also mean that risk interpretation is distilled from brokered conversations between actors, conversations that might include outsiders, even if those are suspicious in public discourse. Gaps in observation and observational infrastructures can be recognized in the same way. Networking and familiarity with the larger world are useful, and where observational infrastructure needs to be built, finding resources, and contriving new uses for existing policy tools and organizations come in handy. Sustainability leadership working on observational capacity is obliged to consider long-term perspectives already. Even if collective strategy is not on the horizon yet, discovering and convincing others that environmental interactions deserve more systematic scrutiny require a story about the long term (Douglas & Wildavsky, 1982).

Self-Observation

Playing the role of stupidity foe might be fun, but as Socrates found out, it's a rather risky job. Being a Machiavellian can be thrilling, but, as Machiavelli himself found, not without risks either. Hence, assessing such risks for oneself, and relating this to the assessment of environmental risk, might mean continuous calculation (Foucault, 2003). Scolding someone for their stupidity, then pushing them aside, might not be an effective tactic. However, the stupidity foe might also be experienced as a liberator from oppressive thought, a breath of fresh air, while the skilled Machiavellian will play a long-term game where those sidelined will feel they gain something, will feel at least respected in their basic values and aspirations.

Therefore, revealing limitations on thinking, as precondition for reflexivity, enrolls a variety of leadership functions. Storytelling toward a reframing of what is known and familiar, toward a rethinking of ways of thinking, opening up new vistas, can all play a role. Networking, both in the community and elsewhere, can lead to the discovery of discursive openings, of ways to show the relevance of other perspectives and the limits of ways of thinking engrained in governance. Travel, bringing in guests, public discussion, even mild comedy can bring preconceptions to the surface, and might encourage new modes of self-reflection (Flyvbjerg, 2011). Turning routine meetings into moments of reflexivity, first ad hoc, later structurally, building institutions to enshrine and amplify reflexivity, and to safeguard places and moments for discussion and debate, will be a collective leadership effort, where several functions can be at play.

Confronting actors with the problematic implications of their perspectives, with the limitations of the current governance process and structure toward understanding and guiding their own actions, can involve gentle questioning, a questioning made possible by subtle environmental risk assessment with leadership, by their external connections, their assessment of governance limits and dependencies. New ideas, on governance and its reflexivity, on environmental relations, can thus be brought in by presenting them or by guiding a process of self-discovery with others (Schön, 2017).

Where reflexivity is less valued in society and governance, challenges are substantial. Nevertheless, chances are that, when obtuse governance is the issue, somewhere in society, the problem was noticed before. This means that leadership can likely draw on those ideas, and that Machiavellian activities can revolve around their dissemination, in the hope that power relations will shift, and that alternative perspectives can be institutionalized (Hall, 1993). Builders might have to be pragmatic, and repurpose, as in the case of environmental observation, existing institutions and organizations with the aim of furthering self-observation. Not all reflexivity has to be system wide and not all systemic reflexivity has to explicitly recognize that aim – it can be a cultivated side-effect or generalized condition. This, then, will determine which leadership functions come to the foreground – whether one needs more resources, new institutions or networks, stories.

Institutional Capacity

Building institutional capacity is first of all building. We know that the builder might have to be, or collaborate with, a Machiavellian and a sage. Someone needs to take initiative, and this can be the leader as builder, or as the sage, who discerned first what should be built and what could be built. The builder can be Machiavellian, in the process of construction, or she can be preceded by a Machiavellian who cleared most obstacles. The sage might read informal institutions in a more consummate manner, and might see outside influences asserting themselves earlier, which paves the way for the builder (North, 1990). Stories become available to justify the building of institutional capacity, which always comes at a cost, and which is bound to touch stories, values and identities. The need to develop capacity can be questioned on the ground of ideological master signifiers, or where small government or low tax stories do not pose obstacles, there can still be a narrative requirement to delineate a set of risks or opportunities to prepare for, a type of situation or activity that would benefit from increased institutional capacity (Grindle, 2004). And any story told there will be scrutinized through the lens of stories already positioned in governance.

As a builder of institutional capacity, there's not only the cost of resistance to consider. One cannot escape the cost of materials. Leaders as builders thus might be obliged to find resources in unexpected places, to network to that end, to tell convincing stories about sharing materials or to redesign a house intended for someone else. Costs may be hidden, in accounting and in stories, ascribed to activities already occurring, existing policy tools and organizational structures might be creatively reused, efficiencies found and redundancies harnessed (Andrews, 2013). Any feature of governance structure and process can potentially be reinterpreted to enhance institutional capacity, either in general, or toward a set of anticipated occurrences. An accounting department can be restructured so it can assist in thinking through scenarios, a set of policy tools appertaining to one policy domain can be discreetly tested for application beyond, a role traditionally restricted to monitoring could be used to elicit ideas on responses to what was monitored, a discretionary budget can be allocated to a broader domain, an economic development branch can be placed at arm's length, to bypass paralyzing regulation.

As with leadership encouraging systemic observation of environmental relations, builders of institutional capacity benefit from a long-term perspective, hence some will develop such perspective for themselves. It can assist in the construction process, and in convincing others to allow and support the activities. Institutional capacity can be sold as a general infrastructure, and as work that addresses more specific goals and concerns. Long-term perspectives ideally guide institutional capacity development, yet it can happen the other way around, where a governance system builds itself up, and then devises futures to legitimize the development (Weible & Sabatier, 2018).

As a sage, leadership is important in assessing institutional capacity. Figuring out what a governance system can do is more than adding pieces, more than building, and distinct from the tinkering of the mechanic. A different set of functions can come to the fore, including the re-relating of inside and outside, the telling of and listening to stories and the shifting of power relations. The same system can do more if one can re-relate formal and informal institutions, which represents an alteration in power/knowledge, and a modification of the embedding of governance in community. If leadership can reconfigure the discursive and affective environment of governance, or reconnect governance to it through networking, storytelling, brokering, the effects of governance can be amplified (Bennett, 2010; Esposito, 2019).

Adaptive Capacity

Assessing the adaptive capacity of a system requires greater leadership than an assessment of institutional capacity and, we argue, this represents an even stronger case for distributive leadership. Adaptive capacity is a matter of system relations rather than system features, meaning that discerning system, environment and relations is a minimum requirement (Walker et al., 2004). We add that insight in the self-transformation of governance is of the essence, which means that leadership, in assessing and enhancing adaptive capacity is able to recognize the dependencies in governance evolution (see Van Assche et al., 2013).

For leadership to understand adaptive capacity then, is to grasp the dependencies in governance evolution. Leadership must be invoked, as the self-transformation of the system is not that transparent to the system itself, so the stories it tends to tell about its future are usually off the mark. Leadership capable of second-order observation, the observation of observations, and this often means leadership well networked inside and outside governance, can come to a different understanding of the capacity for change (Weick, 1988). Such leadership discerns clearly the sorts of resistance coming with dependencies, hence the cost and risk of change. This risk then must be placed against the risk of nonchange, which can only be gleaned through a keen understanding of system–environment relations (Beer, 2023).

As adaptive capacity requires such observation, the quality of observation in the system needs to be evaluated, and as it also entails reflexivity and institutional capacity, all roles and functions of leadership mentioned there might be at play in the assessment and improvement of adaptive capacity. When systemic reflexivity and observational capacity are insufficient, insightful leadership might still draw the right conclusions regarding institutional capacity, but when institutional capacity is lacking, leadership aiming to reinforce adaptive capacity can likely not compensate and be obliged to focus on capacity building first. When navigating dependencies with the eye on transformation for adaptivity, virtually all leadership functions can become relevant. Storytelling may not need to name adaptive capacity as a goal, as it sounds too abstract to be affectively invested, and the high cognitive and organizational demands on leadership for adaptation thus find a counterpoint in the relative ease of hiding the work. It can be hidden, presented as a series of technicalities in minor administrative reform, associated with stories of greater public relevance, and when larger interventions toward adaptivity are on the menu, they can be primarily covered by other goals and stories (Wiek & Lang, 2016). Leadership functions for such larger interventions (a new organization, a significant change in budget, an important policy change) will require assemblage appropriate for that intervention, rather than the general goal of adaptive capacity.

Transcending dependencies in a way that makes for more adaptive systems means making it less dependent on leadership. A Machiavellian leader may serve as a pivotal figure in restructuring power relations, compelling the development of both observational and institutional capacities. Such a leader may employ a combination of persuasion and coercion, operate through both formal channels and informal networks, cultivate external alliances and initiate a wide range of actions – all with the aim of rendering the system less dependent on the future emergence of similarly Machiavellian figures.

A European country introduced legislation making it attractive to offer employees company cars as part of their compensation package. This was an adaptation to high taxes on labor, a way to offer workers something else. Unfortunately, the adaptation made the system less adaptive in terms of environmental goals, as people got attached to cars and as lowering taxes on labor proved an unfeasible alternative. Increasing adaptive capacity in this case would decouple cars from stories about normal compensation, so a wider variety of environmental policy options becomes available, yet this means facing the resistance of both employers and employees.

Long-Term Perspectives

The leadership functions beneficial for the cultivation of reflexivity and observation most likely prove themselves helpful in the development and institutionalization of long-term perspectives. When a vision is so persuasive, a risk is so threatening, an opportunity so amazing that it warrants long-term perspectives where they did not function before, and the visionary might trigger institutional change. In most cases, the community has enough reasons to cling to the configuration it knows, and if that means a limited consideration of the future, so be it (Nixon, 2011).

Long-term perspectives, to be institutionalized, might rely on leaders to tell stories about the present, and how it could be threatened or how it could be extended to the future, if only some work was put into it. Sometimes, scare tactics might work, stories of doom and gloom, but to mobilize the community to rethink its future and install a future-oriented governance, painting a picture that also presents opportunities might be a better bet. Even if leadership has to be keenly aware of long-term risk before others, and recognizes a threat of existential proportions, not all audiences can be served a story built around this assessment (Marshall, 2014).

If historical references can be identified that illustrate the presence of forward-looking governance – or the consequences of its absence – there may be greater openness among individuals to reconsider their current practices, or at least to permit governance processes that engage with long-term perspectives (Ganz, 2009b). If identity narratives can be reinterpreted, translated, into stories that either depict a future warranting action, or convince the community to look ahead in a more concerted fashion, this might provide an alternative path (Jasanoff, 2004). Brokering groups and their stories represents a further avenue. Stories that might convince a community to cease disavowing collective action for the future can thus be assembled from several others, and those do not have to address the future or the past. Good governance narratives, a latent diversity of identity stories, religious values or shifting leadership ideals can all contribute to a brokered assemblage of ideas that might just move the needle, and render a community more sensitive to the future, and its own power of shaping it (Czarniawska, 2004). If this is possible without instilling guilt about the current system, or prevailing values and identity narratives, chances are even better. A Machiavellian leader might add the more cynical touch of subtle bribery, or finding roles, rewards and honors to sideline or silence those opposing governance change, and convincing other that it won't make a difference.

Long-term perspectives can sneak in or even find institutionalization in a rather quiet manner. Expert roles (such as planners, environmental experts, community or economic development specialists) can be installed in administration, without overt political influence, advisory bodies gathering stakeholders around vital themes can be established. The split administration/politics, or the invocation of broader community interests can bring long-term perspectives to life with less resistance. Once in existence, they have a fighting chance to routinize, then render more important, the consideration of the long term in governance (Fischer, 2009; Haynes, 2015). As with adaptive capacity, the functions of leadership required in mobilizing support will depend on the type of intervention deemed appropriate within the specific local context. If an environmental council is the way to get city council to consider not only the environment but the future as such, this offers a further indication for the leadership skills needed to make this happen. A modest budget might be reallocated, a federal grant is spotted, allies in the community are discovered and external experts bring in ideas, first regarding environmental councils, then regarding the environment and its overlooked problems.

Strategic Capacity

Similar to adaptive capacity, strategic capacity in governance comes about when other qualities are already tangible, and when the belief is there that strategy is possible at all. Chapter 7 will provide more detail, but we can say that the systemic capacity for strategy can be used and developed by leadership. When it must be built up, the strategies of leadership to do so, the leadership qualities involved, can be remarkably diverse. Strategic capacity, like institutional capacity and leaning on it, can be developed gradually and often unnoticed. This process can be strategic and is typically driven by leadership. Elsewhere, events combine in a pattern recognized by leadership as offering opportunities to strategize (Mintzberg, 1994). When this leads to the practice of collective strategy, it can instill it as a habit, enhancing the capacity to strategize in the future.

When strategic capacity is real, and ready to be used, leadership is still relevant, in articulating strategy and during implementation, with a lithe switching between tactics and strategy often observed (Whittington, 2006). Strategies tend not to write themselves, even when all pieces are in place. When they are written, or concocted, leadership will still have to come into action, derive partial strategies per topic, time or place, devise supportive strategies and overcome obstacles. Reliance on procedure or plans outlined by the strategy might not be enough. Indeed, strategies are not plans, as organization theorist Henry Mintzberg noted often enough, and plans can undermine their own unfolding by ignoring the need to link with tactics, to integrate new initiatives and to embed themselves in informal institutions.

As strategy is both narrative and institution, and as those institutions are old and new, leadership functions pertain to those domains (Van Assche et al., 2024). Listening to and crafting of stories, networking, reading the role of informal institutions, thinking creatively about resources, seeing a pattern of threat or opportunity in the environment and a pattern of possible responses with the tools at hand can all be valuable. Weighing the pros and cons of integrating existing policies, plans, or laws, and stories already found meaningful, versus constructing new stories and institutions, is a function of governance that is hard to imagine without leadership (Moore, 1997). Judgment of this sort cannot be replaced by procedure, or rational argumentation. Leadership functions are in demand, and deep knowledge of the system, its reliance on informality and external environments, the legacies of old experiences and stories, its latent institutional and adaptive capacities can all be integrated into what looks like an intuitive assessment or a chaotic discussion of strategy.

Leadership functions involved in the crafting of collective narratives for the long run thus differ from those involved in the building of institutions, while what is beneficial for building new stories and institutions differs from what benefits the discovery and creative reuse of stories and institutions, or the coupling of stories to policy tools that can make them or their implied goals reality (Czarniawska & Joerges, 1997). Alas, communities most in need of strategy are often least interested in and capable of strategy. It is to such cases we will turn in the next section, discussing which leadership roles and functions are a premium under conditions of shock and disaster.

Strategic capacity toward responsible consumption and production can be reinforced indirectly through greater coordination and long-term visioning for public procurement. Strategic procurement can make the government a model to emulate, and can, through sizeable and long-term orders, foster more sustainable production practices, making it worth to invest in research and rethink production lines and supply chains. Strategic procurement can be aligned with key sustainability policies and reinforce them selectively, in messaging and through strategic investment. Procurement, therefore, can be more than a small contribution to sustainable practices; if coordinated internally and externally, it can be a basis for strategy, even where few other powers are available. (Myers, 2020)

Leadership Roles in Rough Seas

When communities are in deep trouble, and not capable of responding strategically, with an eye on their own survival, a specification of the previous analyses is in place. Sustainability looks and feels different when survival is at stake, and the capacity to deal with existential challenges is usually not correlated with the severity of the challenge. In other words, most communities in rough seas are not adapted to those seas, and when they have been left to their own devices for a long time, chances are that what we recognized as good sustainability governance never had an opportunity to develop. Communities where sustainability is an urgent concern often went through shocks, and those shocks tend to leave traces. We propose four leadership roles which tend to show their importance when things get truly heated (Gruezmacher et al., 2025). Most characters we met before. We distinguish the leader as *broker, builder, interpreter* and as *therapist*, and leave the argumentation for their relevance to the relevant passages.

Builder

Communities under immediate and grave pressure have the worry of immediate response but, almost certainly, they got into such deep trouble because their economic, social and political organization could not be supported anymore in that environment. Both immediate response and slow rebuilding are required, which creates inherent tensions between tactics and strategy. The master narratives that oriented community and governance alike deserve reconsideration. Many communities ending up in dramatic circumstances had limited institutional capacity to begin with, which might correlate with ideology, hasty construction, dominance of a few players or other factors (Walker et al., 2004). In other words, we are not just speaking of a mismatch between system and environment, but also a weak capacity to pursue any collective goal, and hence also a limited adaptive capacity (Gruezmacher & Van Assche, 2022). Governance might have looked adequate for a long time. Yet, drama can wake us up not only to the events in the present, but also to a past that made us incapable to respond, and to formulate any future strategy.

A need for immediate response and the uncertainty about the way to build capacity might prevent big decisions about the future from being taken. A possible way out is a temporary focus on *transitional governance*, the limited building activities necessary to respond now without closing options for the future and gradually laying the groundwork for a future strategy (Van Assche et al., 2020, 2024). Transitional governance might have different immediate and intermediate aims, which depend on the seriousness of social and environmental conditions, and the character of governance already in place: What do we have to work with? Is what we are missing, to prepare strategizing, subject expertise, forms of local collaboration and inclusion, or rather administrative structures and policy tools? Transitional governance is custom-made, using the materials at hand, for the situation at hand. Hence storytelling by leadership about short and long term combine, in arguing for an assemblage of transitional governance which can have the additional, possibly intended, benefit of shifting power relations, by bringing in different actors and voices, altering the relevance of old organizational structures, all of which can break open vistas on alternative futures later (Homer-Dixon, 2010; Solnit, 2009).

A builder is sometimes a literal builder. Where a fishing town lost its main pier and dock in a storm, and the town was already shrinking, as fish stocks are declining and the product needs to compete with cheap imports, leadership might be convinced that this is not a moment to wax nostalgically and try to mobilize for a return to the past. At the same time, they understand this is not the time for a lengthy planning process, as experience with such processes and their promises has been mixed at best, as rifts in the community on many subjects would be aggravated, and as people are losing faith. A well-connected and entrepreneurial leadership might be able to mobilize funds, for a reconstruction of the waterfront, honoring the town's maritime heritage, yet opening it up to alternative futures. In other words, building "something" might be symbolically powerful, as symbol of resilience, and the something can often connect to local identity, without locking in old economic futures.

Broker

Brokers come in as shocks might have caused conflict, or because internal rifts might have aggravated the shock. Conflicts might arise from polarized discourse and oppositional politics, and they fuel further polarization. Brokers can thus be peace-builders, or at least truce-makers, where the pressure of time and tragedy might overcome differences only temporarily. If brokers bring together parties in conflict, the qualities expected of brokerage will be distinct, as will be the risks (Fisher et al., 2011). If no trusted insiders are available, perhaps because everybody is associated with one of the factions, external parties might play the role. This, however, only works if relations with other communities or higher-level actors are not too troubled themselves. Trust is of the essence, and if an outsider is selected as broker, his leadership role and term can only be limited (Scott, 2008).

If one is lucky enough to have avoided conflict, and brokering can focus on bringing together parties to forge a way forward, maybe to make initial choices on narratives and institution building, several situations still represent forking paths. Brokering where parties get along but are used to passivity, to nonparticipation in governance requires a different approach from communities where an in-crowd, which might be old or new, actively excluded many. When those excluded, the newcomers, outsiders or forgotten elements have to come to the table toward collective action, a broker will have to draw on many qualities, and her stories, networking and resource-finding missions might take on a feverish character, to bring parties together and get the process moving (Gaventa & Cornwall, 2015). Brokering under such circumstances is obliged to bring latent notions of community in the open, unacknowledged master signifiers. It rests on a willingness or a capacity to engender a willingness to re-examine or at least temporarily suspend deeply held ideas and power relations (Mouffe, 2000).

Not all brokers are cut from the same cloth. There's a crucial difference between brokers who bring together what was separated before and those who have an (initial) vision for a process of community healing, or even for future directions for the community. How much power a broker should hold cannot be decided by outsiders, yet it can suffice to say that powerful brokers rely on trust and that such trust comes with risks. When brokers come with their own agenda, this might be a strategy that is entirely unselfish, and later hailed as visionary, but situations occur when the broker is self-interested, just clever enough to hide it (Ferguson, 1990; Li, 2007).

If our goal is to enhance transparency and accountability at national ministries, there might be entirely different understandings of what that means, how it important it is, and how to achieve it. Transparency and accountability measures can be destabilizing, expensive, counterproductive, ideologically colored and insensitive to the discretion and flexibility needed for effective and strategic governance. Political fault lines might be visible, as in party ideologies, but also tense relations between the regions and the capital, competition and organizational cultures at and between ministries. When a country must respond to international partners, a former speaker of parliament, less associated with current tensions, embarks on a brokering mission.

Translator

If communities cannot respond to sustainability challenges anymore, it is likely that both a broker and a translator are needed. Parties must be brought together, people left in the shade brought in, rifts healed. Translation finds uses beyond brokering though, as what might be helpful to the community might not be known and understood. Experts and other knowledges might be around but not understood, stories that might already explain the predicament of their community might have been told before, but did not register, as it did not seem relevant (Schön, 2017).

A translator can therefore still act beyond translation itself, as what needs to be translated, how, for whom, can be understood in various ways, which stand for different versions of the role and associate with different qualities. A rather passive expert interpreter might wait for leaders to ask questions, or for experts or knowledgeable locals to seek advice and help in convincing leadership of the value of their understandings. What might occur is the translation of one sort of expert knowledge in simpler terms, or, in more complex cases, the synthesis of diverse types of expertise into a story that makes sense for leadership or community (Czarniawska, 2004). In such situation, we are not dealing with a translation in the literal sense, but with a refitting of knowledge into a different perspective, and the adaptation of the knowledge to the narrative world of the audience. Which could be a process of metaphorization itself, resting on analogies to familiar experiences expressed in known stories (Latour, 2009; Mosse, 2005).

More ambitious, yet common among leadership is for the translator to assemble a truly new story, by bringing in and reinterpreting ideas that are either foreign, or local but misunderstood. The shock of the new is hoped to produce an insight, which tends to work better when building on the familiar, to come to an entirely unexpected conclusion (Foucault, 2003). What was felt as logical can be shaken up, new characters introduce themselves, moralities are turned upside down, yet the defamiliarizing narrative cannot ignore or belittle the local lifeworld. A story questioning local values and traditions, possibly community identity, must come from a deeply trusted translator, thus from people who have been more than that, and such story has to be deeply rooted in the values and realities of the people they ask to reassess some other aspects of those realities (Ganz, 2009a; Latour, 2018).

Telling stories, knowing the people and the community, developing extensive networks, relating to the outside world and assessing risk thus combine in translators who are leaders in difficult circumstances. The sage, one can say, is often a translator, a translator under high pressure, one not relinquishing ambitions for the community, but realizing that it might have to change. Some leading interpreters take initiative on several fronts, bringing people together who did not speak before, connecting sitting experts with new ones, establishing new links with the larger world and its stories. If there is an initial analysis of the issues and the knowledge missing, the entrepreneurial translator might hunt down people who might hold that knowledge, or who might already provide a first translation of key issues untold in dominant stories. Others might be in a better position than the interpreter to be heard loud and clear, or to offer a version that finds a listening ear (Westley et al., 2009). Possibly, the interpreter is the true author, who finds someone to provide support, in a different language, from a different position, which might just create the resonance that kicks the community into action (Mulgan, 2009).

If encouraging lifelong learning is a sustainability goal, the stories to be told in different directions can diverge significantly, and the function of translator must broaden. Leadership refraining from blunt measures that would antagonize partners needed in the long run, needs creative storytelling that empathizes with the position of each actor. Political ideologues routinely suspicious of government spending and power might be sensitive to the argument that robust economies nowadays are dynamic economies, and that both policy and education must adapt, that more, newer and more diverse skills are needed.

Therapist

Sometimes, the role of interpreter slides into that of a therapist. For us, a therapist aims at reinterpretation of problems, of community and environment, by the community itself, without imposing any external perspective. When leaders assist and guide the community as translator by offering an interpretation of the situation that makes systems relations and futures visible, by forging stories that make sense of sustainability, we would still call such role translator. When a leader seemingly offers more question than answers but uses those questions to engender and guide a process of self-reflection, with the community, within governance, within leadership itself, we would speak of therapy (Gruezmacher et al., 2025). Self-reflection can be a matter of a few deep or difficult conversations within leadership, and it can take the form of a more structured self-analysis in the community, which can include public debate, conversations in smaller circles and organizations, exhibitions, theatre and historiography. Leadership can trigger forms of organizing to enable and sustain such activities (Scharmer, 2009; Wheatley, 2010).

Not every community is interested in or ready for therapeutic leadership and readiness is not correlated with the depth of the troubles people are in. On the brink of disaster, communities might cling to unsustainable activities, ideas and stories, forms of governance more than ever. What might also transpire is the opposite, a new opening for reflection, cracks appearing in the certainties that have been constructed, maybe over generations (Giddens, 2009). If people feel they are lectured, especially by leadership only half trusted or felt as semi-outsider, this can aggravate distrust or alienation. When this lecturing turns into a questioning of core community values, things get ugly quickly. A therapist role, then, hinges crucially on an accurate reading of the situation, and on the ability to allow for *self*-reflection within groups, for most answers and many questions to arise from a group dynamic where a series of minimal interventions can gently enable the continuation of analysis and lead to a deeper interrogation of self (Homer-Dixon, 2010).

Self-analysis can bring leadership, governance and slowly, through intermediaries, the whole community to a reinterpretation of identity narratives, of stories about past and future, relations with the environment (Campbell, 1992). Blind spots, questionable or now untenable assumptions can reveal themselves, trust in parties and people that never deserved them can finally crumble, while marginalized voices and alternative stories can come to the surface. The reasons for neglect and marginalization, for misplaced and denied trust might assert themselves; affects and master signifiers disavowed for a long time might rear their head, become recognizable, as objects of reflection (Cottam, 2018). Cracks in master narratives offer opportunities for new narration. Self-analysis, with some guidance, endeavors to bring about reinterpretation of self, to get unstuck from mucky stories and to overcome self-limitation. Indeed, stories enable and disable; they open up worlds and close paths to the future (Mouffe, 2011).

Communities, in this manner, can disentangle the narratives they live. They might trace the coupled narratives and metaphors shaping their thinking and organizing. As this can be painful, leadership must be sensitive to signs that people are ready to ask questions, to submit to doubt and interrogate what has defined them (Butler, 2004; Erikson, 1994). Even without asking poignant questions, and even where conditions for a structured self-reflection are not there, leadership can be helpful in a therapeutic sense, by *refraining from confirming master narratives*, by withholding reassurance of the sort people might be asking for (Scharmer, 2009). No, we are not certain that all will be good, and we will not say that our traditions and truths might give the answer. Maintaining hope and optimism is possible without dwelling in the false safeties of an old narrative home (Bion, 2003; Zizek, 2011).

Concluding: Analyzing and Crafting Stories

Sustainability leadership, as it appears gradually in our analysis, relies on interpretation, and it requires interpretation. Stories and metaphors help us to understand sustainability leadership, and they help sustainability leadership to understand governance and sustainability, and to convince people of necessary interventions and policy directions. Leadership becomes possible in coupled traditions of thinking and organizing but often succeeds in modifying those traditions (Barrett et al., 1995). Which roles of leadership are possible and desirable appears in those traditions, which leadership functions come at a premium is determined through these coupled lineages (Czarniawska, 2004). Roles that make sense in a context can be grasped through

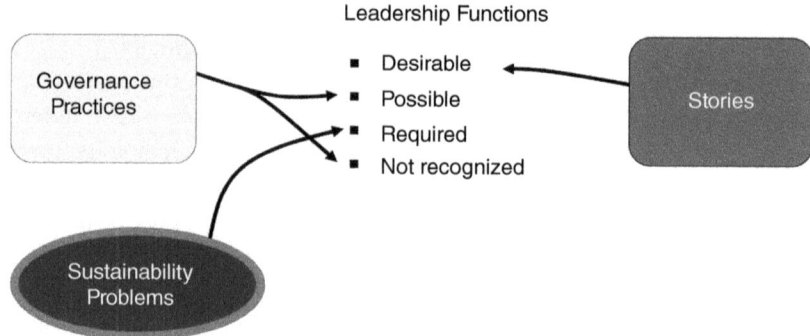

Figure 6.4 Stories will influence the desired leadership functions, while existing governance practices determine which leadership functions are feasible, including some that may not yet be recognized as such. Furthermore, sustainability challenges will shape the leadership functions that become necessary or required.

metaphors, and those metaphors can be for internal consumption, for use by leadership, or rather, for communities to make sense of the leadership they have and desire (Alvesson & Spicer, 2010; Bevir, 2013; Thornton et al., 2012) (Figure 6.4).

Sustainability leadership takes place in and for sustainability governance, as steering communities in a more sustainable direction happens in and through governance. Where good sustainability governance does not exist, leadership assists in bringing it into being, and where it does exist, it contributes to its functioning, to the articulation and implementation of policies, plans and laws that rebalance communities and their environment. It means that sustainability leadership first of all needs to understand what the basic conditions of good sustainability governance are, and how they can be built, contextualized and put into action (Van Assche et al., 2024).

Traditions of thinking and organizing, paths of governance and their dependencies need to be firmly grasped by aspiring sustainability leadership. Assessing which leadership roles and functions are active, which ones are missing and realistic, will be part and parcel of leadership itself, as simply stepping into current patterns of roles and functions is likely not enough to move a community in a more sustainable direction. Roles might be assembled, transformed, or even created, whereby new stories might inspire new roles and vice versa. If not stories but current practices are partly aligned with sustainability goals, those practices can inspire new stories and possibly leadership roles (Scharmer & Kaufer, 2013; Westley et al., 2011).

Leaders analyze and craft stories. Crafting without analyzing will cause a misfiring of initiatives, and analyzing without crafting will engender its own problems, including a risk of blind technocracy. Some stories and metaphors can be tested in small circles and limited applications, while the crafting of other stories is a rather open and continuous process. What we can call *narrative judgment* brings together a set of related qualities: Discerning which stories are relevant for the topic at hand, which ones are harder to dislodge than others and how and where crafting of alternative stories might take place. Analyzing stories thus supports the crafting of stories and analyzing them has to consider the contexts of governance and community (Boje, 2008). Understanding governance and community, their relations, as well as the social-ecological relations relevant to sustainability, supports navigating governance and community, and, from there, possibly transforming them.

Some of the leadership functions we discussed as helpful in building and managing what we recognized as good sustainability governance pertain more to the analysis of stories, others to the study of governance and community or to their navigation and transformation, an effort where the crafting of stories comes into play again. Each feature of good sustainability governance comes with different pressures for leadership, in terms of building it, or translating it into sustainability action. As we discussed, some features rely heavily on the others, and the closer we come to the issue of strategic capacity, the more we must assume regarding the other conditions (Folke et al., 2005; Walker et al., 2004). When sustainability leadership recognizes the need for strategy, yet capacity is weak, it faces the daunting task of building institutional, observational, reflexive and adaptive capacity as well, since all these features function as imbricated infrastructures for strategy. Cunning Machiavellians might be able to push the right levers and tell the right stories to get a strategy accepted and under way yet considering long-term sustainability will still bring back the question of strategic *capacity*, to enable new initiatives, rooted in solid observation and self-observation.

While communities, in democratic polities, decide for themselves what sustainability could mean, how important it is and how to pursue it, we would argue that leadership envisioning sustainability cannot escape the duty to make collective futures, as threats and as alluring possibilities, visible to the community (Giddens, 2009; Jonas, 1984). Threats without hope cannot inspire collective action consistently, while overly emotional discourse and deep self-reflection cannot be maintained over the longer term either, just as broad and intensive public participation can be harnessed only selectively, at defining moments, for key decisions. In this task, stories come front and center, and familiarity with the fabric of narrative and affect upholding the community makes it easier to discern which stories might be foregrounded, so what ensues is neither slumber nor mayhem, neither technocratic utopianism nor misguided denial or defeatism. Taken literally, sustainability leadership is a utopian enterprise. Understood in interpretive perspective, it knows the dangers of literalism, technocracy and utopianism alike.

References

Agrawal, A. (2005). *Environmentality: Technologies of Government and Political Subjects*. Duke University Press.

Alvesson, M., & Spicer, A. (2010). *Metaphors We Lead By: Understanding Leadership in the Real World*. Routledge.

Alvesson, M., & Spicer, A. (2016). *The Stupidity Paradox: The Power and Pitfalls of Functional Stupidity at Work*. Profile Books.

Andrews, M. (2013). *The Limits of Institutional Reform in Development: Changing Rules for Realistic Solutions*. Cambridge University Press.

Arendt, H. (2019). *The Human Condition*. University of Chicago Press.

Barrett, F. J., Thomas, G. F., & Hocevar, S. P. (1995). The central role of discourse in large-scale change: A social construction perspective. *The Journal of Applied Behavioral Science*, 31(3), 352–372.

Beck, U., Giddens, A., & Lash, S. (1994). *Reflexive Modernization: Politics, Tradition and Aesthetics in the Modern Social Order*. Stanford University Press.

Beer, M. (2023). Developing a sustainable high-commitment, high-performance system of organizing, managing, and leading: An actionable systems theory of change and development. In *Research in Organizational Change and Development* (world; Vol. 30, pp. 95–128). Harvard Business School Working Paper, No. 23-016, September 2022. Emerald Publishing Limited.

Bennett, J. (2010). *Vibrant Matter: A Political Ecology of Things*. Duke University Press.

Berkes, F. (2017). *Sacred Ecology* (4th ed.). Routledge.
Berkes, F., Colding, J., & Folke, C. (Eds.). (2002). *Navigating Social-Ecological Systems: Building Resilience for Complexity and Change*. Cambridge University Press.
Bevir, M. (2013). *A Theory of Governance*. University of California Press.
Bion, W. R. (2003). *Experiences in Groups: And Other Papers*. Routledge.
Boje, D. M. (2008). *Storytelling Organizations*. SAGE Publications Ltd.
Butler, J. (2004). *Precarious Life: The Powers of Mourning and Violence*. Verso.
Campbell, D. (1992). *Writing Security: United States Foreign Policy and the Politics of Identity*. U of Minnesota Press.
Cottam, H. (2018). *Radical Help: How We Can Remake the Relationships Between Us and Revolutionise the Welfare State*. Little, Brown Book Group.
Czarniawska, B. (2004). *Narratives in Social Science Research*. Sage.
Czarniawska, B., & Joerges, B. C. (1997). *Narrating the Organization: Dramas of Institutional Identity*. University of Chicago Press.
Dobson, A. (2007). *Green Political Thought* (4th ed.). Routledge.
Douglas, M., & Wildavsky, A. (1982). *Risk and Culture. An Essay on the Selection of Technical and Environmental Dangers*. University of California Press.
Dryzek, J. S. (2013). *The Politics of the Earth: Environmental Discourses*. Oxford University Press.
Erikson, K. (1994). *A New Species of Trouble: Explorations in Disaster, Trauma, and Community*. Norton.
Esposito, R. (2019). *Politics and Negation: Towards an Affirmative Philosophy* (Z. Hanafi, Trans.). Polity.
Ferguson, J. (1990). *The Anti-politics Machine: "Development," Depoliticization and Bureaucratic Power in Lesotho*. CUP Archive.
Fischer, F. (2009). *Democracy and Expertise: Reorienting Policy Inquiry*. OUP Oxford.
Fisher, R., Ury, W. L., & Patton, B. (2011). *Getting to Yes: Negotiating Agreement Without Giving In*. Penguin.
Flyvbjerg, B. (2011). *Making Social Science Matter: Why Social Inquiry Fails and How It Can Succeed Again* (S. Sampson, Trans.; 13. printing). Cambridge University Press.
Folke, C., Hahn, T., Olsson, P., & Norberg, J. (2005). Adaptive governance of social-ecological systems. *Annual Review of Environment and Resources*, *30*, 441–473.
Foucault, M. (2003). *Society Must Be Defended: Lectures At the College de France, 1975–76*. Allen Lane The Penguin Press.

Ganz, M. (2009a). *What is Public Narrative: Self*. Harvard Library.
Ganz, M. (2009b, March 1). *Why Stories Matter*. Sojourners.
Gaventa, J., & Cornwall, A. (2015). Power and knowledge. In H. Bradbury-Huang, (Ed.), *The SAGE Handbook of Action Research* (Vol. 3, pp. 465–471). Sage Thousand Oaks, CA.
Giddens, A. (2009). *Politics of Climate Change*. Polity.
Grindle, M. S. (2004). Good enough governance: Poverty reduction and reform in developing countries. *Governance, 17*(4), 525–548.
Gruezmacher, M., & Van Assche, K. (2022). *Crafting Strategies for Sustainable Local Development*. InPlanning.
Gruezmacher, M., Vodden, K., Lowery, B., Hudson, A., & Assche, K. V. (2025). *Reimagining Resources and Community Development: Lessons from Newfoundland and Labrador*. Routledge.
Hall, P. A. (1993). Policy paradigms, social learning, and the state: The case of economic policymaking in Britain. *Comparative Politics, 25*(3), 275–296.
Haynes, P. (2015). *Managing Complexity in the Public Services* (2nd ed.). Routledge.
Homer-Dixon, T. (2010). *The Upside of Down: Catastrophe, Creativity, and the Renewal of Civilization*. Island Press.
Jasanoff, S. (2004). *States of Knowledge: The Co-Production of Science and the Social Order*. Routledge.
Jonas, H. (1984). *The Imperative of Responsibility: In Search of an Ethics for the Technological Age*. University of Chicago Press.
Latour, B. (2009). *Politics of Nature*. Harvard University Press.
Latour, B. (2017). *Facing Gaia: Eight Lectures on the New Climatic Regime*. John Wiley & Sons.
Latour, B. (2018). *Down to Earth: Politics in the New Climatic Regime*. John Wiley & Sons.
Leichenko, R., & O'Brien, K. (2008). *Environmental Change and Globalization: Double Exposures*. Oxford University Press.
Leiserowitz, A. (2006). Climate change risk perception and policy preferences: The role of affect, imagery, and values. *Climatic Change, 77*(1), 45–72.
Li, T. M. (2007). *The Will to Improve: Governmentality, Development, and the Practice of Politics*. Duke University Press.
Lorenzini, S. (2022). Barbara ward and the transformative power of the Stockholm conference at the birth of sustainable development. *Annals of the Fondazione Luigi Einaudi, 56*, 91–108.
Luhmann, N. (1989). *Ecological Communication*. University of Chicago Press.
Luhmann, N. (1990). *Political Theory in the Welfare State*. De Gruyter.
Luhmann, N. (2017). *Risk: A Sociological Theory*. Routledge.

Marshall, G. (2014). *Don't Even Think About It: Why Our Brains Are Wired to Ignore Climate Change*. Bloomsbury Publishing USA.
Merriënboer, J. C. F. J. van. (2014). Sicco Mansholt and "Limits to Growth." In C. Hiepel (Ed.), *Europe in a Globalising World: Global Challenges and European Responses in the "long" 1970s* (pp. 319–342). Nomos.
Mintzberg, H. (1994). *Rise and Fall of Strategic Planning*. Simon and Schuster.
Moore, M. H. (1997). *Creating Public Value: Strategic Management in Government*. Harvard University Press.
Mosse, D. (2005). *Cultivating Development: An Ethnography of Aid Policy and Practice*. Pluto Press.
Mouffe, C. (2000). *The Democratic Paradox*. Verso.
Mouffe, C. (2011). *On the Political*. Routledge.
Mulgan, G. (2009). *The Art of Public Strategy: Mobilizing Power and Knowledge for the Common Good*. OUP Oxford.
Myers, D. H. (2020). *Sustainability in Business: A Financial Economics Analysis*. Palgrave Macmillan.
Nixon, R. (2011). *Slow Violence and the Environmentalism of the Poor*. Harvard University Press.
North, D. (1990). *Institutions, Institutional Change and Economic Performance*. Cambridge University Press.
Reed, P. (2016). *Acid Rain and the Rise of the Environmental Chemist in Nineteenth-Century Britain* (0 ed.). Routledge.
Scharmer, C. O. (2009). *Theory U: Learning from the Future as It Emerges*. Berrett-Koehler Publishers.
Scharmer, O., & Kaufer, K. (2013). *Leading from the Emerging Future: From Ego-System to Eco-System Economies*. Berrett-Koehler Publishers.
Schön, D. A. (2017). *The Reflective Practitioner: How Professionals Think in Action*. Routledge.
Scott, J. C. (2008). *Weapons of the Weak: Everyday Forms of Peasant Resistance*. Yale University Press.
Seidl, D. (2016). *Organisational Identity and Self-transformation: An Autopoietic Perspective*. Routledge.
Shiva, V. (2018). Earth democracy: Sustainability, justice, and peace. *Buffalo Environmental Law Journal, 26*, 1.
Solnit, R. (2009). *A Paradise Built in Hell: The Extraordinary Communities That Arise in Disaster*. Penguin Books.
Stirling, A. (2010). Keep it complex. *Nature, 468*(7327), 1029–1031.
Thornton, P. H., Ocasio, W., & Lounsbury, M. (2012). *The Institutional Logics Perspective: A New Approach to Culture, Structure, and Process*. OUP Oxford.

Van Assche, K., Beunen, R., & Duineveld, M. (2013). *Evolutionary Governance Theory: An Introduction*. Springer.
Van Assche, K., Beunen, R., & Gruezmacher, M. (2024). *Strategy for Sustainability Transitions: Governance, Community and Environment*. Edward Elgar Publishing.
Van Assche, K., Gruezmacher, M., & Deacon, L. (2020). Land use tools for tempering boom and bust: Strategy and capacity building in governance. *Land Use Policy, 93*, 103994–103994.
Walker, B., Holling, C. S., Carpenter, S. R., & Kinzig, A. (2004). Resilience, adaptability and transformability in social–ecological systems. *Ecology and Society, 9*(2), 5: [online] URL: www.ecologyandsociety.org/-5
Weible, C. M., & Sabatier, P. A. (2018). *Theories of the Policy Process*. Routledge.
Weick, K. E. (1988). Enacted sensemaking in crisis situations. *Journal of Management Studies, 25*(4), 305–317.
Welzer, H. (2017). *Climate Wars: What People Will Be Killed For in the 21st Century* (P. Camiller, Trans.). Polity.
Westley, F., Olsson, P., Folke, C., Homer-Dixon, T., Vredenburg, H., Loorbach, D., Thompson, J., Nilsson, M., Lambin, E., Sendzimir, J., Banerjee, B., Galaz, V., & van der Leeuw, S. (2011). Tipping toward sustainability: Emerging pathways of transformation. *AMBIO, 40*(7), 762–780.
Westley, F., Zimmerman, B., & Patton, M. (2009). *Getting to Maybe: How the World Is Changed*. Random House of Canada.
Wheatley, M. J. (2010). *Turning to One Another*. ReadHowYouWant.com.
Whittington, R. (2006). Completing the practice turn in strategy research. *Organization Studies, 27*(5), 613–634.
Wiek, A., & Lang, D. J. (2016). Transformational sustainability research methodology. In H. Heinrichs, P. Martens, G. Michelsen, & A. Wiek (Eds.), *Sustainability Science: An Introduction* (pp. 31–41). Springer Netherlands.
Zizek, S. (2011). *Living in the End Times*. Verso Books.

7 | *Sustainability Leadership and Strategy*

Community Strategy and Narrative Leadership

Sustainability appears in discourse when underlying issues become evident – particularly when multiple challenges reveal their interconnected nature. Responding to complex and interrelated problems requires a strategy that integrates policy instruments and stories that engage with a wide range of concerns, interests and sensitivities (Ostrom, 1990). Strong emotions will flare when stories and values are touched that framed a reality believed to be stable. A community strategy, as we introduced it, is a story and an institution, a way of thinking and organizing an institution moreover that integrates a set of other institutions, some old and some new, which support a series of policy directions embedded in the narrative (Figure 7.1).

If we forget the institutional side and focus on the content of the story or the rousing effect on the masses, we might lose track of the connectivity with existing implementation tools. A story might have to be modified when it implies the existence of institutions that in reality still must be enacted. Some such tools might not be legal, others might be politically costly to get accepted, and in other cases, the tools might be there but less powerful than imagined. Policies might be in place that theoretically could cohere in strategy, but in practice represent incompatible constituencies and ideologies, in governance and beyond.

A narrative thus needs support from institutions in the pursuit of a desired community future. Conversely, a narrative might endow institutions with the appearance of cohesion and might even show absences in the institutional framework as deplorable and illogical gaps (Czarniawska, 2004; Wagenaar, 2011). Stories can mobilize affect and move the passive to action. Institutions can appear as logically connected but also as imbued with emotion when they seem to sprout from driving narratives. Stories, we know by now, connect

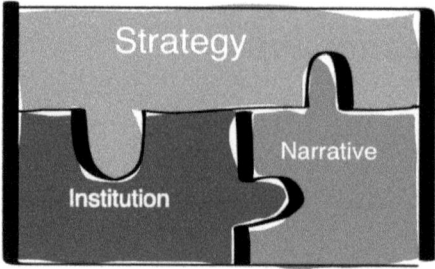

Figure 7.1 A strategy goes beyond being just a story or a set of instructions for achieving a goal. It must function as an institution, serving as a tool for coordination in governance that typically involves other institutions. At the same time, it needs to be a compelling narrative supported by the institutions intended to contribute to a desired future for the community. This narrative should establish a logical connection among these institutions – policies, laws and plans – making them appear as a cohesive framework rather than a disjointed series of efforts. Furthermore, the narrative must be persuasive, resonating with governance practices and with the community itself. This means it should align with the community's understanding of problems, concepts of good governance and their reality.

thinking and organizing through more than one thread, which makes them powerful in shaping our communities and our identities. They link cognition and affect, make sense of past and present, and allow us to look at the future as a community.

All of which renders it natural that a story should be at the heart of community strategy. It also suggests strongly that the pressures on such a story to perform are exceedingly high. Stories driving strategy must be persuasive in governance and in the community, so connectivity to circulating interpretations of problems, of good governance is prime (Hajer, 1995; Leach et al., 2010). In the end, the task is an unlikely yet possible one: Transforming reality as felt in the community, even changing the idea of community, while maintaining myriad threads to the realities of thinking and organizing in that community.

What is crafted by strategists as a story of sustainability must thread another narrow path; that between the particular and the universal. While a sustainability story needs to be contextualized, it needs to invoke the universal in at least two ways. Communities might be proud and stubbornly attached to their identities and understandings of the world and might go against the grain even where this risks

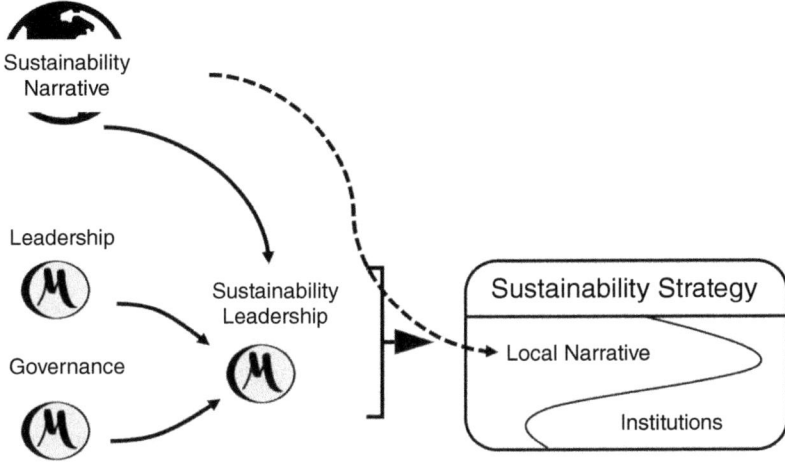

Figure 7.2 Sustainability strategies require a localized sustainability narrative, and the process of localization, of crafting a context-sensitive version of sustainability, is not an easy one. More generally widely circulating sustainability narratives can be an input, but crafting a local strategy resting on a localized narrative has to go through governance, where other narratives are persuasive and requires sustainability leadership, as the governance structures and procedures by themselves are unlikely to produce a viable strategy. The metaphors structuring the understanding of leadership, governance, and sustainability leadership will affect this process of crafting new narratives and strategies.

disaster (Figure 7.2). Yet an exhortation to change in the name of sustainability cannot restrict itself to local arguments. Yes, we need to see and feel for ourselves what is so urgent and why we need to transform our communities, but the authority cannot solely rest on ourselves (Jasanoff, 2016; Sen, 2008).

External authorities trusted to represent a truth or neutral intelligence reinforce our local stories, and if international scientific and policy networks are distrusted or happily ignored, people turn to God or an alternative science to guarantee the compatibility of the particular and the universal. The second path to the universal is more direct, when we need to feel that we can also experience directly the truth of our stories, that we don't merely *say* something but also *see* it, experience it more directly (Giddens, 2009). Narrative worlds can be closed, but never perfectly so; they can be cohesive, but only to a degree. One can identify with them, but only so far. Which means that cracks, insecurities and dissociations can always assert themselves, and one way of maintaining internal cohesion and identification is to lean on the larger world, either through bigger stories endowed with authority, or through a story that stories can be bypassed, that we can know for ourselves when something is real and telling us it needs new stories. Hence, local realities ignoring sustainability issues can still crumble under the weight of experience and stories in the environment, while a sustainability narrative under pressure can lean on these sources of confirmation.

Doubt can easily creep in when an old order shows cracks, but a new one is not in sight locally. A Canadian forestry community dependent on an organization around large paper mills employing most of the population, controlling vast tracts of forest and indirectly, local government, is shaken up by the gradual closing of the mill. The population shrinks, tax revenue plummets and two sets of consultants and entrepreneurs show up: one arguing for a future revolving around tourism and a reinvented forestry, the other one focusing on innovation. As the story of reinvented forestry, less reliant on central players, giving more space to ecological principles and diversity, to non-timber products and to recreative use, sounds utterly alien and no trusted authorities are in place to convince locals, they reject it. Tourism does not register as a real economy, rethinking forestry feels impossible and lingering trauma of the mill closure contributes to its rejection. Meanwhile, "innovation" is utterly unclear, but vague and different enough to invite projection and desire, and it seems backed up by Provincial authorities and their strategies, counting on innovation to diversify the economy. (Gruezmacher & Van Assche, 2022)

Both localization and universalization are finicky affairs, where leadership with narrative finesse cannot be missed. Widely circulating stories about sustainability or any of the problems the signifier tends to cover can serve as input and support, but, even if small leadership circles create the narrative, it needs to go through governance, where other narratives and concerns play out. Sustainability leadership almost certainly will have to play a role in the crafting of narrative, either inside or outside larger governance networks, and in piloting the story through those networks without overly modifying it, or watering down its capacities to discern problems and offer solutions (Dobson, 2007; Eckersley, 2004).

Retelling, repackaging, splitting and recombining with other persuasive stories are part of the repertoire of leadership. Styles, media and genres can be diversified, and this applies to all stages of the strategy process. Preparatory stages, where leadership has to convince governance of the need for strategy, even of the building of strategic capacity, can see a mobilization of media, a harnessing of research, an encouragement of self-organization in society, all aiming to persuade governance and community that, yes, we finally need to look forward and address our problems collectively (Fischer, 2003; Latour, 2009). More articles appear on our damaged environment, old ministry reports are suddenly released and friendly civil society organizations make demands.

Proliferating initiatives of this sort serve more than one purpose. They reinforce and extend the networks knowledgeable and supportive of the strategy. A whiff of clientelism might be detected, as many versions and customized fragments, applications and specifications of the narrative embody a client-centered approach to governance: "What can our strategy do for you? What does it mean for your situation?" Sometimes, lines blur, and customizing stories becomes crafting of stories for customers, which can undermine the strategy. A third reason for a flurry of stories is that it can create an impression of pervasiveness and, it is hoped, irreversibility. Both the goal of contextualized sustainability, and the path, represented by the strategy, can acquire an aura of unavoidability.

Soviet collectivization in agriculture was sold as a precondition for communist development. In an early stage, agriculture had to support industrial development, which in turn could drive the modernization of Soviet society, a modernization which was deemed essential to stabilize the regime. The grand communist experiment, in other words, was considered unsustainable without modernization, or, as Lenin put it "electrification." Industrialization, large infrastructure works, education and research were floating, in early Soviet times, on the cork of collective agriculture. Problem was that everybody hated it. Coercion was necessary to remove people from their land and relocate them into agro-industrial villages. This process was far from smooth, leading to hunger as exports were prioritized over feeding the population. Sustainability of the state, with the state a guarantor of better future, prevailed over hunger in the present. Soviet authorities were not entirely dependent on coercion, and they flooded the zone with more panache than anyone: propaganda was everywhere, from school education to factory learning, labor organization, research, in canteens, youth organizations, media, literature and movies. Novels about collectivization, movies about the perfect farm, about villainous old landowners or lazy peasants, reinforced messaging about progress and loyalty at farm meetings. Irreversibility of the process had to be naturalized. (Fitzpatrick, 1992).

Naturalization, Reality Effects and Goal Dependencies

Naturalization, or the gradual reconstruction of contingent discourse as natural and uncontestable, can come about in many ways. Cultures naturalize their realities by telling stories and developing sign systems believed to be anchored in external reality (Jasanoff, 2004; Stone, 2012). Governance systems can naturalize by force, by accident or by reflecting and reinforcing what people already believed. Governance crafts and tells stories and encodes them in institutions that add a patina of necessity, endow them with an absolute and sometimes timeless character. Before that, the community needs to be convinced that such institution is required, and in the case of a sustainability strategy this might take effort, as one might only perceive the need when dominant narratives and master signifiers have been weakened.

Leadership thus must discern carefully what is more prone to naturalization, and extensive networks and cultural sensitivity prove helpful here too. What appears most in line with what people already believe, or what they might want to believe, can be the problem definition espoused by strategy, but elsewhere the solutions offered, the method of analysis, or the broad outlines of the story about the future can be starting points for an acceptance of the idea of strategy, or a particular strategy. Each can serve as support for the strategy, by offering rather easy naturalization of one element of the strategy, a base from which the rest can be built.

What can serve as a jumping off point, and a spot of blue, for strategy might also be a place of comfort or discomfort, a crack in the certainties of the community which opens minds for exploration, or rather a feeling of profound ease with the culture, and the achievements of the community, inspiring confidence that "we can manage this." Maybe paradoxically, both overconfidence and creeping doubt can prove productive in the exploration of new challenges. Doubt can allow for a questioning of certainties, a weakening of master narratives, and from there an acceptance of further self-analysis, which can be the basis of a reorientation to sustainability (Bevir, 2011). Overconfidence, on the other hand, might inspire action, a courageous head-on approach to new problems on the horizon, and a willingness to mobilize resources and devise new coordination mechanisms along the way. Of course, not all overconfidence is productive; we are not talking about blunt denials of sustainability as a problem, or blithe ignorance about the need for collective action (Schön, 2017; Sunstein, 2005).

Curiosity might be a driver, as it can sit well with an openness to discover both problems and opportunities, or just to refine a collective understanding of the world. If curiosity is a shared value, chances are that people share a basic awareness that the world is a big place, and that social-ecological systems are rather complex. Curious communities tend to guard themselves naturally against the worst excesses of naturalization, against the tyranny of master signifiers. Absolute certainties rarely appear when one is curious, and closure of the minds and the community as such less likely to manifest itself (Landes, 1999; March, 1994). Not being an easy prey to Machiavellian naturalization, they can be supportive of the exploration of new horizons, which might, alas, lead to the discovery of sustainability issues ignored heretofore.

What the community sees, feels and desires as reality thus greatly affects its susceptibility to sustainability strategy, an insight priming leadership to finely attune to those realities. An unwillingness to recognize new realities, to stray from codified problem definitions, might require leadership to probe that unwillingness first, to trigger hopefully a new curiosity or flexibility, associated with either doubt or confidence, even overconfidence. If leadership is convinced that sustainability is a real issue, and we believe it should, the moral imperative to take it seriously asserts itself, the obligation to convince community and governance that a strategy is needed.

Where communities are aware of problems, and open to question assumptions about community and environment, anxiety might produce restless discourse and obstacles to collective action. Here, leadership has openings to intervene more forcefully, through new narratives which can offer interpretation and direction. Stories can anchor affect, provide emotional stability, when they acknowledge the anxiety, yet offer clear alternatives, in delineation of problems and solutions. Sustainability leadership is often allaying of anxieties, through listening and storytelling, trust building and gradual opening of perspectives with fears settling down (Macy & Johnstone, 2012; Senge et al., 2010).

When economies collapse, and poverty is on the horizon, tempers understandably flare. Old ethnic and religious divisions, which might have been patched up in a collage state where each was granted dominion over certain territories, governmental actors and policy domains, assert themselves with vigor, reviving old conflicts. Sustainability policy in the most obvious sense here is not to speak of sustainability, a distraction, but to manage conflict and stabilize the state. State collapse and civil war will undoubtedly deteriorate the economic situation, heralding times of hunger and hatred, of foreign alliances and interventions that make the internal differences unbridgeable.

Governance systems, in many of their manifestations, have the power not just of telling stories and writing rules, but also of shaping physical environments. Hence, we speak of *reality effects* of strategy as more than discursive naturalization (Van Assche et al., 2024). Reality effects, aligning here with evolutionary governance theory, are both discursive and physical in nature. If strategy transforms an environment, this can support not only the idea that the strategy works, or at least does something. It can also signify that the version of reality represented by the strategy, is *the* reality. Discursive and material reality effects can be mutually reinforcing, as when a discursive consensus or coalition has formed around strategy narrative, and the early results of the strategy seem to confirm it. Both the nature of the solution ("well under way") and the character of the problem can be reaffirmed; both can consolidate in conjunction (Dean, 2013). Each intervention in the name of strategy can focus the attention of media, government experts, academics and consultants on the problems looked for, the problems as framed in the strategy.

Reality effects can be intentional and otherwise; they can align with the intention of the strategy or not. Even when they are intentional, they can be interpreted in various ways, as the materialization is always more and always less than what existed in the mind of the strategist or her more technical assistants. It is more, because material realities provide more details and context than one can predict, and less, because what is imagined is colored by fantasy and takes on a hue that will not shine through completely in the document, and less so in a physical product or intervention (Zizek, 2011). As the strategy narrative might not have a complete hold on the collective imagination, alternative master narratives likely linger on, and quite divergent interpretations are sparked. If people believed from the start that the strategy was a terrible idea, they will look for signs of failure, and each physical trace of the narrative will attract negative interpretations.

Whereas reality effects are signs of the strategy that alter the perception of reality in the community, goal dependencies (Van Assche et al., 2013) are the effects of strategy on current governance. They can be direct or indirect, indirect meaning that they take a detour via the community, where approval, critique and resistance can trigger responses in politics and administration. Direct goal dependencies are variegated themselves, as what appears in practice, within governance, is certainly not restricted to alignment with the strategy. Strategies can engender new discursive coalitions within governance, which then support yet reinterpret them; they can reshuffle power relations, with unpredictable effects in discursive competition. Enemies can be made in governance as easily as outside, and bureaucratic obstruction can quietly undermine the story about the problem and solution, or hamper implementation in its progress through complex and lengthy procedures.

Leadership in strategy for sustainability occupies a central role in efforts to naturalize a complex and inherently elusive issue. When such strategies are ambitious and involve significant transformations in governance, the issue becomes particularly challenging to address. Power relations will shift, stories will unravel and identities will be touched. We can understand strategy skills for sustainability leadership in a more precise way now and speak of a necessary and subtle management of reality effects and goal dependencies. If we want to affect the beliefs and actions of people, if we need to undertake a wide variety of physical interventions to flank this push for sustainability, we need to be aware of reality effects and goal dependencies (Van Assche et al., 2021). Managing them entails attempts, first to discern the internal and external effects of strategy, and second, to align them with strategy goals. If this proves impossible, adaptation of either goals or means of strategy is in sight.

Transitions and Trade-Offs

A second quality of sustainability leadership which can be placed under strategy skills is the *navigation of dilemmas*. If transformation of society requires transformation of governance, a restructuring beyond policy choice, the nature of institutional design and redesign will impede any simple progress. Choices must be made, and they come with trade-offs. We observed that adaptive capacity is not one-dimensional, and that neither a state of adaptation or great flexibility were virtues per se. What was stabilized by design or contingency cannot easily be transformed and dependencies in the governance path make certain transformations unlikely.

Sometimes, therefore, a trade-off becomes a dilemma, as polarized choices cannot be avoided, while each polarity comes with benefits (Van Assche et al., 2024). Institutionally favoring rapid response can reduce the quality of the response or weaken checks and balances that can protect from takeover by technocrats or populist backlash. Strategies might find momentum through centralization yet gain legitimacy and contextualization in a more local and participatory approach (Axelrod & Cohen, 2008; Meadows, 2009). Leadership entails the recognition of dilemmas and making a distinction with false polarities. False polarities appear regularly in ideological discourse, where stark choices are imposed on the audience: "you are either with us, or we go to hell" – hell being the place where an opposing ideology reigns. In such schematic stories, qualities and weaknesses of each ideology are overlooked, and real possibilities to combine elements of both are not in the picture (Zizek, 2019).

False polarities and real dilemmas are sometimes difficult to distinguish, especially in a polarized environment, where little reflexivity is allowed on either side. If leadership is interested in sustainability, it cannot solely identify with one of the discourses, if this prevents them from observing options for strategy implementation and useful varieties of institutional design. An additional dilemma appears here, as leadership might only become leadership by (pretending to) identify completely with one of the factions (Selznick, 2011). Once in power, in a position to shape strategy, this leads to two problems: Alienating the base by deploying ideas suspiciously related to enemy discourse, and reaching out beyond that base, to build support for the strategy. Easy solutions are not available, and sometimes polarization is such that even the most gifted, open-minded and subtle leadership team will lose support and face backlash.

Other dilemmas can emerge in the process of reform inspired by strategy, or in the articulation of strategy. When to open discussions and how, where to rely on more radical participation and what to formalize, in terms of decisions, and in terms of policies, plans and laws, benefits from experienced judgment. Assessing trade-offs can bring in expertise of the most diverse kinds. Technical experts, in sustainability issues and in governance reform, economists, business people can all be brought into the conversation, and leadership can benefit. Those voices can also derail the process; much consultation must happen discreetly.

Leadership Roles

Strategy and reform are unlikely to materialize without leaders as *strategist, Machiavellian and sage*. Leaders will be active as *builders*, enhancing strategic capacity, and guiding implementation and governance transformation. Some might have to play the role of *therapist*, without forgetting that is not they but the community that is interrogating assumptions and stories. *Broker and translator* roles are typically subsumed, under such conditions, by those of *storyteller*. Other roles can be integrated under this label, as strategies are assembled around a narrative core, and as sustainability itself comes within our collective grasp through new stories enabling new observations and orientations.

Leadership for sustainability, we argued, cannot make itself vanish, but is perfectly capable of stepping back once a strategy is in place. They themselves can switch roles, or make place for a new generation, attuned to the demands of a community already aware of issues, and able to live with the idea of collective strategy. Neither for them, nor for us, as observers of leadership, it is reasonable to expect that possible and desirable roles are always clear and stable. We, as outsiders, can only observe which roles seem to be helpful under which conditions, and we can metaphorically label them. We can recognize builders and therapists, sages and Machiavellians.

The capacity to listen, interpret and craft narrative takes central place for sustainability leadership, and this applies to narratives which can appear far removed from the topic of sustainability (Boje, 2008; Wheatley, 2010). Communities and governance systems understand themselves through narrative and are marked by a coevolution of stories and institutions that limit their response to problems and their susceptibility to leadership roles. Coevolution brings narrative connections into the remit of sustainability leadership that seem far-fetched for outsiders; they can render a leadership style totally unacceptable because of moves that look out of line only for insiders, that implicate stories not noticed by others.

Sustainable development can get stuck in various kinds of mud. One elementary requirement is legal identity for all, including birth registration. If legal identities are not unambiguous, all other aspects of administration and governance become ambiguous, and more prone to manipulation. If identities are not clear, people can be marginalized and mistreated more easily. If rural populations are not understood, shadow populations and shadow powers can persist, organization and representation at higher levels are less robust, which can benefit national elites. Sustainability leadership can, under such conditions, in a very real way, be represented by a small circle of people from the villages who rather quietly promote registration in places where this is not common, allay fears of retribution or abuse, and find resources to reinforce municipal administration with that very limited but essential aim. (World Bank, 2024).

Sustainability leadership, in the perspective developed in these pages, needs to assist a community in achieving good sustainability governance, and once such conditions are in place, in guiding a governance process that makes the community more sustainable. Such process entails the assemblage and implementation of a sustainability strategy, and it is more likely to succeed when strategic capacity is there, a feature of good sustainability governance which implies the presence of other features – observational, institutional and adaptive capacity and the presence of long-term perspectives in governance (Figure 7.3). Strategic capacity presupposes all others, and a central task of leadership is to build up governance to the place where it is

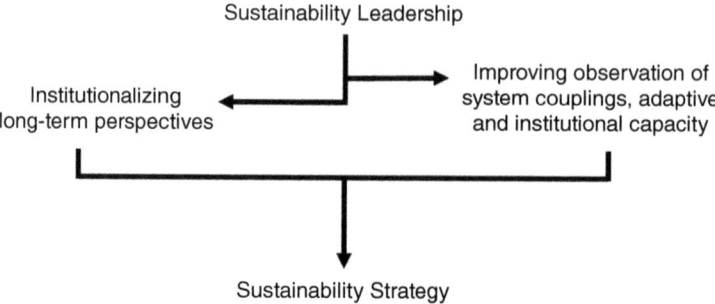

Figure 7.3 While sustainability leadership may take different forms in various communities, requiring distinct governance functions, we can identify three essential aspects of leadership that are inherent in sustainability leadership. These functions, in our opinion, are independent of the context, dominant sustainability narratives and metaphors. Sustainability leadership needs to aim at institutionalizing long-term perspectives in governance, enhancing governance and its environments' observation and articulating and implementing community strategies for sustainability.

capable to strategize. Each feature comes with its own difficulties for leadership, in terms of building and management and asks for different leadership roles and functions.

Roles, Stories and Metaphors

Metaphors help to structure our understanding of complex processes of leadership, governance and sustainability leadership, and they underpin the crafting of new narratives and strategies in this domain. Strategy stories tend to rely heavily on metaphors as they must make many assumptions and engage in complexity reduction on several terrains (Figure 7.4). Leadership is often obliged to condense, condense and condense, to get the message of a strategy or the need for strategy across with unwelcoming and disparate audiences (Denning, 2005; Weick, 1995). Metaphoric understandings of the good and real community, of good governance, leadership and sustainability are implied and deployed.

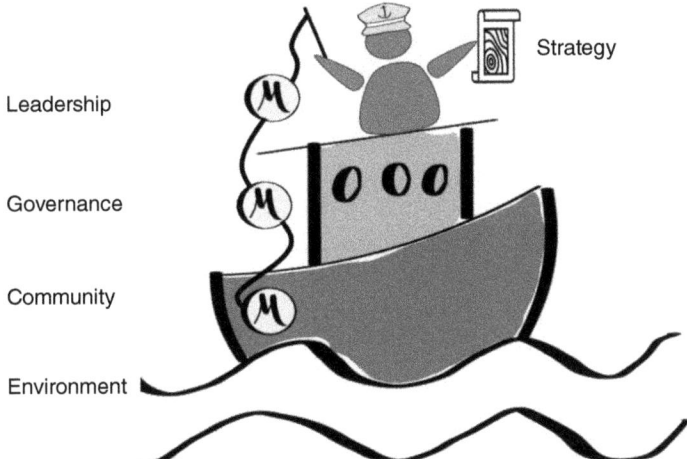

Figure 7.4 Metaphors are a common structure of governance strategies. However, it's less well-known that these strategies, such as those for sustainable development, are shaped by various metaphors. These metaphors focus on concepts like the (good, real) community, (good) governance and (good) leadership. They often revolve around other ideas and can shape our understanding of existing and desirable relationships between leadership and governance, governance and the community and the community and the physical environment.

Ideas on desirable and possible relations between governance, community and environment, and thus the balancing between them are suggested by stories and metaphors. Stories flow and connect thanks to metaphors, while they hold the power to assemble new metaphors (Lemke, 2010). Understanding the way communities relate to their environment, and which roles leadership could play in redefining that relation, is simply impossible without the simplifications of stories and metaphors. Simplification, we must remind ourselves, is not a pale reflection of a reality so much better known by science or other forms of knowing, but a process marking the human mind. Forgetting this and endowing some discourses with the power of the absolute, can only come back to bite us in the unsustainable butt.

How we are entangled with our environment cannot be established in perfect transparency and full detail, as our ways of knowing are limited, shaped by signs, and by that same environment (Luhmann, 1989). We know enough, however, to see that we are in real trouble, and that our governance systems are not equipped to discern the depth of problems we are in, let alone the way to solve them. Leadership is not a panacea, and leaders are not superhumans or angels capable to show us a brighter destiny, yet a re-examination of leadership and how it relates to the narratives that give meaning to our world, is worth the effort. Virtues and qualities of individuals and leadership networks *can* make the decisive difference, and no story about perfect institutions or mechanistic strategy should distract us from that.

In his *Discourses* (Machiavelli, 2012 [1517]), rethinking Livy's history of Rome and his ideas on the sustainability of different regimes, Machiavelli comes to an idea of distributed leadership that still functions as leadership, and to the productivity of tension: between leaders and citizens, between leaders and their administrations, between them and the structures and processes of governance upholding and assisting them. New sustainability stories ought to be tried and tested in such web of productive tensions, a hallmark of imperfect yet healthy governance. Some will be driven by plot, others more by character. Sometimes, leaders appear as main characters, as visionaries, drivers of change, even where this is only partially true. What leaders can do stems from traditions of thinking and organizing, how they are understood stems from those same traditions, and sometimes, the leadership roles that emerge as appropriate to support sustainability strategy can grossly overestimate what they can actually do (Figure 7.5). Other

Roles, Stories and Metaphors

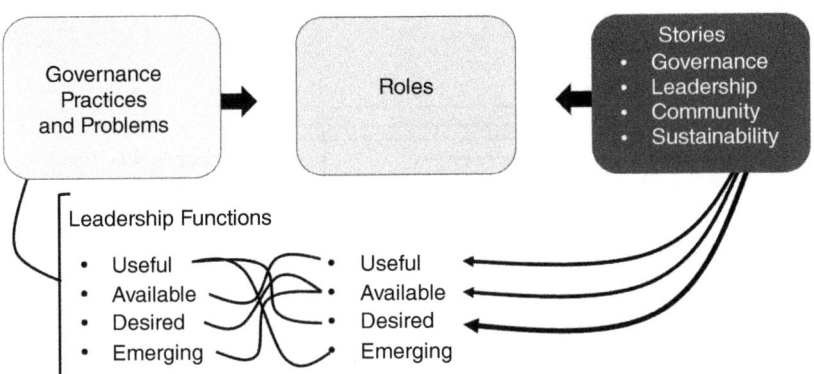

Figure 7.5 In this diagram, we do not intend to represent an ideal, smooth functioning, but rather unavoidable tensions that arise from the influence of stories on both leadership roles and functions.

conditions will make it harder for people to see that leaders can do anything, even if certain roles could greatly enhance community sustainability, would fit the specific problematic of systems relations and the governance configuration in place.

Our interpretive perspective on sustainability leadership makes a double argument for its own relevance. Understanding discursive dynamics is utterly helpful in understanding the entangled evolutions of thinking and organizing in a community, of stories, metaphors and institutions, and of governance, community and environment. From there, it helps to delineate how change comes about, and which leadership roles and functions are in existence, in the practice of governance, and in the stories on governance and community. Second, it can prove itself of value in a future-oriented way, both for leadership trying to understand its own options, and for others interested in the fate of the community. The same analytic perspective that gives insight in current leadership roles and systems relations can provide orientation to those wishing for new leadership roles, toward better environmental policy, sustainability strategy, or the reform that might be in order first. Risk is always involved, and nothing can be prescribed in terms of leadership roles and ideal policies. The risk associated with sustainability strategy not emerging at all, of feckless initiatives not daring to question routines, power relations and master narratives, can be far greater than the risk of reshuffling power relations and questioning assumptions (Gardiner, 2011) (Figure 7.6).

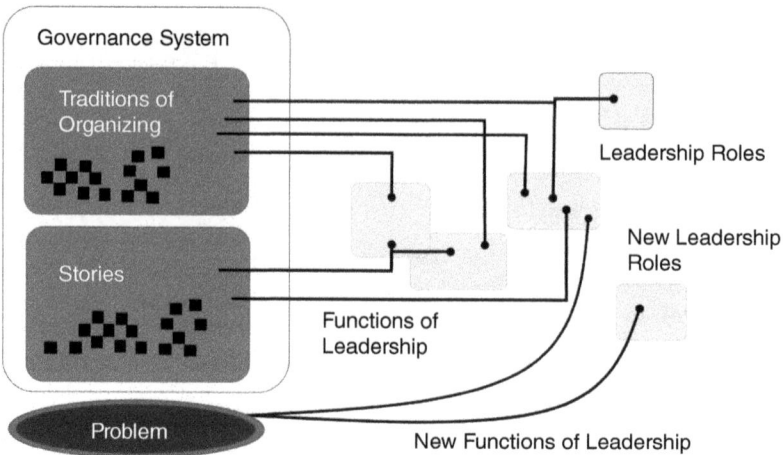

Figure 7.6 Understanding discursive dynamics is crucial for comprehending the intertwined evolution of thinking and organizing within a community. Narratives, metaphors and institutions coevolve within governance, defining leadership functions and roles. New leadership functions and roles can emerge from problems, defined also by narratives not only within governance but also existing in the community more broadly.

Each community must decide for itself, with the assistance it determines to seek, what sustainability could look like, which form of governance this requires, what kind of reform and next whether stronger leadership is helpful and acceptable. Moral dilemmas cannot always be avoided, as leadership might want to *convince* the community that sustainability is a problem and that reform is necessary, so the question arises whether this is still a community freely deciding for itself. Here, we might want to remind ourself that a governance system cannot unequivocally reflect the unified will of the people (Arendt, 2019). What a community believes it wants is always mediated by what people believe to be real, possible and desirable, and this is brokered by the governance system itself.

References

Arendt, H. (2019). *The Human Condition*. University of Chicago Press.
Axelrod, R., & Cohen, M. D. (2008). *Harnessing Complexity*. Basic Books.
Bevir, M. (2011). The logic of the history of ideas – Then and now: The author responds. *Intellectual History Review*, 21(1), 105–119.

Boje, D. M. (2008). *Storytelling Organizations*. Sage Publications Ltd.
Czarniawska, B. (2004). *Narratives in Social Science Research*. Sage.
Dean, M. (2013). *The Signature of Power: Sovereignty, Governmentality and Biopolitics*. Sage.
Denning, S. (2005). *The Leader's Guide to Storytelling: Mastering the Art and Discipline of Business Narrative*. John Wiley & Sons.
Dobson, A. (2007). *Green Political Thought* (4th ed.). Routledge.
Eckersley, R. (2004). *The Green State: Rethinking Democracy and Sovereignty*. MIT Press.
Fischer, F. (2003). *Reframing Public Policy: Discursive Politics and Deliberative Practices*. Oxford University Press.
Fitzpatrick, S. (1992). *The Cultural Front: Power and Culture in Revolutionary Russia*. Cornell University Press.
Gardiner, S. M. (2011). *A Perfect Moral Storm: The Ethical Tragedy of Climate Change*. Oxford University Press.
Giddens, A. (2009). *Politics of Climate Change*. Polity.
Gruezmacher, M., & Van Assche, K. (2022). *Crafting Strategies for Sustainable Local Development*. InPlanning.
Hajer, M. A. (1995). *The Politics of Environmental Discourse: Ecological Modernization and the Policy Process*. Clarendon Press.
Jasanoff, S. (2004). *States of Knowledge: The Co-Production of Science and the Social Order*. Routledge.
Jasanoff, S. (2016). *The Ethics of Invention: Technology and the Human Future*. W. W. Norton & Company.
Landes, D. S. (1999). *The Wealth and Poverty of Nations: Why Some Are So Rich and Some So Poor*. W. W. Norton & Company.
Latour, B. (2009). *Politics of Nature*. Harvard University Press.
Leach, M., Stirling, A. C., & Scoones, I. (2010). *Dynamic Sustainabilities: Technology, Environment, Social Justice*. Taylor & Francis.
Lemke, T. (2010). Beyond Foucault: From biopolitics to the government of life. In *Governmentality* (pp. 165–184). Routledge.
Luhmann, N. (1989). *Ecological Communication*. University of Chicago Press.
Machiavelli, N. (2012). *Discourses on the First Decade of Titus Levius*. Hardpress Publishing.
Macy, J., & Johnstone, C. (2012). *Active Hope: How to Face the Mess We're in Without Going Crazy*. New World Library.
March, J. G. (1994). *Primer on Decision Making: How Decisions Happen*. Simon and Schuster.
Meadows, D. (2009). *Thinking in Systems: A Primer*. Earthscan.
Ostrom, E. (1990). Analyzing long-enduring, self organized, and self-govern CPRs. In *Governing the Commons: The Evolution of Institutions for Collective Action* (pp. 58–101). Cambridge University Press.

Schön, D. A. (2017). *The Reflective Practitioner: How Professionals Think in Action*. Routledge.
Selznick, P. (2011). *Leadership in Administration: A Sociological Interpretation*. Quid Pro Books.
Sen, A. (2008). The idea of justice. *Journal of Human Development*, 9(3), 331–342.
Senge, P. M., Smith, B., Kruschwitz, N., Laur, J., & Schley, S. (2010). *The Necessary Revolution: Working Together to Create a Sustainable World*. Crown.
Stone, D. (2012). Transfer and translation of policy. *Policy Studies*, 33(6), 483–499.
Sunstein, C. (2005). *Laws of Fear: Beyond the Precautionary Principle*. Cambridge University Press.
Van Assche, K., Beunen, R., & Duineveld, M. (2013). *Evolutionary Governance Theory: An Introduction*. Springer.
Van Assche, K., Beunen, R., & Gruezmacher, M. (2024). *Strategy for Sustainability Transitions: Governance, Community and Environment*. Edward Elgar Publishing.
Van Assche, K., Duineveld, M., Gruezmacher, M., & Beunen, R. (2021). Steering as path creation: Leadership and the art of managing Dependencies and Reality Effects. *Politics and Governance*, 9(2), 369–380.
Wagenaar, H. (2011). *Meaning in Action: Interpretation and Dialogue in Policy Analysis*. M.E. Sharpe.
Weick, K. (1995). *Sense-Making in Organizations*. Sage.
Wheatley, M. J. (2010). *Leadership and the New Science: Discovering Order in a Chaotic World*. ReadHowYouWant.com.
World Bank. (2024). ID4D Global Dataset *2021: Volume 3* – Trends in Identification for Development (Text/HTML No. Vol 3). World Bank Group. www.documents.worldbank.org/en/publication/documents-reports/documentdetail/en/099031924132035631
Zizek, S. (2011). *Living in the End Times*. Verso Books.
Zizek, S. (2019). *The Sublime Object of Ideology*. Verso Books.

Glossary

Actors: individuals, organizations or groups with an influence on governance, on collective decision-making, formally or informally. Actors can do what their formal role description says or something quite different. They can enter governance circles, transform through participation in governance and become actors by observing governance and aspiring to take part in it. Sometimes, governance deliberately creates new actors, through decisions and through new institutions. Who is an actor is always in interpretation, an ascription of agency?

Adaptive capacity: the capacity of governance systems to adjust to change. Adaptive governance can aim at stabilization of communities but can also signify adaptation of the community at large to change. Adaptive capacity of the community does not solely emerge through governance, as self-organization certainly contributes, but without adaptive governance, resilient communities are hard to imagine. Well-adapted and stable systems might be rigid; hence, the importance of adaptive capacity, beyond adaptation. Adaptive capacity is hard to assess and cannot be understood as one-dimensional, which also means that it cannot be reasonably quantified. Any version of adaptive capacity correlates with a range of circumstances to adapt to.

Affect: emotion, as felt and expressed by individuals and groups. Narratives can be invested with affect, while they can amplify and disseminate affect. Reality for people is what they know through stories, what they know to be true and what feels true. Rational arguments make less of an impression if they do not connect to stories and their affective value. Desire can trigger affect and vice versa but cannot be reduced to each other. Sustainability discourse can form through strong affect but can also face strong affective backlash.

Analogy: similarity between phenomena, as observed by people. Analogies can be seen, and they can be expressed in storytelling for rhetorical effect. Metaphors rest on analogy, as something similar is noticed between dissimilar things, which enables one to explain the other.

Arena: a place or an organizational setting where a group of actors discuss and debate regarding collectively binding decisions. Some arenas are more open than others, as direct participation might combine with power through representation. We do not speak of actors when people participate rarely in such participatory processes.

Assets: something of value for a community. Assets become assets because of valuations enshrined by stories and practices inspired by stories and technologies. Gold only has value because we attribute value, and tar sands become exploitable because we told stories that fossil fuels were the future and developed the technologies to use them and exploit them. For a community, something can become an asset in a vision for the future, and if a strategy is formed around it, chances are higher of this becoming a reality.

Audience: governance has many audiences, and the stories selected and crafted for them and the genres, media and styles chosen depend on an audience, the role it plays in governance and community and the relation between storyteller and audience. Not all stories in governance are intended for the rest of the community; some are intended for the ears of an opposition party only, for friendly media, outside observers, or for an in-crowd sharing an interest and an organizational culture – maybe a crowd defining an actor.

Coevolution: where two systems or entities influence each other, relate to each other and shape each other over time in a significant respect. Actors coevolve in governance, discourses coevolve and societies coevolve with natural systems within social-ecological systems. The result of coevolution is that coevolving entities cannot be understood without reference to each other, and that transformation of either must be seen against the background of transformation of the coevolving configuration. What happens to either is limited and structured by the pattern of coevolution, which reveals modes of transformation?

Community: a group that shares a narrative foundation, as in shared values, a shared (imagined) history, or a desired future. People living together are not communities per se, and administrative boundaries do not necessarily coincide with community or cultural units. Over time, governance can create cohesion in culture and can create identification and shared values, but this cannot be predicted or assumed. Communities can be tolerant to diverse perspectives, or less so. For governance, such diversity is essential for adaptive capacity and for maintaining checks and balances.

Complexity reduction: it happens all the time. We cannot understand and navigate realities without it, and stories help us greatly. Metaphors have special powers of complexity reduction, not in the first place through its connecting of dissimilar phenomena, but through its capacity to synthesize a world of narratives in an image, which likely underpins other metaphors. Humans create complex systems too, including systems of politics and administration, and societies as overarching social systems. Stories are helpful in creating this complexity, and reducing it again, to enable communications about governance and society, and to assist people in navigating them.

Concentration problem: an issue prevalent in closed communities, marked by rigid identity stories and limited discursive diversity. Governance tends to simplify and ossify under such conditions, and self-transformation becomes unlikely. Where communities have been dependent on one resource, or devoted to one activity, under one type of leadership, institutions and stories that might have enabled change tend to shrivel and wither away.

Condensation: powerful reduction of complexity, as through metaphors. Metaphors and master signifiers can synthesize a knot of stories, or, as in the case of master signifiers, diverging interpretations, and a metaphor or another sign can come to stand for a great many things. Condensation works best if many stories are shared, and the more inside knowledge one has access to, the easier the unraveling of the knot. However, there's another path of persuasion, where little is known, but the fascinating sign intimates a world of meaning and makes one curious.

Dependencies: rigidities in the evolution of governance. Rigidities stem from coevolution in governance and do not account for determinism. Governance paths cannot be predicted, but they are constrained. We distinguish path dependencies, goal dependencies, interdependencies and material dependencies – see elsewhere in this glossary for explanation. As indicated by material dependencies, governance is located in a double context of community and ecological system, in a social-ecological system in other words, and coevolution shows itself in all relations.

Desire: what communities want, even if they are not aware of it. Communities express desire through stories, disavow desire and create desire through stories and decisions, which change social, economic and physical landscapes. Communities learn what they desire through stories, through observation of and comparison with others and through construction of pasts and futures.

Dialogic: a quality of a text or any other communication, in that its interpretation always takes place in a dialogue with other texts, which cannot always be grasped or predicted by those trying to communicate something. A text appears in a context, and that context is always a multiplicity, in the sense that not only the whole world could potentially influence the interpretation of a sign, but also the history of sign uses and the traditions of a genre, style, and medium. A novel, even if written by a barely literate person, will resonate for others with other stories in the literary tradition, and if the writer was so illiterate that any resonance fails, the thing would not be recognized as a novel.

Discourse: a conceptual structure that makes it possible to grasp something in reality. Discourses can take narrative form, they are born and die, travel in between those points and transform and change others in coevolution. Discourses can reinforce each other's truths in configurations and coalitions.

Discursive configuration: a configuration of discourse that finds connectivity, in governance or beyond. Discursive configurations make up our reality, and we are lucky that their mutual stabilization is never perfect. They never capture our ideas, feelings and desires completely and lose their persuasive capacity for reasons we never fully understand. As stabilization of communities is a core function of governance, it relies on discursive configurations and coalitions. A narrative fabric is a particular form of, and usually a part of, a discursive configuration.

Discursive coalition: a coalition of discourses associated with a set of actors and interests. Actors can create a discursive coalition, and such a coalition can catalyze the recognition of interests and the formation of actors. Discursive coalitions come, therefore, in different guises, where one side of the configuration (actors or discourse) can be more clearly structured than the other.

Discursive migration: the movement of discourse through time and place, and across boundaries of culture, genre, style and medium.

Discourse can travel in parts and wholes; discursive fragments can show up in new contexts and transform that context. Fragments can travel through paths of association and sharing between stories, in configurations and coalitions and through shared affect.

Environment: communities are an environment for governance systems, and actors in governance have each other as tightly coupled environments, meaning that they cannot ignore each other that easily. Material environments, broadly defined as ecologies, shape and are shaped by societies, at least in part through governance and coordinated action.

Environmental interactions: social and ecological systems interact, and social systems are capable of observing those interactions. Sustainability appeared as discourse when something went awry in environmental interactions, with ecosystems suffering more than expected from human activities, and societies being surprised by the social and economic effects of that deterioration and unanticipated change.

Familiarizing/defamiliarizing: stories and metaphors can achieve effect by making things look more similar or dissimilar. Making things similar brings them within the grasp of individual and collective cognitive abilities, reduces anxiety, and enables connectivity with other stories and ideas. Defamiliarization can open the eyes to new features of what was routinely overlooked. Both mechanisms can lead to innovation and exploration, yet also to critique of an existing order, or its confirmation.

Formal/informal institutions: communities structure themselves through formal and informal institutions; governance systems cannot operate on formal institutions (policies, plans and laws) alone. Formal institutions can derive from existing informal coordination mechanisms, and they can align with them. Informality can also function as an alternative to formal institutions, and this can have both positive and negative effects. A positive effect appears when the formal institution does not function anymore, loses support, or is undermined by governance actors or societal forces, and informal coordination offers a solution. A sustainability strategy unaware of the world of informality will find it hard to rethink the relations between system and environment.

Genre: a type of communication, usually narrative, that comes with formal and substantive traditions and requirements. Stories and real-life situations are often through the lens of genre, even where one is not aware of it. Genres and their conventions come about in a history where they differentiate from other genres, and new examples of a genre are interpreted through those conventions and comparison with earlier examples: what is new or interesting here, what is typical?

Goal dependencies: effects of visions of the future, or more limited goals set, on the reproduction of governance in the present. Goal dependencies can entail a variety of phenomena, including internal alignment and capacity development to support goal-oriented actions, selective observations of governance and environment of parameters supposed to indicate progress, but also transformation of goal and strategy, shifting of discursive coalitions, rebalancing of power relations, internal resistance and effects on internal competition. Effects can be indirect through societal effects of strategy or goals, which then trigger a response in governance.

Governance: the process of taking collectively binding decisions in a community. Governance is a process and a structure; it rests on coevolving configurations of actors and institutions, with formal and informal institutions coupled on the institutional side. Power/knowledge configurations make up the second coevolving configuration, where both actors and institutions can represent and use power and knowledge, and where shifts in actors, institutions and their relations are bound to have effects in power/knowledge. Governance is always there and always extends beyond the confines of a recognizable set of governmental actors. Actors never stick to their formal role, and some are not supposed to be there, in which case we can speak of informal actors.

Governance paths: unique evolutionary paths of communities in terms of their governance. Coevolution in complex configurations produces unique features and paths, marked by modes of self-transformation which are not entirely within the grasp of community and governance. This is an important observation, pertinent to any kind of directed change, including change toward more sustainable societies. Any transformation has to be conscious self-transformation, and every instance will come with unanticipated effects. Rather than ignoring or denying such effects, enhancing observation and self-observation are viable tools of self-management. Each community, moreover, will produce different responses to a policy or strategy imported from somewhere else.

Identity: both a narrative and a process. Identity is a narrative, as people and groups know themselves and each other through stories. Organizations, too, tell stories about themselves and know themselves through stories. Identities can be tied to roles, in an organization, of an organization, roles in governance, in society or in groups, providing another coupling between thinking and organizing. One can also speak of spatial identity, when communities assign meaning to places and identify themselves through places. Social identities can construct narratives of history, and vice versa, such narratives can have a creative and brokering power in relation to groups and societies. Governance reflects identity and contributes to the maintenance and creation of identity, using powers delineated by its own self-understanding. Identities frame the evolution of power/knowledge configurations in governance. They are also the expression of a process of self-reproduction, a result of coevolution that is not entirely conscious. An identity is not fully accessible; therefore, observation by others can be helpful to come to more complete self-images.

Ideology: bigger stories, meaning stories portending to explain a larger domain of life. Ideologies give direction to governance, toward a particular set of social values, and an ideal form of social, political or economic organization. Some ideologies start from economic ideals, others from political, economic, moral, or religious ones. Ideologies are never neutral and never fully grounded in other stories, meaning that they have to contain a circular element, a tautology – things are because they are, they should be because they should be. Questions that guide and structure governance, including the question of what good governance is, which idea of the community, which version of the community is embodied by governance, aimed for by governance, are of an inherently ideological nature. Ideologies are thus not tied to political parties, and they are not restricted to the formal domain of the political; they become political when they have an effect in governance and from there on decisions regarding the desirable organization of society. Thus, knowledge becomes ideological when it enters governance or is framed by stories that aim to mobilize for change in society, while knowledge more generally is always ideological in a second sense, as it is rooted in a bigger story about the state of affairs in the world, and ultimately, the nature of reality. Reflexivity, in governance and for leadership, requires a reflection on the ideological nature of stories and assumptions deployed, and strategy can be undermined, supported and shaped by ideology.

Institutions: tools of coordination between actors in governance. Simple institutions are rules, complex and composite institutions are policies, plans and laws. Institutions are formal when they are the ones supposed to guide an interaction, informal when they are anything else, Thus, informality can be what is unwritten, or elsewhere, an unwritten rule or coordination mechanism that is not the one formally sanctioned, imbued with power. Institutions are produced by actors, enacted and legitimized in governance, supported by other institutions which enable and delimit their power and content. Actors craft institutions and coordinate through institutions, and institutions guide the interpretation and application of others. Strategies are institutions that integrate and coordinate a set of other institutions and are provided cohesion by a narrative. Sustainability leadership will have to familiarize itself with the variety of institutions in existence, the capacity to produce and implement institutions through governance, and the power relations associated with institutions one hopes to get rid of.

Institutional capacity: the capacity of a community to organize governance and society through institutions, and to pursue common goods. Institutional capacity cannot be quantified, and careful assessment is required in any attempt at change. Sustainability leadership most likely will have to develop institutional capacity, either to enable strategizing, or as an intermediate goal of strategy, and, as such, needs to grasp precisely what institutional capacity would be in the present, and how modes of self-transformation might increase it in precise ways. Importantly, leadership has to distinguish between cases where it is institutional capacity that needs to be improved, or rather the creativity of governance systems in crafting, using and combining institutions. Goals can be reached in many ways, using different formal and informal tools, through different coalitions and stories, and leadership functions and roles will diverge between capacity building and creative crafting.

Institutional imperfection: the imperfection of governance systems to do what they are expected to do and what they say and hope to do. Institutional imperfection has many forms and causes, including the necessarily imperfect cohesion between institutions, the presence of hidden agendas, incomplete self-understanding and understanding of society, discursive dynamics in governance and society, the only partial translation of thinking into organizing and the effect of master signifiers to unite while dividing. Procedures introduce blindness and rigidity, organizational cultures can engender risk aversion and passivity, dominant roles and narratives can make governance diverge from what it wants to do or what society is expecting. Leadership is necessary to partially overcome these deficiencies and, with that, help communities to cultivate long-term perspectives, reflexivity and the other features of good sustainability governance.

Interdependence: the mutual reliance of actors on each other, on institutions and of institutions on other institutions. Without grasping interdependence, one cannot discern goal dependencies and reality effects; we need to understand the supports in governance to get things done, the supports that keep actors and institutions in place and enable them to have an effect. Leadership will have to assess its own interdependence in order to assess its scope of operations, its degree of autonomy.

Interpretation: the art and craft of understanding anything through assigning meaning. What can be interpreted might be a conscious communication by someone else, or a state of the world. People can interpret landscapes, histories, other people and what they say. Governance systems, actors, their performance and stories, their actions and decisions will be interpreted by others in governance and society. Interpretation works through signs, and everything can become a sign of something. Signs do not exist in nature and start to mean something when people see them as standing in for something else, referring to something else, a meaning. Meaning can form when signs refer to other signs, in systems of delineated signs that are connected to concepts or meanings, which refer to other meanings. Without a landscape of signs, and a landscape of meanings, signs and meanings, or concepts, cannot meaningfully relate to each other. Signs operate in sign systems, where spoken and written language function in conjunction with other sign systems to complete the interpretation of anything happening in governance: how is the leader dressed? What is this occasion really, this space, this food offered, the music playing in the background? Stories structure interpretation, and stories can become signs themselves, can become seen as significant, saying something about their time and context, their users and their uses.

Intertextuality: the conscious and unintentional connection of text through other texts, of expressions through other expressions and the history of sign use. Texts refer to other texts, by intentional reference, accidental borrowing from a concrete model or reference to a genre, style, period or author. Bigger stories, ideologies, can shimmer through a text, and it can also reveal its meaning through assemblage. Text can refer to others by showing themselves as an assemblage of chunks of meaning or structure already produced, attributable to an author or to a tradition. Knowledge of author and context, interpretations, shape the recognition but also interpretation of intertextuality: is this just clumsiness I perceive, in seeing this jumble or mash up of stories and signs and formats I know, or is it a crafty combination of things, an adaptation to audience? What shimmers through, which other texts can be recognized, thus hinges on the reader, or interpreter, the speaker or author, the text or combinations of signs itself and the context. Sustainability leadership always operates in a world of stories and signs, in a governance system deploying a variety of signs; it has to be masterful in interpreting the world and discerning how the world interprets.

Leadership: in governance, leadership is almost always distributive, meaning that it is exercised by a group of individuals, who might not consider themselves a group, and in some cases might not see themselves as belonging to leadership. Leadership is always necessary, as institutional design is always imperfect, prone to passivity and governance systems tend to take themselves as a reference, as reality itself, after a while. Leadership can be coordinated, if the group is aware of itself as a group, and if coordination is aimed at. Besides individuals, organizations can take up leadership roles in governance just as organizations can become actors.

Leadership functions: things that people and organizations do in governance, and that enable governance to overcome its own limitations and imperfections. What leadership would do is thus specified from the start by the goals and imperfections of governance. Leadership, moreover, can contribute to the articulation of collective goals, and the selection and crafting of institutions that might help it move in that direction. Common leadership functions include the creative use of institutions, finding resources, establishing and navigating new networks, re-relating inside and outside of governance, bringing in new ideas, new observations of self and environment, building new coalitions, telling and crafting stories that can build support for sustainability, linking tactics and strategy. These are common leadership functions as these are activities where routines and procedures are often insufficient.

Leadership roles: combinations of leadership functions that enable individuals or organizations to overcome a problem or imperfection in governance, by cohering into a role that can make a difference in that context. Leadership roles can be recognized in practice, can be crafted in practice and discerned as possible by insiders or outsiders in governance. One way of making such roles communicable and understandable is through metaphors, indicating the role, suggesting a combination of activities, and position in larger systems. Some leadership roles can revolve around one core function, others must be more diverse; individuals can shift roles and roles can be taken up by more than individuals. Leadership roles we distinguished as realistic and relevant for sustainability governance include the leader as storyteller, broker, builder, therapist and visionary. We downplayed the importance of the visionary if that person acts independently, without flanking by other leadership roles, and we argued that a role can entail that other functions come to serve one central to that role.

Master narrative and signifier: master narratives are stories that keep other stories in place, by confirming their truth, identifying their characters, defining origins and goals, supplying core values, providing context. Ideologies can become master narratives but not every ideology is successful; some maintain a life in a small niche or remain isolated from other aspects of life. Governance requires master narratives to maintain a degree of cohesion, legitimacy and purposefulness, yet some governance systems are keen to reduce their potential, and the understanding of that potential, through master narratives. Master narratives can be structured around master signifiers which can have a metaphorical character, but not necessarily so. Master signifiers do refer to a variety of things and give the impression to communities grasping with elusive realities, or people trying to find communicative common ground, that they found a hard reference point, a shared one. Sustainability is itself a master signifier, which can harness the power of coalitions formed through a feeling of mutual understanding.

Material dependence: the effects of material environments, both natural and human made, on the current reproduction of governance. Material environments can hold great powers of shaping, enabling and delimiting human activities taking place in them; they indirectly hold power over their governance systems, by gearing them toward activities, risks and livelihoods. Sustainable communities need to redefine their relationship with the material environment, so they ought to be as fully aware as possible of their entanglement with that environment. Reflexivity comes at a premium. Sustainability strategies can reduce the dependence on an environment, as a way to enhance resilience, but can also choose for adaptation, even dependence, if this is possible without damaging self and environment, and if it is possible to avoid the concentration problem, that is, without reducing adaptive and institutional capacity. In such a case, one cannot espouse a master narrative of small government and absolute efficiency, as capacities need to be maintained that are not visibly used for a long time. Grasping the way an environment shaped thinking and organizing in governance is essential for each path, as it can elucidate real limits in reorganization, as well as self-limitation that might not be necessary.

Medium: a material or virtual substrate of communication that co-determines form and content of such communication, as well as modes of circulation and types of audiences. Not every medium is as apt to accommodate the same genres, reach the same audiences and reproduce the same discourses. Printed books come with limitations that some virtual media do not have, printed media are more flexible in their reproduction and adaptation than books, and capable of capturing an audience with different stories about different aspects of reality. A medium is also an intermediate, and not a sign system itself; dance is a sign system, that can be read about, seen on television, or more directly, as a performance. Media come with different limitations therefore, different implications for social embedding and functioning, and weaker or tighter couplings with genres, styles and sign systems. Architecture is a sign system but does not accommodate complex narratives well.

Metaphor: a rhetorical figure which reflects the way we create meaning more generally. Metaphors do not merely serve as decoration but serve to familiarize or defamiliarize: they establish connections between two semantic domains, which helps to explain one in terms of the other. Metaphors can help to explore new terrain, to innovate, but also to reinforce what we know; to make the unfamiliar familiar, or the other way around. We speak of a source domain and a target domain, where the source domain is the familiar one, and the target domain that which we try to understand. Metaphor rests on analogy, on features found comparable, and these can be concrete or abstract, few or multiple; the selectivity established by the analogy guides us through new terrain. If A is like B because of x and y, then x and y will help us to discover more features in A. Over time, the analogy can expand, and more similarities can be found, so more can be explained. Metaphors can condensate narratives or complex realities, which is a function beyond establishing connectivity, and in the case of sustainability leadership, metaphors assist in the management of complexity both in grasping sustainability and possible roles for leadership to mobilize governance toward enhancing sustainability.

Metaphor family: metaphors can start a family, and if a metaphor underpins many other metaphors, and supports many narratives, one can call it a root metaphor. Metaphor families appear when the analogies recognized first prove very helpful in explaining a variety of things, or when the analogy is expanded. Back-and-forth exploration of features of source domain and target domain can bring people to the recognition of a more extensive analogy, or allow for the detailing of an analogous feature: if society is a ship, the sea is a dangerous environment, so maybe the waves mean something? Maybe a more modest economic disruption is a wave?

Metaphoric slide and stretch: metaphors can be used to explain broader phenomena. They can travel to new contexts, find application in new target domains. They can also stay in place, yet stretch up, so more and more things are considered similar. Stretch is not identical to expansion, as here, the core metaphor is not necessarily forming a family, but covering a larger target domain, to the extent it is creating a problem. The analogy doesn't really hold anymore, and the explanatory value shrivels to very little. Stretching is not the only reason for losing value, and ossification (see below) is another one. Metaphoric slide refers to the weakening for analogy in any sense, as when the signifiers slip off the concepts, or when something in either target or source domain has shifted, to the extent that the reality of either side feels less convincing.

Modernism: a philosophy of progress, finding its roots in eighteenth-century European enlightenment thinking. Modernism is founded on a positivist idea of science, meaning that we can know reality objectively, through science. Positivism and modernism thus differ from postmodern, constructivist, structuralist and poststructuralist approaches, and from interpretive perspectives, such as the one we developed in this book. Modernism proved very attractive for the builders of nation-states and their bureaucracies in the eighteenth and nineteenth centuries, as it promised leadership an objective overview of the state of the nation, its problems and solutions, seen through technical and statistical lenses. Modernism often supported the colonial enterprise, as it could uphold the pretense that the colonizers brought progress. In a modernist perspective, governance design can be optimized, policies can always be objectively tested, strategy does not need to rest on reflexivity, and systems relations can be known and objectively stabilized. Sustainability leadership appears then as the building of a modernist bureaucracy which can decide on sustainability problems and solutions through technical means and possibly guard its smooth functioning.

Myth: a myth can be a story that communities use to explain themselves and the world around them. We would use the concept of master narrative for such mythologies. In this book, myth is a pejorative term for a story aspiring to be a master narrative yet misleading the community in its search for sustainability. Myths can contain a kernel of truth, or more than a kernel, but are nevertheless misguided, as they bring communities to embrace policies that will not bring about the desired goals, either through misrecognizing societal values or through misapprehending the functioning of governance and leadership.

Narrative: a discourse that is structured in a way that is recognizable as a story, with episodes, characters and often a morality, that makes it more persuasive. Stories can compel to action, can form community, affirm identity and consolidate realities. Order is introduced on discursive materials, suggesting by inference an order in external reality. The order can be temporal, spatial and affective. Stories assist people to interpret themselves and the world, and leadership is under high pressure to discern, understand, select and craft stories, in convincing governance and community of sustainability problems and solutions. Affective investment in stories makes them more real, endows them with a mobilizing power. While stories can generate affect themselves, amplify it, support its circulation. We know what to feel because of stories, and we know how to relate to stories because of affect.

Narrative fabric: communities and their governance systems understand themselves and the world not through single narratives or collectives of narratives, but through an interweaving, or fabric of narratives. Stories can connect or couple to each other, support and validate each other, produce new ones, and the connectivity can take place literally, through shared concepts, narrative fragments and inferences, or figuratively, which often means through metaphors. Metaphors thus contribute to the stability of a narrative fabric, and more generally of discursive configurations and discourse coalitions. Sustainability leadership has the difficult task to be deeply familiar with and respectful to the narrative fabric of the community, while simultaneously understanding the need to transform aspects of it, to enable a reorientation of governance and behavior.

Naturalization: the process of becoming reality, of appearing as natural rather than contingent. Naturalization can be unintentional, a contingent process itself, and it be engineered, by actors inside and outside governance. Naturalization can rest on persuasive metaphors and narratives, on power relations which exclude alternatives, and which attempt to depoliticize, and dehistoricize what is historical and political. Governance systems are given greater or smaller powers of naturalization through their own master narratives regarding good governance, and through the congruence with narratives, aspirations and affect in society. If people want it to be true, it is easier to present it as truth.

Observational capacity: the capacity of governance systems to observe themselves and their environment. In the case of self-observation, we can speak of reflexivity, and if some self-observation succeeds in observing the way the system makes distinctions and observes, one can speak of second-order observation. Second-order observation can take place from outside the system, or from within, if alternative system references are available, and a degree of autonomy from the dominant distinctions and modes of observation. For sustainability leadership, reflexivity and the capacity to observe the entwining with environments is essential, as are the skills to develop systemic capacity of observation.

Path Dependency: the effect of legacies of the past on the reproduction of governance, hence a rigidity that has to be acknowledged when contemplating reform. Path dependence can be cognitive or institutional, found in the sphere of narrative and knowledge, or rather in the domain of policy tools and organization. Patterns of couplings between thinking and organizing can be inherited, while reform toward sustainability strategy might assume different patterns, or an easy modification of such patterns. Leadership, as always, benefits from a deep familiarity with formal and informal system features, to assess what can be changed at what cost.

Performance: the existence of stories and their position in governance does not fully explain their effect. Affective investment can fluctuate because of discursive shifts, migration, shocks and unexpected events. And there is the performance, the telling and performing of the story, where leadership can make a real difference, and find the right story in the right version and telling for the appropriate audience. Performance can modify stories, and even create an audience, maybe as a discursive coalition capable of supporting sustainability transition.

Polyphony: related to intertextuality, polyphony is a concept that expresses the interplay of voices in a text or other expression. Polyphony can be overt and covert, intentional and unintentional. A novel, as theorized by Bakhtin, can resist synthesis, as it might contain truly diverse voices or perspectives, an example of intentional and overt polyphony. Policy documents, political speech and academic literature on policy and administration tend to be polyphonic in a more covert fashion, which can be intentional or unintentional. Policies, plans and strategies can be assemblages recognizable as such only for insiders, and stories about alluring futures can appeal consciously to different audiences, by crafting carefully a polyphony that does not reduce coherence to a degree that becomes too observable.

Power/knowledge configuration: governance paths are marked by unique, identifying, power/knowledge configuration. By this we mean that the way stories, ideas and forms of expert knowledge are positioned in governance is unique, and uniquely influencing the formation, interpretation and use of institutions. Power/knowledge, similarly to actor/institution, has to be understood as a unity, since, in governance, each shift on the discursive side triggers alterations in discourse, and/or the potential of discourse to change things, to create new realities or to make people do things differently. New actors or institutions, conversely, will have an impact on the stories and perspectives in governance. If new policy tools are entering governance, if other tools are re-evaluated and found useful in new ways, this, unfailingly, will come with consequences for modes of thinking and their positioning. Power here emerges, as with Foucault, not as an effect of thinking or organizing separately, as both stories and institutions can make people think differently and change the outside world. Power/knowledge functions in a particular way within governance, as governance holds the potential to change the community and its environment.

Real: that what pushes back against signification from the outside, and that what, from the inside, shapes our thinking and observing without our knowledge. The concept is borrowed from Jacques Lacan, psychoanalyst, and complements an interpretive perspective that acknowledges there are realities, inside and outside us, that can push back against interpretations that do not work, and that have a grip on us. Governance, when ambitious, can hit the Real in many ways, and sustainability governance is almost certain to be confronted with limits of governability, some of which will be encounters with the Real. This, however, is no reason to be daunted, as governance is also an eminent to craft new stories, include new perspectives, reconsider and reorganize relations with our environment. What helps in avoiding tripping over the Real is reminding ourselves of the nature of the enterprise, the always precarious exercise of sustainability strategy. If we aim at an ideal balance between system and environment, one can predict this will be an imaginary one.

Reality effects: those effects of governance that alter the realities of residents, either through discursive effects or material changes. Governance can reshape the realities of residents in various ways, and convincing them of different goals, problems and solutions, new topics of relevance belongs to that repertoire. Reality effects can align with the intentions of governance, or not; stories promoted by governance, or style of performance can irritate, create resistance and backlash. Or effects can be neither aligned nor oppositional to strategy, but simply unexpected.

Resilience: the capacity of systems to bounce back after a shock, without losing essential system functions or features. To what extent social systems can be resilient, how this could be assessed and whether it is good to be resilient, rather than, say, transformative, is hard to say. One can see that some ecological systems are more resilient than others, that some landscapes, ecosystems and environments we appreciate most are less resilient than they used to be. We can also say that adaptive capacity of governance systems is for most circumstances more valuable than refined adaptation, and that adaptive capacity is a key to resilience. Adaptive capacity, however, can also generate strategies of transformation, of governance, society and environment.

Rhizome: the productive connectivity that generates realities, through relations that can form simultaneously. A material object, its spatial context, an idea, an affect can form an assemblage that is meaningful for us, and we are formed in the same process. Rhizomes can produce new offshoots, in places that are unexpected if we have a more hierarchic idea of the system. Affects can spread through the rhizome, can extend it by generating new stories, objects and encounters. Stories can engender subjectivities not anticipated by any storyteller or any system taking the story as reality. Rhizomes will be grasped in different ways by different observers, each observing only part of the assemblage.

Semiotics: the study of signification and interpretation, the study of sign systems. We can interpret a variety of sign systems, each with different competence. Telling stories relies on several sign systems, and navigating the world necessitates the understanding and use of various modes of signification. Not all sign stories are as easily understood and used as others, and not all sign systems lend themselves as easily to the construction or reading of complex narrative. Sign systems can be consciously combined, as in art forms, but also in the art of governance, where reality and authority have to be conquered through signs.

Social-ecological systems: the most encompassing sort of system, where social systems relate to ecological environments. Sustainability can be grasped in different ways, without assuming an optimal relation between social and ecological systems. It is possible to recognize problematic relations without inferring the existence of a perfect relation. Metaphors of equilibrium, health and services can all be helpful but have to be understood in that context: they are metaphors expected to generate and support narratives that help us to imagine and test system–environment relations. Such relations can be imagined differently, ideas of problems and solutions will change.

For the example of the balance metaphor: we are bound to come to new versions of a balanced relation, while the idea of balance might prove less palatable in new perspectives on social-ecological systems.

Strategy: a process and a form, where communities attempt to imagine and organize a desirable future. This book argued that good sustainability governance entails the development of first strategic capacity, where necessary, and next the articulation of sustainability strategy. Strategy at the community level has to pass through governance and has to be both a narrative of desirable future and a set of institutions, old and new, unified through that narrative. Thus, a strategy functions as an institution, a recognizable tool of coordination itself. Strategic capacity in governance rests on institutional capacity, adaptive and observational capacity.

Sustainability: a relation between social and ecological systems that is interpreted as sustainable. We emphasize the circularity because we cannot know what is sustainable, what is an optimal impact of social on ecological and vice versa. In other words, we cannot know what an ideal way of using, navigating or relating to an ecological environment would be, since our needs and desires, our ideas and identities will evolve and since environments respond to us and our interventions in them in unpredictable ways. The amount and quality of the metaphorical "services" provided by an environment, and the nature of a service, cannot be predicted or pinpointed; therefore, we can more easily proceed from a path of negatives: something appears as a negative in the narrative frames available, and we can decide to accept it, or to intervene in social or ecological systems to avoid future negatives of a similar sort.

Sustainability governance: in a broad understanding of sustainability, good sustainability governance can still be defined, and a set of features has been used as a red thread throughout this book's narrative. Institutional, adaptive and strategic capacity we can identify as necessities for sustainability governance, as strategizing requires the other capacities. Reflexivity and observation of system–environment relations are basic functions of governance if sustainability is an overarching goal, as is the articulation of long-term perspectives, a basis for strategy which in turn assumes an interest in the future state of social and ecological systems.

Temporality: systems have their own temporalities, which are not always easily coordinated or even known. Elections provide a clear structuring of time for the political system, yet governance systems include many other actors, and their temporality is structured in many more ways, through procedures, meeting schedules, policy agendas, hierarchies, tactics and strategies. Natural rhythms, starting with seasons, weather patterns and animal migrations can entangle with governance temporalities, as can temporalities in the social system, not in the least place economic cycles and episodes, and the mood swings of customers, voters and students. Stories create their own temporality and allow us to grasp and organize other temporalities: we can understand society and environment through stories that allow us to discern their rhythms and structure the temporalities of governance to adapt to or transform those rhythms. Strategy can translate temporality of a narrative future into the temporalities of governance, and through governance, society. Sustainability strategy has to envision an environment with different systems temporalities, and re-relating society and environment means recoupling temporalities.

Transition: we speak of transitions when we believe we need to do something about sustainability, and we are aware that our societies and governance systems are in need of serious modification. Transitions toward sustainability cannot follow one path toward one goal, as governance paths are marked by different dependencies and modes of self-transformation, as systems relations differ and as what is imagined as a desirable state will vary. A strategy for sustainability can end up as transition strategy, and if institutional redesign is on the table, this comes with a series of dilemmas and tradeoffs: goals can come with incompatible requirements for institutional design, and risk reduction in one area can increase risk elsewhere.

Transitional governance: a temporary governance arrangement where strategizing is not possible yet. Transitional governance can aim at building strategic capacity, either directly or indirectly, by addressing issues in reflexivity, institutional or observational capacity, while sometimes, urgent environmental problem-solving or conflict management is the first priority, the structuring force of transitional governance. Leadership will likely be more involved in transitional governance than elsewhere, even if the transitional configuration is more deeply participatory. Sustainability leadership will have to balance short-term sustainability goals and the development of systemic capacities to articulate sustainability strategy.

Index

adaptive capacity, 6, 17, 90, 134, 154, 156, 161–162, 186, 196, 202, 223
affect, 17, 40, 44, 48, 54, 59, 74, 79, 107, 109, 111, 116, 149, 196, 207, 215, 221
authoritarian, 9, 12, 119, 125, 130, 134

backlash, 107, 147, 162, 224
Bakhtin, Mikhail, 51
Barthes, Roland, 31–32, 34

civil society, 8, 150, 169, 183, 219
Club of Rome, 19, 186
cohesion, 39, 46, 88, 215
complexity, 48, 75, 80, 163, 227
   management, 6, 57, 146
   and metaphors, 82
conflict, 4, 51, 72, 78, 183, 203
corruption, 93, 158
creativity, 39, 168
critical
   observation, 2, 128
   perspectives, 133, 136, 165

democracy, 50, 71, 95, 109, 111, 115, 130, 135, 148, 156, 163, 209
desire, 43, 125, 163–164, 188
   community, 4, 18, 23, 41, 50, 221
   governance, 7
   leadership, 12, 17, 208
discursive coalition, 149, 223
discursive migration, 81

Eco, Umberto, 31, 52
experiment, 53, 59, 160, 219

fantasy, 24, 105, 222
Foucault, Michel, 15, 34–35, 83–84

genre, 30, 39, 50–54, 76, 218
global south, 4, 121
goal dependency, 220, 223
governance, 2, 12–18, 33, 45, 58, 95, 108, 128
   actors in, 53
   adaptive, 111
   dependencies, 17, 90, 126, 134, 170, 194, 196
   evolutionary governance theory, 17, 222
   good, 23, 30, 95–96
   governance configuration, 14, 22–23, 87, 144, 146, 168, 229
   governance path, 17, 134, 144, 224
   imperfect, 6, 59, 96, 131, 146, 162, 228
   and leadership, 4–6, 87, 92, 96
   and leadership functions, 7
   metaphor, 71, 77, 88, 92, 94–95, 117
   observation, 22
   power/knowledge, 49
   reform, 47
   routines, 8
   stories, 3, 39, 48, 56, 72, 86, 118, 128
   sustainability, 7, 18, 22–23, 127, 129, 133, 135–136, 147, 160, 172, 181, 208–209, 226
   temporality, 127
   thinking and organizing, 1
   and time, 57
   transitional governance, 202

identity, 30, 35–36, 39–40, 46–47, 58, 95, 112, 116, 126, 130, 149, 153, 188, 198, 202, 206, 225
insider/outsider, 17, 92, 149, 203, 225
instability, 74, 124, 158

253

institutional capacity, 58, 134, 151, 156, 162, 185–186, 194–196, 199, 201
institutions, 1, 3, 14, 49, 56, 87, 128, 133, 146–147, 161, 166, 190, 193, 200, 215, 220
  evolution, 14
  formal/informal, 7, 158, 162, 194
  narrative, 215, 225
  perfect, 144, 157, 228

knowledge, 8, 15, 34, 59, 82, 84, 187, 200
  expert, 15, 36, 52, 204
  formal/informal, 7
  governance, 33
  integration, 148
  local, 148, 161

Lacan, Jacques, 32, 42, 80
leadership functions, 6–11, 200, 207
  and adaptive capacity, 197
  and roles, 190
  and strategic capacity, 200
leadership roles, 10–12, 92, 208, 229
  broker, 183, 192, 196, 201, 203, 230
  builder, 181, 183, 185, 187, 194, 201–202, 225
  captain, 10, 128
  cyborg, 90, 151, 183, 192
  and functions, 190
  hero, 37, 151, 163, 168, 184
  Machiavellian, 186–189, 192–194, 197–198, 225
  in rough times, 201
  sage, 186–187, 194
  and strategy, 225–226
  storyteller, 46, 108, 181, 185, 188, 191, 225
  sustainability governance, 182
  therapist, 201, 206, 225
  translator, 183, 185, 187, 204–205, 225
  visionary, 91, 182, 186, 198, 204
learning, 18, 183, 205, 219
Levi-Strauss, Claude, 31, 35
long-term perspective, 10, 58, 122, 127, 147, 151, 155, 188, 190, 195, 198–199, 226
Luhmann, Niklas, 56

master signifier, 42–43, 56, 78, 79, 108–110, 114–117, 126–127, 194, 207, 221
media, 3, 51–52, 54, 115, 218
medium, 30, 33, 50
metaphor, 10, 24, 39, 68, 85, 87, 106, 112, 122, 144, 153, 207, 227
  family, 74–78
  governance, 92–97
  and leadership, 89–92
  and meaning, 69–74
  mutual metaphors, 118
  negative, 114
  ossification, 78–82
  root metaphor, 74–78
  and simplification, 82, 85
  and sustainability, 109
  sustainability governance, 127–132
  traveling, 78–82
modernism, 112, 124, 128, 147, 159–160, 171, 186, 219
myth, 22, 39, 86, 93, 144
  leaders and innovation, 167–171
  leaders and money, 152–156
  leaders and morality, 163–167
  leaders and perfect institutions, 156–163
  leaders as experts, 147–152

narrative, 21, 30, 50, 68, 88, 98, 107, 145–147, 150, 188, 225, 228–229
  community, 44
  and discourse, 36
  identity, 46, 198
  invisible, 114
  master narrative, 30, 42, 47, 56, 73, 77–78, 86, 130, 153, 185, 187, 201, 222
  master signifier, 108
  metaphor, 106, 161
  migration, 38
  narrative fabric, 40, 72, 116
  narrative judgment, 209
  narrative time, 57–59
  negative, 114, 116
  and strategy, 200, 222, 227
  structure, 36, 40, 59

and sustainability, 114, 120, 127–132, 147
theory, 30–36
and time, 55, 58
naturalization, 220–221
nature, 21, 36, 39, 106, 108, 117, 125, 130, 145, 161, 188

observation, 16–17, 22, 96, 98, 130–131, 134, 161
observational infrastructures, 183, 192
second-order, 196
self-observation, 18, 22–23, 155–156, 167, 184, 209
system-environment, 183, 191, 195
opacity, 115

participation, 6, 13, 34, 45, 54, 95, 130, 158, 203, 210
planning, 8, 15, 35, 126, 153, 186, 189, 202
polarization, 44, 79, 203, 224
policy integration, 84, 151
policy tool, 3, 8, 15, 47, 115, 130, 134, 188, 195, 200
procedure, 5, 7, 9, 13, 149, 157, 162, 172, 200
public discourse, 55, 72, 114, 120, 124, 183, 192

reality effects, 220, 222–223
reinvention, 115, 126

risk, 9, 19, 78, 123, 147, 149, 157, 159, 167, 170, 187, 192, 196, 203, 205, 229
routine, 5, 8–9, 13, 17, 57, 98, 146, 189, 193, 229

self-organization, 69, 84, 168, 219
semiotics, 31, 35
Claude Levi-Strauss, 35
C.S. Peirce, 69
infinite semiosis, 69
Michel Foucault, 35
Roland Barthes, 31–32
Umberto Eco, 31–32
social-ecological, 14, 19, 21, 105, 111, 115, 117, 122–123, 133, 147, 160, 221
strategic capacity, 134, 188, 199–200, 225–226
strategy, 7, 9–10, 23, 55, 90, 95, 105, 128, 131, 135, 153, 155, 170, 192, 199, 202–203, 215, 218, 220–222, 224
leadership, 190, 200, 215, 223, 225
sustainability, 166, 189, 209, 228
systems time, 57–59

trade-offs, 68, 115, 135, 224
transition, 11, 23, 90, 110–112, 150, 170
transparency, 204, 228

uncertainty, 42, 117, 161, 202

For EU product safety concerns, contact us at Calle de José Abascal, 56–1°, 28003 Madrid, Spain or eugpsr@cambridge.org.

www.ingramcontent.com/pod-product-compliance
Ingram Content Group UK Ltd.
Pitfield, Milton Keynes, MK11 3LW, UK
UKHW021928120426
469821UK00020B/449